Government-Linked Companies and Sustainable, Equitable Development

The debate over how far governments should intervene in economies in order to promote economic growth, a debate which from the 1980s seemed settled in favor of the neoliberal, non-interventionist consensus, has taken on new vigor since the financial crisis of 2008, and after. Some countries, most of them in industrialized Asia, have survived the crisis, and secured equitable economic growth, by adopting a developmental state model, whereby governments have intervened in their economies, often through explicit support for individual companies. This book explores debates about government intervention, assesses interventionist policies, including industrial and innovation policies, and examines in particular the key institutions which play a crucial role in implementing government policies and in building the bridge between the state and the private sector. The countries covered include China, India, South Korea, Malaysia, and Taiwan, together with representative countries from Europe and Latin America.

Edmund Terence Gomez is Professor of Political Economy in the Faculty of Economics and Administration, University of Malaya, Malaysia.

François Bafoil is Senior Research Fellow at the CNRS, Sciences Po, France.

Kee-Cheok Cheong is Senior Research Fellow at the Faculty of Economics and Administration, University of Malaya, Malaysia.

Routledge Malaysian Studies Series

Published in association with the Malaysian Social Science Association (MSSA)

Series editors:
Mohammed Hazim Shah, University of Malaya
Shamsul A. B., University Kebangsaan, Malaysia
Edmund Terence Gomez, University of Malaya

The Routledge Malaysian Studies Series publishes high-quality scholarship that provides important new contributions to knowledge on Malaysia. It also signals research that spans comparative studies, involving the Malaysian experience with that of other nations.

This series, initiated by the Malaysian Social Science Association (MSSA) to promote study of contemporary and historical issues in Malaysia, and designed to respond to the growing need to publish important research, also serves as a forum for debate on key issues in Malaysian society. As an academic series, it will be used to generate new theoretical debates in the social sciences and on processes of change in this society.

The Routledge Malaysian Studies Series will cover a broad range of subjects including history, politics, economics, sociology, international relations, geography, business, education, religion, literature, culture, and ethnicity. The series will encourage work adopting an interdisciplinary approach.

Government-Linked Companies and Sustainable, Equitable Development

Edited by
Edmund Terence Gomez, François Bafoil,
and Kee-Cheok Cheong

Routledge
Taylor & Francis Group

LONDON AND NEW YORK

First published 2015 by Routledge

2 Park Square, Milton Park, Abingdon, Oxfordshire OX14 4RN
711 Third Avenue, New York, NY 10017

Routledge is an imprint of the Taylor & Francis Group, an informa business

First issued in paperback 2017

British Library Cataloguing in Publication Data
A catalogue record for this book is available from the British Library

Library of Congress Cataloging in Publication Data
Government-linked companies and sustainable, equitable development /
edited by Edmund Terence Gomez, François Bafoil and Cheong Kee-Cheok.
pages cm – (Routledge Malaysian studies series ; 16)
Includes bibliographical references and index.
1. Economic development–Government policy–Developing countries.
2. Industrial policy–Developing countries. 3. Government business
enterprises–Developing countries. I. Gomez, Edmund Terence, editor.
II. Bafoil, Francois, editor. III. Cheong, Kee-Cheok, editor. IV. Mani, Sunil.
Economic liberalization and the performance of public sector enterprises in
India. Container of (work): V. Series: Routledge Malaysian studies series ; 16.
HC59.7.G688 2015
338.9'27091724–dc23
2014021502

ISBN: 978-1-138-80145-5 (hbk)
ISBN: 978-1-138-57809-8 (pbk)

Typeset in Times New Roman
by FiSH Books Ltd, Enfield

Contents

Illustrations

Figures

Tables

Contributors

Alvaro Artigas is Researcher at Sciences Po, Paris, France.

Jong G. Back is Professor at Gyeongsang National University, South Korea.

François Bafoil is Senior Research Fellow at Sciences Po, Paris, France.

Kee-Cheok Cheong is Senior Research Fellow at the Faculty of Economics and Administration, University of Malaya, Malaysia.

Edmund Terence Gomez is Professor of Political Economy at the Faculty of Economics and Administration, University of Malaya, Malaysia.

Michelle F. Hsieh is Assistant Research Fellow at the Institute of Sociology, Academia Sinica, Taiwan.

Lee Hwok Aun is Senior Lecturer at the Faculty of Economics and Administration, University of Malaya, Malaysia.

Li Ran is a PhD candidate at the Faculty of Economics and Administration, University of Malaya, Malaysia.

Sunil Mani is Professor at the Centre for Development Studies, Trivandrum, Kerala, India.

Elsa Satkunasingam was Senior Lecturer at Monash University Malaysia.

Zhang Miao is a PhD candidate at the Faculty of Economics and Administration, University of Malaya, Malaysia.

Preface and acknowledgements

The debate whether the state or the market should serve as the primary driver of the economy has long been a topic that has preoccupied economists. Mainstream economic theory was built around the supremacy of the market. However, the devastating social and economic consequences of the 1929 Great Depression threatened this dominant idea that the market should be recognized as the primary engine of growth, giving credence to John Keynes's more interventionist approach to economics. This respite, involving state intervention, including in key business sectors, was short-lived, undermined by the emergence of stagflation in the 1970s and the administrations of Ronald Reagan in the United States and Margaret Thatcher in the United Kingdom in the 1980s, the policies of which were based on what is now termed the neoliberal model of growth. The primary tenets of neoliberalism were proposed by Friedrich von Hayek, a key proponent of the need for "small government" and a deregulated market to allow private enterprises to foster economic growth. The Asian Financial Crisis of 1997, attributed to the problems accruing from active state intervention, further signaled the need to privatize government-owned institutions and de-regulate the economy. The post-1997 period represented the high tide of neoliberalism with its "let the market rule" mantra, a strategy that had been pushed, ironically, by the Bretton Woods institutions that Keynes had helped create.

However, recent events have re-ignited the debate about the need for state intervention to drive equitable and sustainable growth. This renewed interest in state intervention in the economy emerged following the eruption of the Global Financial Crisis in 2008 which brought the world economy to the brink of collapse. This crisis has been blamed on deliberate lack of regulation of the financial system by the US Federal Reserve helmed by Alan Greenspan, a strong advocate of neoliberal policies.

But the state–market debate has far more significance today than when Keynes crossed swords with Hayek over it in the 1940s. In the last quarter of the twentieth century, a number of developing economies achieved unprecedented rapid economic growth, emerging as highly-industrialized middle-income countries. Countries in East and Southeast Asia, which the World Bank referred to as "high-performing Asian economies," had adopted what was defined as the developmental state model, whose tenets were major departures from those advanced by neoliberalism. The development of these Asian economies, especially those in Japan, South Korea, and Taiwan, and arguably the most successful of all, China, have collectively undermined the case for neoliberalism as the development model to pursue. These alternative models of development are important not only in relation to the Keynes-Hayek debate but also in advancing an understanding of the role of the state and its relations with society. But such debates about economic development were not limited to countries in Asia. Eastern Europe, gripped by the Big Bang theory of market liberalization, suffered, as did countries that constituted part of the former Soviet Union. In both cases, the peoples of these regions encountered considerable pain before economic conditions stabilized. And in Latin America, where US influence had waxed and waned, the economies of this region had also experienced active bouts of neoliberalism, but with uneven results.

Further, even after the Asian Financial Crisis, Asian governments in general and those that suffered its direct impact in particular were not convinced of neoliberalism's merits. Malaysia chose not to call in the International Monetary Fund (IMF) for aid, resorting instead to capital controls. While dissatisfaction with the government of Thailand's Chatichai Choonhavan over his handling of the financial crisis had led to his ouster in 2001, his successor Thaksin Shinawatra's pursuit of neo-Keynesian counter-cyclical policies showed him to be no neoliberal. And Indonesia was an example of a case where neoliberal policies were imposed by the IMF on "unwilling countries." Indeed, these governments regretted earlier efforts to liberalize their economies.

More fundamentally, the 2008 crisis forced governments and the development community alike to review the models of economic development amidst growing calls for the construction of an agenda to protect and consolidate the well-being of the domestic economy. This crisis drew attention to issues such as the degree of state intervention to spur industrialization, upgrade technology, and enhance services; the extent of public ownership and control of the banking sector; the effective and productive employment of government-linked companies which retained a ubiquitous corporate presence in many developing economies; the scale and scope of regulation of the economy; the mechanisms to nurture domestic firms, particularly entrepreneurial small and medium-scale enterprises; and the volume of infrastructure development spending to sustain efforts to reduce poverty.

This volume is targeted at examining these key debates about models of development as well as reviewing the outcomes of government policies that entailed intervention in the economy along with attempts to liberalize the market. In most of industrialized Asia, governments had adopted a mix of developmental state and neoliberal policies, a situation also seen in parts of Eastern Europe and Latin America. With our focus on government-linked companies (GLCs), this study draws attention to a group of key institutions that play a key role in implementing government policies while also providing the bridge between the state and the private sector. In doing so, this study speaks to state-society relations, revealing complexities that are seldom if ever discussed in existing theories about public enterprises. It also addresses areas of government intervention, such as industrial and innovation policies, that go far beyond what has been elucidated in neoclassical theories of the role of government. And, it sheds much light on the evolution of this group of institutions themselves, GLCs, an issue not covered in any analytical depth in academic publications. Finally, with coverage of countries in several parts of the world, this book provides an empirical basis for comparisons of the states' choice of development strategies, all the while reminding the reader of the importance of context.

The funding for this study was obtained from the Malaysian government's Ministry of Higher Education. This ministry's focus was then on the role that the Malaysian government could play to aid the development of under-industrialized countries in Southeast Asia, with particular focus on Cambodia, Laos, Myanmar, and Vietnam. This endeavor by the Malaysian government was proposed in 2010, not long after the 2008 economic crisis and during a period when there were animated debates worldwide as well as in Malaysia about the need to construct a new model development. We had made the following argument to obtain funding for this project: given the role that the state had played in developing East Asia by employing GLCs, most evident in Malaysia, Singapore, Taiwan, South Korea, and Indonesia, there were important lessons to be learnt from them by countries in Indo-China. During the course of the discussions about reviewing models of development that had been adopted by under-developed countries to quickly transform themselves into thriving economies, it was also proposed that we include case studies of countries in Eastern Europe and South America. Our primary concern was to embark on a comparative study of the role of GLCs in developing economies, a clear gap in the literature and a topical issue given the debates then about how such enterprises could be properly deployed to help deal with the impact of the 2008 crisis. We are extremely grateful to the Ministry of Higher Education, recently re-named the Ministry of Education, for awarding a grant to the University of Malaya to undertake this project.

One part of this initiative to aid the development of Indo-China was to include bureaucrats from this region in this project. Discussions were subsequently held with bureaucrats and academics in Cambodia, Laos, and Vietnam about participating in this project. During our visit to the region, the administrators at the University of Southeast Asia, situated in Siem Reap, in Cambodia, expressed a keen interest to host a conference that we were planning to review our research topic. The conference was convened in Siem Reap on February 9–10, 2012 and the participants included academics and bureaucrats from Cambodia, Vietnam, and Laos. The academics at Siem Reap played a major role in planning and hosting the conference and ensuring that bureaucrats from Cambodia and the region were invited to this forum. These Cambodian academics also initiated a country study on this topic, with the help of academics from the University of Malaya as well as François Bafoil who has done extensive research in the region. We are grateful to Rous Bunthy, the Vice President of the University of Southeast Asia, and his colleagues for organizing and hosting the conference. We wish to mention, in particular, Dina Delos Santos Dela Cruz, and Nuon Vireak, academics based at the University of Southeast Asia who played a major part in hosting this conference.

The participants at the conference included, apart from the contributors to this volume, academics from Indonesia, Japan, South Africa, and, as mentioned, from Laos and Vietnam. While we could not include in this volume all the papers that were presented at this conference, we wish to acknowledge with much gratitude the contribution of the following academics: Riant Nugroho, Saykham Voladet, Ganief Bardien, Lumkile Mondi, and Tran Dinh Lam. Many of the issues they raised at the conference have been included in this study.

I wish to acknowledge my enormous debt to François Bafoil and Kee-Cheok Cheong for graciously accepting my invitation to help me edit this volume. They did so even though they were aware of the enormous volume of work that was required of them. They have been unstinting in their assistance to ensure that this project was completed.

I acknowledge, with much gratitude, the academics who have contributed chapters to this volume. They were active participants at the conference in Siem Reap and they responded promptly to our numerous requests to improve their chapters when they received our comments. We have learnt much from our discussions with them.

It would be remiss of me not to mention Peter Sowden, the commissioning editor at Routledge. Peter responded very positively when the proposal for this study was sent to him. And, he has endeavored to ensure that the book was published promptly. We remain indebted to him for his support for this project.

Edmund Terence Gomez
University of Malaya
December 1, 2013

Introduction: The state's return to business

Government-linked companies in the post-crisis global economy

Edmund Terence Gomez, François Bafoil, and Kee-Cheok Cheong

Economic crises, developmental state, neoliberalism

The debate about the role of the state in the management of an economy has ebbed and flowed, punctuated by the contrasting positions taken by Thomas Jefferson and Alexander Hamilton, and more recently, between the prominent economists John Maynard Keynes and Frederick von Hayek.[1] The latter debate occurred as the world economy was recovering from two epochal events: the devastating 1929 Great Depression and the Second World War—and had appeared to be settled in favor of Keynes, but the intervening years have not been kind to him. The emergence of stagflation in the 1970s discredited Keynesianism, while the Asian Financial Crisis of 1997 seemed to signal the high tide of neoliberalism with its "let the market rule" mantra, a strategy that had been proposed, ironically by the Bretton Woods institutions that Keynes himself had helped create, since the 1980s.

However, recent events have reignited the argument on state intervention, suggesting that the Hayek–Keynes debate is far from being dead and buried. This renewed interest has emerged following the eruption of the global financial crisis in 2008 which brought the world economy to the brink of collapse. Following this crisis, a vigorous critique of neoliberalism emerged, bringing to the fore debates about models of development and the role of the state in processes to generate growth in an equitable and sustainable form.

The 2008 crisis forced governments to review their model of economic development in response to growing calls for the construction of an agenda to protect and consolidate the well-being of the domestic economy. This crisis drew attention to issues that required deep consideration, such as the degree of state intervention to spur industrialization, upgrade technology, and develop services; the extent of public ownership and control of the banking sector; the effective and productive employment of government-linked companies (GLCs); the scale and scope of regulation of the economy; the mechanisms to nurture domestic firms, particularly small and medium-scale enterprises (SMEs); the methods to foster research and development (R&D) through public agencies; and the volume of infrastructure development spending to sustain efforts to reduce poverty. These issues encompassed matters fundamental in arguments that had transpired between Keynes and Hayek. While Keynes advocated state intervention as a necessary complement to the private sector to ensure employment and growth, Hayek (and the neoliberal movement he would inspire) saw the government's role as one limited to law enforcement and the provision of—minimal—social welfare, with no interference in market forces. However, much of the post-2008 crisis literature about the Keynes versus Hayek debate grappled inadequately with the concept of power, which had come to be concentrated in the hands of big business, with state support, following the promotion of neoliberalism. This recent literature also dealt inadequately with other core issues such as the importance of involving labor in discourses about effective and equitable development processes.

Usually forgotten in the heat of debate is the fact that Keynes and Hayek were discussing developed economies. A large body of work on development, with theories of economic dualism, balanced (Nurkse 1961) and unbalanced growth (Hirschman 1958), linear stages of growth (Rostow 1962) and economic catch-up growth (Gerschenkron 1962), all posit the significant role of the state. This is equally true of schools of economic growth that are alternatives to if not in competition with mainstream (neoclassical) growth theory, namely the evolutionary growth school inspired by Joseph Schumpeter, and the institutional school that argues institutions, not more or less government, are the key. Yet, these theories have greatest relevance for East Asia, the most dynamic region in the world since 1980, as well as other members of what has been called "emerging market economies".

What is evident is that long before the 2008 credit crisis, governments worldwide, including those in rapidly industrializing East Asia, such as South Korea, and Taiwan, as well as the current group of high performing developing economies (i.e. China, Brazil, Russia, and India), have employed GLCs, or state-owned enterprises, to generate economic growth and employment, and nurture highly entrepreneurial enterprises. In industrialized East Asia, state-led development was responsible for the rapid emergence of Japan's economy as the second largest in the world, despite its decimation during the Second World War. South Korea, Taiwan, and Singapore replicated to varying degrees post-war Japan's form of economic development—well-known as the "developmental state model" (Johnson 1982)—in order to cultivate domestic enterprises and industrialize their economies. Numerous Southeast Asian countries, including Malaysia, Thailand, and Indonesia, influenced by East Asian corporate models, specifically Japan's *zaibatsu* and *keiretsu* and South Korea's *chaebol*, with their emphasis on the close links between the financial and industrial sectors to advance industrialization and develop local entrepreneurial capacities, would rapidly emerge as high performing economies. China would follow in this tradition with its own unique forms of state-business nexus to promote industrialization. In these Asian countries, the state's role in the economy was patently fundamental, evident too in the significant presence of GLCs in key economic sectors.

"Big push" policies introduced in the USSR during the 1930s had similarly resulted in massive investments in state-owned enterprises (SOEs) in Central and Eastern Europe (CEE). However, unlike the East Asian experience, the poor productivity rates and inefficiencies of these SOEs had contributed to several crises during the communist period. In 1989, this huge economic inefficiency, combined with very wide feelings of political illegitimacy precipitated the end of this political economic mode of development.

In spite of industrialized Asia's unprecedented rate of development—the World Bank (1993) referred to it as the "East Asian miracle"—the active partici-pation of GLCs in economies worldwide has long remained a much deliberated topic. Perhaps more than the collapse of the Soviet Union, which occurred around 1990, a core reason for this deliberation was that, in tandem with the rise of industrialized Asia, neoliberalism as a model of development was being actively fostered in the industrialized West. In Britain, as the economy struggled with a recession, a huge public debt burden, and escalating unemployment, a major reform ensued from the early 1980s during the administration of the Conservative Party's Margaret Thatcher. Her staunch support of Hayek's ideas led Thatcher to advocate policies that favored private over public enterprise and minimal state intervention. The foundation of Thatcher's support for neoliberal policies was her belief that they would engender far more efficient employment of key resources. Arguments supporting "small government" would subsequently be adopted and propagated in the United States by her close ally, the Republican president Ronald Reagan, who similarly argued that the government should dissociate itself from business. While the state in East Asia focused on ownership and control patterns, monitored the pattern of development of private enterprise, and disciplined "winners" picked to drive industrialization, the proponents of neoliberalism drew no attention to the influence that big business could come to have in a highly de-regulated economy.

In the CEE, implementation of neoliberal reforms was supported by what was called "standard theory". This approach had been developed in the 1980s and 1990s by monetarist scholars who represented important "epistemic communi-ties" throughout the world. Many members of the ruling elite in the new East European states subscribed to this school of thought; for instance Balcerowicz, the Polish minister of finance in 1990 had studied in Britain in the 1980s. This approach postulated the radical failure of the communist system and the absolute capacity of human beings to satisfy their own interests provided there were no obstacles, such as the state, trade unions, or other social intermediaries (Bafoil 2009). This approach was lent greater credibility by the failure of the Soviet-type state in establishing legitimate institutions. All institutions of the communist period had to be destroyed and all former civil servants, fired. This approach was evident in the "Balcerowicz Plan" in Poland, which intended to simultaneously solve macro issues (exchange rates), meso issues (privatization), and micro issues (cutting off state subsidies to firms) (Balcerowicz 1995). But if the first level of the reform was successful, the two other levels encountered strong resistance from stakeholders because appropriate institutions to implement privatization were missing and there was little knowledge of market rules (Orenstein 2000).

In policy terms, the key features of neoliberalism involved, apart from the merits of liberalization and deregulation, a strong endorsement of privatization (Harvey 2005). Deregulation was endorsed to facilitate liberalization of the functioning of key financial institutions such as banks. Trade and import liberalization was to accompany financial liberalization, and government expenditure would focus on education, health, and infrastructure, specifically transportation and communications, key factors that would smooth the development of private enterprise by reducing the cost of production and providing the human capital for product upgrading. Given neoliberalism's strong emphasis on wealth accumulation and individualism, the role of trade unions had to be impeded while "flexible" work and wage systems were introduced.

The core tenets of neoliberalism was best encapsulated in what Williamson (1990, 1997) termed the "Washington Consensus", a set of market-driven dictates designed to facilitate the intensification and expansion of capitalist markets and trade. The primary elements of this Consensus included the contention that economic growth could only be achieved through a combination of deregulation of the market, fiscal discipline, reduced public expenditure, including through privatization to encourage competition, tax reform, competitive exchange rates, promotion of foreign direct investments (FDI), secure property rights, and trade liberalization (*ibid.*).

Subsequently, major international financial institutions such as the World Bank and the International Monetary Fund (IMF) in which the United States and Europe exercised effective control through shareholding, began adopting and espousing neoliberal ideas, a key factor that hampered state intervention in developing economies and one that eventually led to the dismantling or sale of public institutions to private enterprises. This was facilitated by structural adjustment programs (SAPs) in which "structural adjustments" (liberalization) were key conditions for loan approval. SAPs actively promoted the idea that to sustain economic growth, a liberalized private sector was imperative. These programs were structured ostensibly to allow a developing country to generate income, pay off debts, and industrialize its economy.

The European Commission started to disseminate these ideas of liberalization after having adopted the Unified Market Act in 1986 which postulated the freedom of flows of goods, services, and people. The telecom sector was the first to be liberalized and privatized. Then, in the 1990s, other public infrastructure sectors such as the railways, the post, and energy were privatized. The European Commission favored the division of the main activities of each public monopoly, by separating production, transport, trade, and services. These EU directives led to the emergence of an oligopolistic market dominated by the strongest Western enterprises which used these liberalization opportunities to become "national and European champions". The fall of communism in Eastern Europe was a fortuitous opportunity for these oligopolies to extend their business reach to the new East.

These arguments about the private sector's crucial role to drive growth would gain currency with the significant weakening of left-leaning political parties with the fall of the Berlin Wall. Kymlicka and Banting (2006) have noted that in

European countries where left-based parties are out of power and unions are weak, there has been a decline in support for state intervention including for welfare purposes.

In countries that adopted the SAP framework, new problems emerged, including the creation of private monopolies in sectors previously under public control. Privatizing public services tended to concentrate control over utilities, services, and resources in developing countries in the hands of multinational companies (MNCs) or of powerful vested interest groups, while government oversight in these sectors was also reduced considerably. From the late 1980s, after Latin American governments actively began privatizing their assets to generate money, privatizations secured by foreign firms led to an inflow of US\$ 13 billion in the region between 1988 and 1994 (Vernon 1998: 79). Following these privatizations, MNCs were also accused of "exploiting the weaknesses of the Latin Americans" (*ibid.*)

Another crucial dimension of the SAPs, involving financial and investment liberalization in developing economies, greatly aided the activities of MNCs. These provisions entailed, among other things, the entry of FDI, the removal of controls on currency speculation, and the right of foreign investors to acquire or hold 100 percent equity ownership of domestic firms. With these provisions in place in developing economies, MNCs were able to easily purchase land, invest, and remove unlimited amounts of money, and establish enterprises in key sectors of the economy, driving out local competitors. To encourage increased foreign investment, countries competed with each other using various incentives including tax exemptions, relaxed labor, and environmental standards, and free trade zones. Conditions in developing countries implementing such policies were particularly attractive to MNCs, due to limited corporate regulation and government oversight in key sectors, such as extractive industries and construction, which are often the most profitable and least regulated activities available to foreign firms. Currency crises would soon feature large in Latin America.

The economies of East and Southeast Asia of the late 1980s and 1990s posed a challenge to this approach, however. While subscribing to some degree of liberalization, governments have maintained a strong economic role. This mixture of market discipline and state support, far from meeting a sticky end as predicted by neoliberal theories, produced stellar economic growth, with the World Bank itself acknowledging them as "High-Performing Asian Economies" (HPAEs) (World Bank 1993). Neoliberal ideologues would nevertheless argue that it was adherence to market principles that begot the "East Asian Miracle". So, in 1997, when the Asian currency crisis occurred, these ideologues pointed to the misguided hand of the state that precipitated the collapse. Other scholars, however, pointed to the opposite—the de-regulation of capital flows and unchecked growth of debt by large enterprises, a number of which required government bailouts, had brought the house down (Gomez 2002).

It was, however, the financial crisis that erupted in the United States and Europe in 2008 that would bring into open question the viability of this neoliberal model of development, one that had long been critiqued as having contributed to new and serious wealth and income disparities.[2] This crisis led to a growing call for governments to institute reforms within a new institutional framework. This call for reforms entailed more than the short-term measures introduced by governments involving the drawing in of FDI and the assembling of economic stimulus packages that presumably would help increase domestic spending and promote projects with high multiplier effects. Other issues that equally required deep consideration included the controversial role—mainly in the United States, though to a lesser extent in Britain—of the extent of government ownership and control or lack thereof, of key sectors, specifically the banking industry, and the effective and productive employment of state-owned enterprises (SOEs) and GLCs.

Employing government-linked companies

In the United States, the involvement of the government in business in the post-crisis period was seen as imperative to rectify problems created by inadequately regulated financial enterprises. This was a historic moment, for when the United States asserted the need for greater state intervention in the economy, governments around the world slowly began to accept the need to employ GLCs far more effectively and productively.

However, just as neoliberalism's viability was critiqued long before the onset of the global crisis, this idea of keeping government out of business, including through GLCs, was being reconsidered because they had begun acquiring a reputation for outstanding business performance. There was ample evidence that many GLCs in developing countries had emerged as "best practices" companies, compared to those in the private sector. GLCs in Brazil, Russia, Mexico, China, South Korea, Taiwan, Singapore, Malaysia, and Indonesia have proved that they are capable of becoming leading enterprises in the region, even in the world. Singapore Airlines and Singapore Telecom have been acknowledged as "world class companies". Malaysia's Petronas is in the list of the most prominent companies in the Fortune 500. Telekomunikasi Indonesia was quoted on the New York Stock Exchange. China Petroleum is one of the world's leading oil and gas enterprises. This suggests, in the post-global economic crisis period, the core debate should focus on the most pragmatic approach to be adopted by governments to ensure that GLCs perform better as business entities to promote economic growth.

Because of their links with government, GLCs had been criticized as softer versions of SOEs, which a range of theories, from agency to public choice, argue to be inefficient by nature. Thus, early assessments of GLCs contend that privatization was an effective approach to reform poorly performing firms in many countries. Numerous studies of Britain's public enterprises, as well as those subsequently conducted in other countries, contend that privatization was the only panacea to GLCs that were thwarting economic growth. However, the subsequent generation of privatization studies revealed that the transfer of GLC ownership to private individuals did not guarantee improved company performance. Some GLCs performed just as poorly after privatization while fairly well-functioning government enterprises were run aground under private owner-ship.[3] Debates about the efficacy of this neoliberal policy heightened after disclosure of severe failure of privatized basic public services, especially water supply, leading in some cases, as in Bolivia, to a revolution that overthrew the government and the re-nationalization of this sector (Sawyer and Gomez 2012).

These studies and the lessons of the global economic crisis draw attention to the important role that GLCs are now required to play in an economy. What remains, however, is how governments can ensure that GLCs, particularly under-performing firms, are revamped to enable them to contribute to economic growth. The efficacy of these reforms has much to do with the nature of state intervention, the form of governance of GLCs, including the level of autonomy accorded to their professional managerial team, the volume of investment in R&D to nurture innovation and foster upgrading of technology, and the creation of social compacts involving the state, capital, and labor to ensure a more equitable form of economic development.

Researching government-linked companies: key themes

This study's primary objective is to assess prior to and after the 2008 global finan-cial crisis the changing nature of the relationship between government and business, to facilitate expansion of domestic enterprise and develop key economic sectors. The mode of development of an economy remains a contentious issue for national governments. While different developmental inclinations exist within every society, it is the preferences of the most powerful groups that often take precedence. Whether supported by the state or international institutions, the path-way to development that is ultimately chosen is generally in the interests of powerful groups who provide the necessary financial support. Since power distri-bution across society is vastly asymmetrical, those who lack power and representation seek to pursue contrasting conceptions of development, a factor contributing to different modes of development in countries. The different modes of development adopted in countries, employing their capital base in different forms, is best captured in the varieties of capitalism (VoC) literature.

A major contribution of the VoC literature, seen particularly in the works of Peter Hall and David Soskice (*Varieties of Capitalism*), and Bruno Amable (*The Diversity of Modern Capitalism*), is the attention they draw to the heterogeneity of capitalism in practice among economies worldwide. Hall and Soskice (2001) proffer two major types of capitalist models, the coordinated market economy, and the liberal market economy, while Amable (2004) presents five: market-based, social democratic, Asian, continental European, and south European.

In spite of the attempt by VoC theorists to draw attention to the heterogeneous forms of capitalism, this literature can be critiqued as being rather "essentialist" in nature. The concept of VoC as employed by these theorists suggests, for exam-ple, that Asia has basically one common form of capitalism while Europe has a greater variety. This is a false dichotomy. The form of capital development within Europe and Asia, and within countries in these two continents varies far more considerably than the VOC theorists suggest. While Britain's pattern of private capital development is akin to that of the United States, GLCs have a phenomenal presence in the French economy. Germany's social market economy has its own unique features involving co-ownership of key enterprises by the state, trade unions, and families, while the Scandinavian countries have a social democratic structure that has had a major bearing on state–capital–labor relations which has hugely influenced forms of enterprise development. The competitive strength of Italian firms in global markets is due to the role of small and medium-scale enterprises (SMEs) and industrial districts that have operated in labor-intensive industries producing consumer products. Among companies in the industrialized West, Alfred Chandler Jr. (1990, 1997) had noted different styles of managerial capitalism; its form in Britain is personal, while in the United States it is competitive, and in Germany it is seen as co-operative. How GLCs function within these models of development vary as do how they relate with large firms or SMEs.

In Asia, the developmental state model employed in Japan is characterized by a state–capital–labor compact that has not been replicated in other Asian countries that are reputed to have adopted a similar mode of development, including South Korea, Taiwan, Singapore, Malaysia, Thailand, and Indonesia. China's form of economic and enterprise development, which is now apparently emulating ideas offered by the developmental state model but retains its distinctiveness in important ways, is vastly different from the form of capital development in India. Corporate ownership and control patterns and business systems in Asian countries differ significantly. Japan's *keiretsu* system involves extensive interlocking ownership ties between industrial firms and banks. In South Korea, the highly diversified *chaebols* are basically family-owned enterprises, while in Taiwan, the driver of growth are the SMEs which constitute nearly 98 percent of the economy. In Southeast Asia, the conglomerate pattern of enterprise development is popular, while these economies depend heavily on FDI to generate growth.

A close assessment of economies worldwide would indicate that there are varying degrees to which the state intervenes in countries to promote domestic enterprise. The pattern and extent of state intervention in these economies have been crucial in determining the type of capital that has secured a prominent presence in each country. Economic growth in the post-Second World War Europe was driven by GLCs, seen in particular in France, Italy, Norway, Finland, and Austria. Leading European enterprises in the industrial sector have been under government control and ownership. In France, internationally recognized firms linked with the state include those in a range of industrial sectors such as Renault (automobiles), Alcatel (telecommunications), Usinor (steel), and Thomson (electronics).

In Asia, South Korean GLCs such as the Pohang Steel Company (POSCO) and the Industrial Bank of Korea have similarly driven industrialization while Taiwan's early industrialization endeavors during the 1950s were led by state enterprises. In spite of active privatization, by 1990, six of Taiwan's top ten companies, in terms of assets, were GLCs. In Malaysia, at the turn of the century, seven of the top ten publicly listed firms in terms of market capitalization were GLCs, even after the extensive practice of privatization. Similarly in Singapore, where privatization is much promoted, the leading enterprises are GLCs (Tipton 2009). In China, too, despite the perception of the pervasiveness of SOEs, the important group classified as "state-holding enterprises" in which the government has minority ownership but retains control are in fact closer to GLCs than to SOEs.

However, with the exception of China, Asian GLCs' relatively poor presence in manufacturing raises questions about the state's capacity to cultivate large competitive enterprises in this sector. Given the limited presence of their GLCs in the industrial sector, Malaysia and Singapore have heavily cultivated foreign investment to encourage manufacturing. GLCs, however, have shown little ability to deal with foreign firms, with whom joint ventures in the industrial sector were created. It also appears that during the involvement of these GLCs in joint ventures, their primary concern was only with advancing industrialization, not developing entrepreneurial capacity.

Following the crises in Asia in 1997 and in the United States and Europe in 2008, one common outcome has been the need for governments to take over ailing but important economic institutions, in particular major financial enterprises. This has raised concerns of the manner in which GLCs will link with these different types of capital. To assess the reforms required, insights are required into how GLCs can be productively deployed to sustain economic growth. This study involves a historical assessment of the role of GLCs in India, China, Taiwan, South Korea, Malaysia, Poland, and Chile and Brazil.

In this comparative study, an in-depth assessment is provided of the nature of the relationship between political and economic forces in historical perspective, how this shaped the mode of the state's intervention in the economy as well as the outcomes of the links created between governments and different types of business enterprises. There are two dimensions to this study. The first set of chapters assesses the evolution of the roles of GLCs and related state-owned agencies, emerging as major holding companies with a growing domestic and global presence, including as wealth sovereign funds (China, South Korea, Malaysia, Brazil and Chile). The second set of chapters deals with the role of the state in driving industrialization, nurturing key sectors of the economy, and facilitating the development of domestic enterprises, including SMEs (Taiwan, India, Poland). The primary objective in both sets of studies is to assess the roles of GLCs and how they will—or can—function in the post-crisis period.

In this history, specific attention is paid to the mode of development, involving types of economic and social policies created to drive industrialization (see the differences between Brazil and Chile in Chapter 7 of this volume, as well as Poland in Chapter 6 and India in Chapter 1; see also the cases of Taiwan and South Korea in Chapters 3 and 4). This history focuses on key themes such as the *role of government-linked financial institutions*, specifically how the banks, or finance-related public institutions, such as developmental-type banks, were deployed to channel funds to domestic firms to drive industrialization (Taiwan, South Korea, and Malaysia), while also reviewing the development of commercial banking enterprises and their role in the developmental process (Malaysia).

A review of the financial sector, including an assessment of development-based financial institutions and commercial banks, provides important insights into the *links between industrial and financial capital*. This assessment reviews interesting forms of public-private partnerships that were created to drive industrialization or nurture new economic sectors (Brazil and Chile, specifically the differences between the two, as well as Poland, Malaysia, Taiwan, South Korea). This assessment of government institutions includes a review of those that were employed to support domestic firms, specifically SMEs, in terms of providing them with a proper infrastructure and financial incentives to *promote R&D* (India and Taiwan). An evolution of these government institutions allows for an assessment of the changing nature of the relationship between government and business.

The history of the relationship between political and economic forces became more complicated with neoliberal forms of globalization, encouraged by the World Bank, IMF, and the various regional multi-lateral development banks such as the Asian Development Bank, and Latin American Development Bank. This focus on the outcomes of neoliberalism, including privatization, and the emergence of powerful MNCs, helps draw attention to the crucial *role of regulatory institutions*. This history of economic development in industrializing countries reveals the imperative need for regulatory institutions to be given greater autonomy, for relevant new regulations to be introduced, and why corporate governance measures are helpful in ensuring a form of development that is transparent, accountable, and sustainable (South Korea, India, China, Malaysia).

The *role of MNCs* is assessed primarily through global trading and manufacturing production networks that were created (Taiwan, China, Poland). While new forms of capital linkages were created between domestic firms and MNCs, specific GLCs were also creating ties with international firms to foster growth in key sectors of the economy that governments were keen to develop. The role of MNCs in domestic economies through *transnational production linkages*, and in *special economic zones* would emerge as a major mechanism through which industrialization was promoted (China, Taiwan, Malaysia, Poland). The role of the state in creating linkages between MNCs and domestic firms to protect domestic interests as well as nurture SMEs would lead to the practice of subcontracting and outsourcing as major forms of business transactions. Subcontracting and outsourcing as new modes of production would have a major bearing of how labor was employed, indicating the need to review the *role of trade unions*. Much attention is therefore paid to the role of labor—the extent to which trade unions were incorporated into, or bypassed, in these development plans (Poland, South Korea).

Core findings

The nature of the state and social compacts

The crucial point emerging from the country studies is that attention should be paid to *political institutions or key actors* who have much influence or hegemony over the state and GLCs as this provides insights into *decision-making processes* involving new modes of development involving state-owned enterprises. The state can act in a unilateral form (Malaysia, China), while others are subject to numerous checks and balances (South Korea, Brazil and Chile, India), a factor that can hinder or promote genuine reforms of GLCs. Since different developmental preferences exist within every society, the pathway to development that is ultimately chosen is generally in the interests of powerful groups, who provide the necessary financial support, indicating the important need for ownership and control of the state-owned banking sector and finance-based development agencies, seen particularly in the case of Malaysia, Poland, Taiwan, and South Korea. Political reforms, including the rise of democracy, would bring about important institutional restructurings that would lead to greater autonomy for state institutions, though with the simultaneous introduction of vigorous checks and balances in government.

This is vital because even in a democratic system the issue of the "revolving door" looms large. A revolving door involves the practice of key personnel circulating among government ministries and domestic enterprises, contributing to the codification and dissemination of specific knowledge and expertise. This revolving door between the public and private sectors shape official understanding of governance and development (Brazil and Chile, Poland, Malaysia, China). Through a revolving door between business and government agencies, including GLCs, key actors use their mutual public and private ties to benefit personal interests. This blurring of the public and private spheres can transform the state into a broker that represents the interests of private businesses while subordinating its public role. It is for this reason that theories that argue for the superior efficiency of private enterprise over SOEs, such as agency theory and public choice theory, which assume a clear separation between the two sectors, have often not been borne out in practice in many countries.

And what of the role of trade unions in transitions between models of development and mode of governance? Political institutions and their democratic functioning are determinant factors for the development and survival of trade unions. Countries with left-leaning parties and strong unions, particularly Poland, Brazil, South Korea, and India, have shown themselves to be supportive of the welfare of workers. In situations where a strong state is present, the role of unions have been deeply circumscribed, seen specifically in the case of Malaysia and China, inhibiting the capacity of labor to obtain a fair wage and decent working conditions. In the United States, the decline of the welfare state has been attributed to the weak position of the left and the unions (Kymlicka and Banting 2006). What is patent in the country studies is that there has been little support for social compacts involving GLCs, unions, and business. Governments are much more open to public-private ties that involve only state-owned enterprises and private firms. In relation to this, social policy is strictly subordinate to the overriding policy objective of economic growth in most countries though in Malaysia and India they go hand-in-hand, through policies such as affirmative action.

What history does indicate in industrialized East Asian and certain European countries is that social compacts have comprised not just government and business, but also labor. Such compacts have provided for much-needed stability in policy planning and implementation. In Japan, Germany, and the Nordic countries, for example, it was social partnerships between employers, trade unions, and the government that helped them register significant economic progress, provide for social protection measures, and reduce poverty appreciably. In these social compacts to help foster development equitably, the importance of the small firm in terms of promoting innovation, developing industrial capacity, generating employment, and redressing spatial and ethnic inequities have been noteworthy. GLCs have played a role here is helping to nurture such SMEs through the provision of incentives, start-up funding, loans at affordable rates, and creation of domestic and foreign production networks, seen specifically in the case of Taiwan.

However, such public–private arrangements can be problematic. One primary reason for this is that the state is an institution fraught with contradictions, undermining its capacity to serve as a neutral arbiter between competing forces within the corporate sector and society. The professed neutrality of the state has been known to be undermined by the phenomenon of institutional capture, a reason why a neoliberal model of development has led to serious inequities and has proven unsustainable. This suggests that the institutional framework within which incentives are created and distributed should allow under-privileged communities an avenue to participate in decisions that would affect their way of life as well as provide for effective and accountable oversight over the implementation of policies.

Mix and match of policies

A fundamental issue that emerges from this historical review of the evolution of emerging economies is that the development models that were employed were usually a consistent mix of developmental state and neoliberal ideas (China, Malaysia, Poland, Taiwan, South Korea). In this mix of developmental models, important social policies such as affirmative action would play a major role (India, Malaysia). The structure of these hybrid modes of development draws attention to the critical point that development models are not static and are subject to change over time. While India, Malaysia, Taiwan, and South Korea would develop their economies significantly through various forms of state intervention involving GLCs, neoliberal initiatives such as privatization were subsequently introduced (cf. also the case of Poland, where the more important institutions were supported both by the state and by the EU funds). What is significant about these transitions in policy planning, involving the inclusion of neoliberal policies, is not merely that this was in response to serious public sector problems such as mounting debts, persistent budget deficits, inefficiencies in the public delivery system, and a bloated bureaucracy. Equally significant was the orientation of key government leaders about the role of the state as well as a recognition that policies such as privatization could serve as a major mechanism for the practice of patronage or for their desire to develop huge privately owned domestic enterprises through the transfer of GLCs into private hands (Malaysia, China, South Korea).

The promotion of developmental state measures clearly helped drive rapid industrialization, create employment, reduce poverty, and foster the rise of a new middle class, while the introduction of neoliberal policies, including de-regulation of the financial sector, contributed to the ascendancy of capital and growing income and wealth inequalities with immense wealth concentration. The particular importance of a "flexible developmental state", involving this mix of neoliberalism and the developmental state, is closely linked to the concept of a "competition state", one which prioritizes the goal of economic competitiveness over that of social cohesion and welfare. In this situation, social policy has been subordinated to the needs of the economy. Meanwhile, the rise of neoliberalism appears to have coincided with the shift from universalism to targeted based policies (Malaysia, South Korea, India). However, as indicated in Taiwan, with its focus on nurturing SMEs, the emergence of a "developmental network state", where government-business ties are not crony-like linkages, routinized interactions between lower level bureaucrats, engineers of public-funded laboratories, and SMEs can lead to multiple connections that drive R&D and foster innovation. Such networks involve a large segment of society, a process that provides for employment and a constant desire to upgrade production methods.

This lesson provided by Taiwan is crucial as other core outcomes of the impact of neoliberalism on society include a weakened relationship between business, labor, and social protection (Brazil–Chile, South Korea, and a few sectors such as transport and health in regions like Silesia in Poland). The growing emphasis on targeted-based initiatives to control social expenditure led to less social protection, though society has greatly opposed privatization. Such protests have contributed to a transition from top-down statecraft to more social dialogue, an indication of the growing importance of social movements (Poland, Brazil and Chile, Taiwan, South Korea). These transitions have also led to the decline of the influence of techno-bureaucratic elites. In India, from the 1980s, a similar mix between neoliberal policies and developmental state-type policies led to a growing nexus between government and business, with increasing evidence of state capture by capital which influenced policy-making, a factor contributing to growing class inequalities, and grand corruption.

In Malaysia, neoliberal policies were introduced but the government also expressed a commitment to the developmental state model. The outcomes of neoliberalism included a shift from pro-poor to pro-business policies with the growing influence of capital, both domestic and foreign, in terms of policy advice, though given the power of the state, businesses do not have considerable policy-making authority, trends similarly noted in Poland and China. The state continues to maintain close links with trade unions in spite of the introduction of neoliberal policies. The Poland, China, India, and Malaysia cases indicate that there is no simple divide between neoliberalism and the retreat of the state, as the latter can still be involved in the economy in different ways.

Government-linked company ownership, institutional reforms, industrialization

One key lesson from the country studies is that institutions matter. Institutions created by the state have played a major role in driving development, either directly or by fostering industrial-financial linkages (Taiwan, South Korea, Malaysia, Poland). Since institutions remain in place even with regime change or following a crisis, it is the types of incentives offered that vary when a new government comes to power. And with the passage of time and as economies develop, institutional reforms are necessary.

The country studies indicate that how GLCs handle governance, with specific reference to the interface between directors, acting also on the dictates of the government, and senior managers requires thoughtful consideration, with useful lessons emerging from South Korea and Malaysia. Other issues of concern include the appropriate level and nature of involvement of the boards of directors in the management of GLCs, as well as the size, qualifications, and role of the board members. What is clear is that formal mechanisms, such as board meetings, and informal mechanisms employed in pursuing key agendas, are important procedures that should be set in place defining when the board should take on a participatory role in the management of the firm, a point most well noted in the case of Malaysia and South Korea. These factors are important as the relationship between management control and various key issues, such as ownership pattern, the nature of business, and sectoral composition, clearly affect GLC performance. The role of the boards of directors and managerial performance is crucial given their responsibility as custodians of GLCs that have a strong presence in key sectors of the economy, including in finance, services, utilities, and agriculture.

The degree to which strategy demonstrates the influence of the board of directors, at both the policy and business levels, provides insights into the role of the government in directing policy for business development within GLCs. These issues are specially pertinent in the case of GLCs with a major presence in *the financial sector*. The country studies cogently indicate that ownership and control of the financial sector is a crucial determining factor as to how an economy evolves (Malaysia, South Korea, Taiwan). How this sector was employed to promote industrialization and nurture new enterprises determines also the pace of economic growth of a country, suggesting the productive linkages of financial and industrial capital, a factor that can also help alleviate poverty when the focus is on rural industries (Malaysia, South Korea, Taiwan). A distinction between development and commercial banks is important with the former focusing on issues with a social and redistributive bent as opposed to the latter's focus on turning a profit while also funding industrial ventures based on public policy planning.

The theme of institutions is central in the extensive literature relating to the factors affecting GLC performance. The growth of new forms of GLCs, such as China's state-private enterprise hybrids and their conglomeration as enterprise groups under state sponsorship is one example. Important questions need to be answered. Since the form of ownership matters and to ensure GLCs play a proactive role in industrial policy under a developmental state or mixed model, there should be some focus on institutional reforms, a point most persuasively noted in South Korea.

New institutional frameworks have been created in South Korea, Poland, and Chile and Brazil to ensure a more transparent, accountable, and equitable form of development. Through *devolution of power* that has led to greater autonomy, the *quality of public institutions* and their capacity to deliver and institute reforms have improved, including to drive industrialization (South Korea, Taiwan). Such institutional reforms have better enabled the government to regulate or coordinate a system of global production (Poland, Taiwan). Crucially too, the case studies reveal that regulation matters, involving adequate checks and balances in the system to ensure transparency and accountability, a factor that also inspires confidence in investors (Malaysia, South Korea, China).

These institutional reforms have also helped foster government-led R&D by large-scale industrial GLCs, for example, the case of BHEL in India and POSCO in South Korea. In Taiwan, government-funded research-based institutions, such as the Information Technology Research Institute (ITRI), have contributed to R&D that have helped SMEs scale up the technology ladder. The role of government-linked holding companies such as Khazanah in Malaysia is an interesting model of promoting R&D through its control over the management of the its vast base of companies, though it has not been as successful as a centrally coordinated research model of the type seen in Taiwan and India. GLCs such as Khazanah help nurture domestic firms given its control over key banking institutions, a factor that has contributed to industrial-financial linkages. These links have, however, not been effectively groomed, a factor contributing to Malaysia's rather poor investment in R&D, constituting only about 0.95 percent of GDP. In China, the rate is 1.5 percent of GPD while in Japan it is 3.4 percent and in South Korea 3.23 percent. This suggests that in Malaysia the collective role that GLCs can play in promoting industrialization has still not been properly institutionalized. The problem is different in CEE countries. In Poland the liquidation of the former SOEs research potential, the radical reduction of the academy of sciences and the fact that the new foreign investors almost never localized R&D to their new Polish plants led to very weak R&D capability: less than 1 percent of the national budget is dedicated to RD despite the fact that the EU Lisbon strategy and the new EU 2020 target for R&D is 3 percent of the EU budget.

Conclusion

The 2008 financial crisis drew attention to the need to assess and change the nature of the relationship between government and business. However, one core conclusion that can be drawn from the case studies is that, in spite of the lessons of the 2008 crisis, which deeply discredited neoliberalism, there has been some reluctance by government leaders to bring to an end related policies such as privatization. While there is much acknowledgement of the role of GLCs in the post-2008 crisis era, given the enhanced role of the state in the economy, it is evident that powerful forces within the global and domestic economies continue to resist greater regulation, particularly of the financial sector.

The historical perspective adopted here and the country studies provide important lessons on the role of the state in the economy leading up to and immediately after the onset of the 2008 financial crisis. What is clear from the country studies is the variety of forms adopted by government to develop a domestic enterprise base and hence the entire economy, a situation seen in particular in Asia, though also evident in the study comparing Chile and Brazil. The pattern and extent of state intervention in these economies has determined the type of capital that has secured a prominent presence in each country, with big business securing ascendancy in post-authoritarian South Korea and Poland, and in democratic India, though SMEs remain a dominant force in Taiwan, while the state continues, through GLCs, to dominate the economies of Malaysia and China.

The country studies provided insights into the role of GLCs in major economic sectors—services, agriculture, banking, and manufacturing—drawing attention to the themes of governance, strategy, and mode of development. The multiple roles of the state, as facilitator of domestic enterprise, as a key actor in national and transnational perspective, and as a regulator of the conduct of business, is revealed in the country studies. A clear separation of the objectives of GLCs should be considered (i.e., involving redistribution and as profit-making entities). Corporate governance measures, involving the role of the board of directors and the autonomy they have to act without political interference is important. A *viable ownership and control model* that can be employed, for example, a "golden share" or "special share", where the decisions of the board of directors of GLCs can be reviewed by the government if they are deemed not to be in the interest of the nation though of much benefit to the firm and to limit political interference in these important enterprise (as a comparison, see the cases of China and Brazil in Chapters 2 and 7 of this volume; see also Chapters 5 and 6 on Malaysia and Poland).

References

Amable, B. (2004) *The Diversity of Modern Capitalism*. Oxford: Oxford University Press.
Bafoil, F. (2009) *Central and Eastern Europe. Globalization, Europeanisation and Social Change*. New York: Palgrave Macmillan.
Balcerowicz, L. (1995) *Socialism, Capitalism, Transformation*. Budapest: Central European University Press.
Chandler, A. (1990) *Scale and Scope: The Dynamics of Industrial Capitalism*. Cambridge, MA: Harvard University Press.
Chandler, A. (1997) "The United States: Engines of Economic Growth in the Capital-Intensive and Knowledge-Intensive Industries." In A. Chandler, F. Amatori, and Takashi Hikino (eds), *Big Business and the Wealth of Nations*, 63–101. Cambridge: Cambridge University Press.
Gerschenkron, A. (1962) *Economic Backwardness in Historical Perspective*. Cambridge, MA: Harvard University Press.

Gomez, E. T. (ed.) (2002) *Political Business in East Asia*. London: Routledge.
Hall, P. A. and Soskice, D. (2001) *Varieties of Capitalism: The Institutional Foundations of Comparative Advantage*. Oxford: Oxford University Press.
Harvey, D. (2005) *A Brief History of Neoliberalism*. Oxford: Oxford University Press.
Hirschman, A. O. (1958) *The Strategy of Economic Development*. New Haven, CT: Yale University Press.
Johnson, C. (1982) *MITI and the Japanese Miracle: The Growth of Industrial Policy, 1925–1975*. Stanford, CA: Stanford University Press.
Kymlicka, W. and Banting, K. (2006) "Immigration, Multiculturalism, and the Welfare State." *Ethics and International Affairs* 20(3): 281–304.
Nurkse, R. (1961) *Problems of Capital Formation in Underdeveloped Countries*. New York: Oxford University Press.
Orenstein, M. A. (2000) *Out of the Red: Building Capitalism and Democracy in Post-Communist Europe*. Ann Arbor, MI: University of Michigan Press.
Rostow, W. W. (1962) *The Stages of Economic Growth*. London: Cambridge University Press.
Sawyer, S. and Gomez, E. T. (eds) (2012) *The Politics of Resource Extraction: Indigenous Peoples, Multinational Corporations and the State*. Basingstoke: Palgrave Macmillan.
Tipton, F. B. (2009) "Southeast Asian Capitalism: History, Institutions, States, and Firms." *Asia Pacific Journal of Management* 26: 401–34.
Vernon, R. (1998) *In the Hurricane's Eye: The Troubled Prospects of Multinational Enterprises*. Cambridge, MA: Harvard University Press.
Wapshott, N. (2011) *Keynes Hayek: The Clash that Defined Modern Economics*. New York: W. W. Norton.
Williamson, J. (ed.) (1990) *Latin American Adjustment: How Much Has Happened?* Washington, DC: Institute for International Economics.
Williamson, J. (1997) "The Washington Consensus Revisited." In L. Emmerij (ed.), *Economic and Social Development into the XXI Century*, 48–61. Washington, DC: Inter-American Development Bank.
World Bank (1993) *The East Asian Miracle: Economic Growth and Public Policy*. Washington, DC: World Bank.

Notes

1 For a recent discourse on that great debate, see Wapshott (2011).
2 In the CEE, criticism of this model predated the 2008 crisis because unemployment rates rapidly rose above 10 percent in most of these countries by the early 1990s. By 2004, it had reached almost 20 percent in Poland and the Slovak Republic.
3 In the European energy sector, the advantages of the liberalization and privatization were presented by arguing of that the price of energy would decline while there woul be greater transparency and competition in the *operations* of these firms which would provide consumers with more choice. However, while there was a reduction in the cost of energy in the first few years after privatization, the price of this commodity has steadily increased.

1 Economic liberalization and the performance of public sector enterprises in India

Sunil Mani

Introduction

There are two specific ways in which the state can intervene in promoting industrialization in the so-called late industrializing or catch-up countries. The first method is for the state to put in place some framework industrial policies, which would support and encourage the market in its industrializing efforts. The second method is for the state to directly intervene in industrialization by setting up its own enterprises. Most countries have followed a combination of the two methods, as is the case with India.

Since the market was not that well developed in the period immediately following her independence, India has been according a fair amount of importance to state-owned undertakings. In fact, public sector enterprises (PSEs) were supposed to be the "commanding heights of the economy" and were charged with the responsibility of promoting not just industrialization, but also balanced regional development and technological self-reliance in a whole host of especially high technology areas ranging from aerospace to machine tools. However, over time the actual performance of PSEs appears to have fallen short of the high expectations that were placed on them by the state. In fact, this disenchantment has manifested itself with the privatization of public enterprises since 1991. The policy on privatization took on various dimensions such as divestiture, deregulation, and contracting out, although divestiture was by far the most prominent method employed. In this context, the purpose of this chapter is to map out the changing position of public sector enterprises in India's economy by focusing essentially on one of the more important rationale for the establishment of public enterprises, namely domestic technology development. I do this by focusing on one area of technology development, namely heavy electrical equipment which is used for the generation, transmission, and distribution of electric power.

The chapter is structured into three sections. The first section will present a quantitative survey of the changing role of public enterprises in India's economy. The purpose of this section is to analyse the more recent changes in the policy towards PSEs and the effect of these policies on the performance of the sector. The second section will map out the relative roles of public and private sector enterprises in the generation of innovations in India's economy. This will be discussed in terms of a number of conventional innovation indicators such as research and development (R&D) expenditure, and patents. This section will also analyze, briefly, the position of one of India's leading high technology PSEs, namely BHEL. The third and final section will sum up the findings of the study and will distil out the policy conclusions that emanate from my analysis.

Changing role of public sector enterprises in India

Right through Independence, public sector enterprises were assigned the exalted position of "commanding heights of the economy." This manifested itself in terms of several areas of manufacturing and services reserved exclusively for the public sector. However, the recent wave of economic liberalization that has been put into effect, albeit in an unstructured and ad hoc manner, has sought to reduce this premier position of the public sector. This was to be done through a combination of policies aimed at reducing areas reserved exclusively for the public sector coupled with a policy of divestiture (read privatization) that sought to reduce the government's equity in government-controlled companies. Consequent to this, the share of public sector enterprises in India's economy has been reduced to about 8 percent of the country's GDP. But there has been a rise in its share of overall investments, thereby implying declining productivity levels (see Table 1.1). This is contrary to what Nagaraj (2006) had observed for public sector[1] as whole until 2002–3 or so.

However, in terms of growth performance, while the private sector has followed the direction of movement depicted by the growth performance of India's economy, the public sector's performance appears to be following an independent growth path. Out of the five years under consideration, its performance is better than the overall macroeconomic performance only in two years (see Figure 1.1). One of the most important developments affecting public enterprises in India has been the government policy on privatization through essentially the divestiture route. This policy, first articulated in 1991, has undergone a number of minor changes (see Table 1.2 for a chronological documentation of this policy on divestiture.)

Table 1.1 Share of public sector enterprises in gross domestic product (GDP) and gross domestic capital formation

Year	GDP	Investment
2004–5	11%	10.8%
2005–6	10.1%	10.75
2006–7	9.8%	10.5%
2007–8	9.3%	11%
2008–9	8.9%	13.5%
2009-10	8.4%	12.6%

Source: Central Statistical Organization (2011)

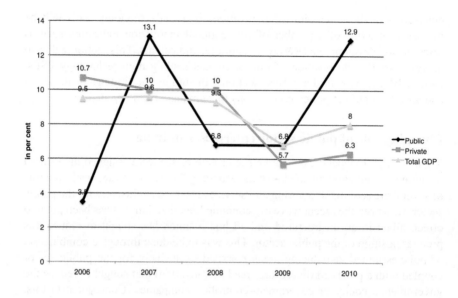

Figure 1.1 Growth performance of public sector enterprises
Source: Central Statistical Organization (2011)

Table 1.2 Evolution of the policy on divestiture since 1991–2

Date	Event
1991–2 Interim Budget	Government announced its intention to divest up to 20% of its equity in selected Central Public Sector Enterprises (CPSEs) in favor of public sector institutional investors.
Industrial Policy statement dated July 24, 1991	In the case of selected enterprises, part of government holdings in the equity share capital of the enterprises will be disinvested in order to provide further market discipline to the performance of public enterprises.
Rangarajan Committee April 1993	It emphasized the need for substantial disinvestment and stated that while the percentage of equity to be divested should not be more than 49% for industries explicitly reserved for the public sector, it should be either 74% or 100% for others.
Budget speech, 1998–9	Government has also decided that in the generality of cases, its shareholding in public sector enterprises will be brought down to 26%. In cases of public sector enterprises involving strategic considerations, the government will continue to retain majority holding. The interest of workers shall be protected in all cases.

Table 1.2 continued

Date	Event
Budget speech, 1999–2000	Government strategy towards public sector enterprises will continue to encompass a judicious mix of strengthening strategic units, privatizing non-strategic ones through gradual disinvestment of strategic sale and devising viable rehabilitation strategies for weak units.
Cabinet decision dated March 16, 1999	CPSEs have been classified into strategic and non-strategic areas for the purpose of disinvestment. Strategic CPSEs would be those in the areas of:
	(a) arms and ammunitions and the allied items of defense equipment, defense air-crafts, and warships;
	(b) atomic energy (except in the areas related to the operation of nuclear power and applications of radiation and radio-isotopes to agriculture medicine and non-strategic industries); and
	(c) railway transport.
	All other CPSEs were to be considered as non-strategic. For the non-strategic CPSEs, it was decided that the reduction of the government stake to 26% would not be automatic. Decision with regard to the percentage of disinvestment (i.e., the government's stake going down to less than 51% or to 26%) would be taken on the following considerations:
	(a) whether the industrial sector requires the presence of the public sector as a countervailing force to prevent concentration of power in private hands; and
	(b) whether the industrial sector requires a proper regulatory mechanism to protect the consumer interest before Public Sector Enterprises are privatized.
Budget speech 2000–2001	Government announced its decision to reduce its stake in the non-strategic PSEs to even below 26%, if necessary. There would be increasing emphasis on strategic sale and the entire proceeds from disinvestment/privatization would be deployed in social sector, restructuring of PSEs and retirement of public debts.
Decision dated June 23, 2000	In order to secure the presence of the public sector as a countervailing force, the government took the decision of not going for disinvestment of GAIL, IOC, and ONGC, and retaining them as flagship companies.
Decision dated September 7, 2002	CPSEs and Central Government-owned Cooperative Societies (where government's ownership is 51% or more) should not be permitted to participate in the disinvestment of other CPSEs as bidder. If in some specific cases any deviation from these restrictions is considered desirable in public interest, the Ministry/Department concerned may bring an appropriate proposal for consideration of the Core Group of Secretaries on Disinvestment.
Budget Speech 2003–4	Details about the already announced Disinvestment Fund and Asset Management company, to hold residual shares post-disinvestment, shall be finalized early in 2003–4.

Table 1.2 continued

Date	Event
Budget Speech 2004–5 (July 2004)	Disinvestment and privatization are useful economic tools. Government will selectively employ these tools, consistent with the declared policy. Government will establish a Board for Reconstruction of Public Sector Enterprises (BRPSE). The Board will advise the Government on the measures to be taken to restructure PSEs, including cases where disinvestment or closure or sale is justified. The disinvestment revenues will be part of the Consolidated Fund of India. While presenting the Budget for 2005–6, report to the House the manner in which the said revenues have been or will be applied for specified social sector schemes.
Decision dated January 27, 2005	(i) Government decided, in principle, to list large, profitable PSEs on domestic stock exchanges and to selectively sell a minority stake in listed, profitable PSEs while retaining at least 51% of the shares along with full management control so as not to disturb the public sector character of the companies. (ii) Government has also decided to constitute a "National Investment Fund" into which the realization from sale of minority shareholding of the government in profitable PSEs would be channelized. The Fund would be maintained outside the Consolidated Fund of India. The income from the Fund would be used for the following broad investment objectives: (a) Investment in social sector projects which promote education, healthcare, and employment. (b) Capital Investment in selected profitable and revivable PSEs that yield adequate returns in order to enlarge their capital base to finance expansion/diversification.
Decision dated November 25, 2005	Government decided, in principle, to list large, profitable CPSEs on domestic stock exchanges and to selectively sell small portions of equity in listed, profitable CPSEs (other than the Navaratnas).

Source: PE Surveys, Ministry of Heavy Industries and Public Enterprises, Government of India (various years)

Privatization of the divestiture route was taken by the state essentially to raise non-inflationary form of revenue for reducing the fiscal deficit. Targets were fixed for each year separately. But the actual divestiture proceeds obtained was woefully short of the targets (see Figure 1.2). Thus, from the fiscal point of view, the privatization efforts in India were clearly not successful. Further, over time the government had sold its equity in its more profitable enterprises thereby reducing the possibility of reducing the dividends and profits that the state could have obtained had it held on to its equity. There exists no systematic evaluation of the divestiture process except for a *White Paper* on it brought out by the

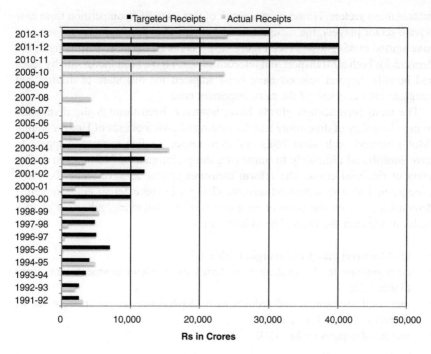

Figure 1.2 Trends in divestiture proceeds in Indian privatization: targets versus actual

Note: 1 crore = 10 million.

Source: www.divest.nic.in/SummarySale.asp (accessed March 8, 2013)

Department of Public Enterprises in 2007. Meanwhile, the performance of most public sector enterprises has actually improved over time. Consider the following facts:

As of March 31, 2012, there were as many as 260 CPSEs (excluding 7 insurance companies). The number of profit making CPSEs increased steadily from 143 CPSEs in 2004–05 to 160 CPSEs in 2007–08. The number of profit making CPSEs as on 2011–12 stands at 161.[2]

Performance of Public Sector Enterprises

Public sector enterprises in India were subjected to two forms of privatization: deregulation and divestiture. Deregulation was the preferred mode, especially for public utilities such as air transport and distribution of telecom services. Due to changes in technology and lowering of barriers to entry, these sectors were opened up to private sector participation. So the public sector incumbents in these sectors were subjected to competition from new private sector enterprises, which entered these sectors. However, as a result of this increased competition from new private sector players, the incumbents in both air transport and telecom services have started making losses (see Figure 1.3). This is all the more surprising as the demand for both air transport and telecom services have been increasing by leaps and bounds. Several reasons have been adduced for this state of affairs, bad management being one of the most important ones.

The main privatization efforts have, however, been through the divestiture route. The policy of divestiture and the signing of a Memoranda of Understanding (MoU) between individual PSEs and their respective line ministries appear to have contributed ultimately to improving the performance of PSEs even during years of financial crisis. The reform measures appear to have made the PSEs stronger and able to withstand adverse changes in the external environment. I demonstrate this on the basis of an analysis of the following indicators of PSE performance over the years. The indicators are:

- total turnover and profit margin (Table 1.3);
- contributions to the exchequer in terms of dividend payments and taxes (Table 1.3);
- increased investment and reductions in dependence on government for its financing (Table 1.4); and
- increased exports (Table 1.4).

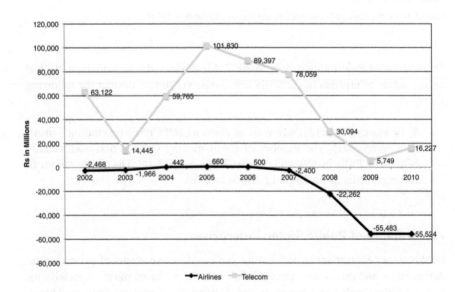

Figure 1.3 Financial performance of deregulated public sector enterprises, 2002–10

Source: PE Surveys, Ministry of Heavy Industries and Public Enterprises, Government of India
(various years)

Table 1.3 Indicators of performance of public sector enterprises (values in Rs crores at current prices)

Year	No. of operating enterprises	Capital employed	Turnover	Profit of profit-making CPSEs	Loss of loss-incurring CPSEs	Profit-making CPSEs (no.)	Loss-incurring CPSEs (no.)	Dividend	Retained profit	Net profit to capital employed (ratio)
2000-1	234	331,372	458,237	28,494	12,841	123	110	8,260	6,551	4.72
2001-2	231	389,934	478,731	36,432	10,454	120	109	8,068	17,902	6.66
2002-3	226	417,160	572,833	43,316	10,972	119	105	13,769	17,382	7.75
2003-4	230	452,336	630,704	61,606	8,522	139	89	15,288	35,835	11.71
2004-5	227	504,407	744,307	74,432	9,003	143	73	20,718	41,394	12.88
2005-6	226	585,484	837,295	76,382	6,845	160	63	22,886	43,435	11.88
2006-7	217	661,338	964,890	89,581	8,526	154	61	26,819	50,129	12.26
2007-8	214	724,009	1,096,308	91,577	10,303	160	54	28,123	48,429	11.21
2008-9	213	792,232	1,271,529	98,488	14,621	158	55	25,501	54,233	10.57
2009-10	217	908,842	1,235,060	108,435	15,842	158	59	33,223	54,220	10.17

Note: 1 crore = 10 million.

Source: PE Surveys, Ministry of Heavy Industries and Public Enterprises, Government of India (various years)

The turnover of the CPSEs has increased at a compound average annual growth rate (CAGR) of 11.6 percent during the period under consideration. During this period, the total number of profit-making CPSEs has increased from 119 in 2002–3 to 158 in 2009–10 and the number of loss-making CPSEs has reduced from 105 in 2002–3 to 59 in 2009–10. At an aggregate level, the CPSEs have recorded an improvement in profitability over the years. On account of increased profitability and scale of operations, CPSEs have recorded considerable increase in contribution to the exchequer by way of dividend payment, interest payment on government loans, and payment of taxes and duties registering a CAGR of 8 percent. However, the overall contribution to the exchequer has declined in the last two years (2008–9 and 2009–10) primarily on account of reduction in contribution towards customs duty which can be attributed to rationalization of duties.

Increased scale of operations and modernization, and adoption of new technology to remain competitive have prompted increased financial investments in PSEs. The cumulative investment (paid-up capital plus long term loans) in all the CPSEs has increased at a CAGR of 8 percent. An assessment of the source of these investments reflect a strategic move by the PSEs to reduce their dependence on central government and increase their reliance on funds from banks and financial institutions as far as financial investments are concerned and internal resources as far as investments in assets are concerned. This in sharp contrast to private sector enterprises, which have been relying on governmental concessions of various sorts, and the tax foregone as a result of these fiscal incentives, now work out to about 18 percent of the corporate income tax collected. See Figure 1.4 for a comparison of the dividends and profits received by the government from public sector enterprises compared to the tax foregone as a result of concessions of various sorts given to the private sector. The PSEs have also managed to maintain their foreign exchange earnings at the same level even during the "crisis" years of 2008 and 2009.

Table 1.4 Trends in financial investments and exports of public sector enterprises (values in Rs thousand crores)

Year	Financial investment	Investments in assets	Foreign exchange earnings
2002–3	333.7 (44.1)	525.3	26.3
2003–4	350 (41.2)	596.7	34.9
2004–5	357.9 (37.8)	649.2	42.3
2005–6	403.7 (36.4)	715.1	46.4
2006–7	420.5 (33.3)	782.7	70.9
2007–8	455.6 (35.6)	862.2	74.3
2008–9	513.5 (30.7)	978.2	74.2
2009–10	579.9 (27.0)	1129.9	77.7

Notes: 1 crore = 10 million. Figures in parentheses indicate central government's share in percentage of these financial investments.

Source: PE Surveys, Ministry of Heavy Industries and Public Enterprises, Government of India (various years)

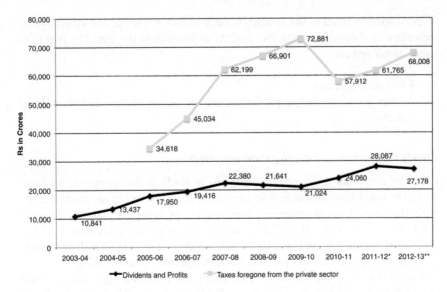

Figure 1.4 Dividends and profits received from public sector enterprises compared with taxes foregone

Note: 1 crore = 10 million.

Source: Union budget, Ministry of Finance, Government of India (various years)

Although admittedly brief, my analysis indicates that the PSEs have improved their performance over the years and the financial crisis does not seem to have affected them that much. This finding is very significant in the sense that despite severe pressure on them in terms of increasing globalization of India's economy and the deregulation that has subjected the PSEs to a fair amount of competition, they have managed to not only withstand it but also improve their performance.

An important aspect of the rationale for establishing a series of PSEs was to hasten the process of technological catching-up that India wanted to do with the West and especially to implement the avowed objective of a planned form of development with technological self-reliance. Although more than six decades have passed, there has not been a systematic inquiry of the role of PSEs in the generation of innovations in the country. I now attempt to analyze this role of public enterprises, first at the macro level, and subsequently at the micro level by taking the case of one specific high technology enterprise, namely the heavy electrical equipment manufacturer, BHEL.

Role of public sector enterprises in generation of innovations

The purpose of this section is to understand the relative roles of public and private sector enterprises in the performance of innovative activity in India. In measuring this I employ two of the conventional indicators for measuring the generation of innovation in India as the country is yet to develop a set of non-conventional indicators as obtained through the conduct of innovation surveys. The two indicators employed are:

- R&D statistics; and
- patents granted to Indian public and private sector enterprises both in India and abroad.

Trends in research and development investments

I start by analyzing the overall investments in R&D in the country as a whole. Trends in R&D investments both at constant and current prices are tracked along with the overall gross domestic expenditure on research and development (GERD)[3] to GDP ratio. Both the nominal and real growth rates have declined since 1991 and the overall research intensity of the country has virtually remained constant during the pre- and post-liberalization periods, at about 0.78.[4]

Care has to be exercised while interpreting these figures, specifically as this means that the overall investments in R&D have actually declined. This is because of certain peculiarities with respect to India's R&D performance. Even now the government accounts for over 63 percent of the total R&D performed within the country although the share of government has tended to come down over time (Mani 2010). This has been accompanied by an increase in R&D investments by business enterprises which now account for about 30 percent, a significant increase from just 14 percent in 1991 (for China, the similar percentage is about 71 percent by business enterprises and research institutes (read government) account for only 19 percent). Increase in the share of R&D performed by business enterprises is generally considered to be a desirable trend as they tend to implement or commercialize the results of their research more quickly than the government sector where much of the research does not translate into products and processes for the country as a whole.[5]

Reducing role of public sector enterprises in research and development performance

Most countries organize their data on R&D according to the norms laid down in the *Frascati Manual*, a two-way classification of R&D expenditure according to sector performance and financing available. However, in the case of India such a two-way classification of R&D data is not prepared and so what we have is only a breakdown according to sector performance. Based on this, I had already noted that the share of industrial R&D is performed by three different sectors, namely public and private sector enterprises, and government research institutes (read as CSIR laboratories in the Indian case). Between these three components, the most important one from the point of view of performance of industrial R&D is private sector enterprises. These enterprises have increased their R&D investments considerably during the post-liberalization period. As will be argued below, this is to a large extent due to the

increased competition faced by the firms in certain specific industries such as pharmaceutical and automotive industries as these industries account for a significant
proportion of the R&D investments in the industrial sector.

It is interesting to note that the share of PSEs, dominated by a number of large
high- and medium-tech enterprises, have steadily declined over time. Considerable
technological capability was built in some of these public enterprises and it will be
instructive to find out as to what has happened to these capabilities in the post-
liberalized phase. For instance, PSEs such as BHEL and HMT had built
considerable innovation capability (being able to conceptualize, design, manufacture and sell state-of-the art equipment) in their respective technologies or
domains, but nothing much is known about these capabilities at present except that
there has been an absolute growth in the R&D expenditures, especially of PSEs
under the ownership of the central government (see Table 1.5). Average R&D
expenditure per enterprise has shot up by as much as 107 percent since liberalization and between 2008 and 2009 there were 64 firms (out of a possible 220)
investing at least Rs 1 lakh in R&D compared with just 47 in 1992–3.

How does this compare with private sector enterprises? Given that an average
private sector enterprise is much smaller in size (in terms of sales or employment)
compared to an average public sector enterprise, a straightforward comparison of
the relative investments in R&D would be meaningless. So I compare the research
intensities (R&D expenditure as a percent of sales turnover) of these two groups
(see Figure 1.5). Both groups spent less than a percent of their respective sales
turnover on R&D although the average research intensity of private enterprises is
almost double that of PSEs for all the years under consideration. So it is not just
in terms of share that the private sector in India expends more but also in terms of
research intensity, while their commitment of financial resources to R&D is significantly higher than that of PSEs. Two important policy changes may explain this
apparent better performance. First is the desire for private sector to invest more in
in-house R&D, as during this period, the market for disembodied technologies had
become rather imperfect (Mani 2002) and therefore the licensing of proprietary
technologies had become extremely difficult. Technology licensing is increasing,
possible only within a large MNC, between the parent firm and its affiliate abroad.
So if you are an unaffiliated company in India or in the South, your chances of
entering into a technology licensing contract are much less in the period since the
1990s. Consequently, firms in both the private and public sectors have no other
alternative but to increase their investments in in-house R&D efforts. Second,
privatization of the divestiture variety has in some sense unsettled decision-
making in public enterprises, especially in strategic areas such as issues related to
technology acquisition. This is reflected in some of the major public sector R&D
spenders such as the telecommunications enterprise, ITI, paying far less attention
to domestic technology development. However, one leading PSE, BHEL, continued to maintain its R&D investments and even increased it substantially. BHEL
also leads in patent applications, which is a measure of output of its R&D efforts.

The veracity of this trend of private sector enterprises leading in R&D investments and in intensity has been questioned on the grounds that businesses

Table 1.5 Research and development expenditure of central public sector enterprises, 1992–3 and 2008–9 (values in Rs lakhs)

Enterprise	1992–3	Enterprise	2008–9
1 Hindustan Aeronautics Ltd	63,583	1 Bharat Heavy Electricals Ltd	69,001
2 Steel Authority of India Ltd	4,466	2 Hindustan Aeronautics Ltd	67,478
3 I T I Ltd	3,637	3 Bharat Electronics Ltd	24,333
4 Bharat Electronics Ltd	3,532	4 Oil & Natural Gas Corporation Ltd	20,750
5 HMT Ltd	939	5 Steel Authority of India Ltd	11,820
6 Projects & Development India Ltd	815	6 Indian Oil Corpn Ltd	11,750
7 Indian Oil Corporation Ltd	677	7 BEML Ltd	3,198
8 Bharat Heavy Electricals Ltd	583	8 Bharat Petroleum Corpn Ltd	3,024
9 Central Electronics Ltd	569	9 I T I Ltd	2,812
10 Electronics Corpn. Of India Ltd	559	10 Electronics Corpn. Of India Ltd	2,423
11 Semi-Conductor Complex Ltd	500	11 National Mineral Development Corporation	2,095
12 Engineers India Ltd	389	12 Nuclear Power Corpn of India Ltd	1,989
13 National Mineral Development Corporation	387	13 Oil India Ltd	1,821
14 Hindustan Antibiotics Ltd	377	14 Hindustan Petroleum Corpn Ltd	1,436
15 Bharat Dynamics Ltd	294	15 South Eastern Coalfields Ltd	1,387
16 Central Mine Planning & Design	286	16 Bharat Dynamics Ltd	943
17 Balmer Lawrie & Co. Ltd	257	17 NTPC Ltd	926
18 Hindustan Petroleum Corporation Ltd	153	18 Engineers India Ltd	811
19 Oil India Ltd	146	19 Central Electronics Ltd	752
20 Hindustan Photo Films Manufacturers Ltd	125	20 Neyveli Lignite Corpn Ltd	603
21 Hindustan Insecticides Ltd	106	21 Chennai Petroleum Corporation Ltd	562
22 Hindustan Cables Ltd	106	22 Dredging Corpn of India Ltd	433
23 IBP Co Ltd	87	23 Goa Shipyard Ltd	378
24 Instrumentation Ltd	82	24 National Aluminum Company Ltd	348
25 Power Grid Corporation of India	66	25 Balmer Lawrie & Co. Ltd	271
26 Manganese Ore(India) Ltd	63	26 Cochin Shipyard Ltd	200
27 Rashtriya Chemicals and Fertilizers Ltd	63	27 Uranium Corporation of India Ltd	186
28 Bharat Heavy Plates & Vessels Ltd	59	28 Manganese Ore(India) Ltd	167
29 GAIL (India) Ltd	56	29 Rashtriya Chemicals and Fertilizers Ltd	167
30 Uranium Corporation of India Ltd	49	30 Indian Rare Earths Ltd	161
31 Fertilizers & Chemicals (Travancore) Ltd	48	31 HMT Ltd	142
32 Bharat Petroleum Corpn Ltd	44	32 HMT Machine Tools ltd	136
33 Hindustan Organic Chemicals Ltd	44	33 Rajasthan Electronics and Instruments Ltd	131
34 Rajasthan Electronics and Instruments Ltd	35	34 Kudremukh Iron Ore Co Ltd	97

Table 1.5 continued

Enterprise		1992–3	Enterprise		2008–9
35	Andrew Yule & Company Ltd	30	35	Bharat Refractories Ltd	90
36	Sponge Iron India Ltd	21	36	Hindustan Latex Ltd	89
37	Praga Tools Ltd	21	37	Nepa Ltd	85
38	NTPC Ltd	19	38	Mangalore Refinery and Petrochemicals Ltd	80
39	Cement Corpn of India Ltd	16	39	Hindustan Photo Films Manufacturers Ltd	76
40	Heavy Engineering Corpn Ltd	12	40	Eastern Coalfields ltd	61
41	Hindustan Latex Ltd	9	41	Airports Authority of India Ltd	61
42	Bridge & Roof Co (India) Ltd	5	42	Housing & Urban Dev Corpn Ltd	56
43	Hindustan Newsprint Ltd	5	43	Bharat Heavy Plates & Vessels Ltd	55
44	Sambhar Salts Ltd	3	44	Power Grid Corporation of India Ltd	50
45	Burn Standard Company Ltd	3	45	Hindustan Paper Corpn Ltd	46
46	Hindustan Copper Ltd	1	46	Scooters India Ltd	45
47	Hindustan Salts Ltd	1	47	Karnataka Antibiotics & Pharmaceutical Ltd	44
			48	Hindustan Cables Ltd	40
Total		*83,328*	49	Fertilizers & Chemicals (Travancore) Ltd	36
Average per enterprise		*1,773*	50	BEL Optronics Devices Ltd	34
			51	Mecon Ltd	32
			52	Hindustan Newsprint Ltd	26
			53	FCI Aravali Gypsum & Minerals India Ltd	23
			54	Biecco Lawrie & Co Ltd	20
			55	NHPC Ltd	15
			56	Sponge Iron India Ltd	13
			57	Burn Standard Company Ltd	12
			58	Bridge & Roof Co (India) Ltd	9
			59	Andrew Yule & Company Ltd	7
			60	Heavy Engineering Corpn Ltd	6
			61	Hindustan Salts Ltd	2
			62	Bengal Chemicals & Pharmaceuticals Ltd	2
			63	Hindustan Insecticides Ltd	1
			64	Artificial Limbs Mfg. Corpn of India Ltd	1
			Total		*233,848*
			Average per enterprise		*3,654*

Note: 1 lakh = 100,000.

Source: PE Surveys, Ministry of Heavy Industries and Public Enterprises, Government of India (various years)

reporting R&D expenditure to the Department of Science and Technology may be tempted to exaggerate such expenditure to obtain tax incentives available in India for any business investing in R&D. These tax incentives are linked to the volume

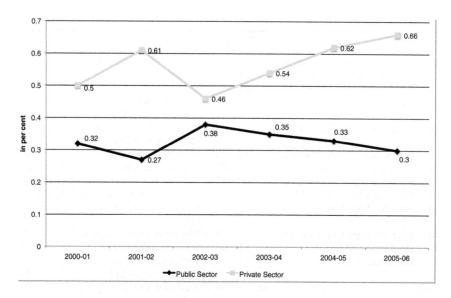

Figure 1.5 Average research intensity in public and private sector enterprises, 1998–9 to 2005–6

Source: Department of Science and Technology (2009)

of R&D performed; hence the temptation to overstate it. However, this suspicion is unfounded. In order to verify this proposition, a comparison was made of R&D investment as reported by the Department of Science and Technology with the dataset available from the Centre for Monitoring the Indian Economy's Prowess for the period 1991–2003. This comparison shows that although the level reported by the Department of Science and Technology is higher over most of the years under consideration than in the early 1990s, the difference has tended to decrease over time. Moreover, both series have gone in a similar direction. The argument that the increase in R&D expenditure by private companies is a mere statistical artefact would is thus not true.

Within the industrial sector, four industries account for the lion's share of investment in R&D, with the pharmaceutical and automotive industries being the biggest spenders on R&D. In fact, it has been said that India's national system of innovation is led by the sectoral system of innovation of the pharmaceutical industry.

Trends in patents

India has improved its patenting record in the United States, with acceleration over the past decade. Most Indian patents are utility patents, defined as those for new inventions. However, most of these patents are in chemistry-related areas and most are being granted to foreign companies located in India, based on R&D projects they have carried out in the country, a growing trend (Mani 2010). Similarly, the number of national patents granted by the India Patent Office has increased tremendously but over three-quarters of these patents are still granted to foreign entities. Once again, most of these patents concern chemistry and pharmaceutical-related areas. Although the TRIPS (Agreement on Trade Related Intellectual Property Rights) compliance of the Indian Patents Act appears to have had a positive effect on patenting by Indian inventors, most of the patents granted to Indian inventors, both in India and abroad, are going to foreign companies.

In terms of ownership of these patents, among the domestic inventors, CSIR continues to be at the top (Table 1.6) although its rate of patenting in the United States, after reaching a peak, has fallen since 2007. Among domestic Indian enterprises, a group that is dominant in patenting are those in the pharmaceutical

Table 1.6 Domestic assignees of Indian patents at the United States Patent and Trademark Office, 2005–9 (cumulative number of utility patents granted)

First named assignee		Cumulative 2005–9
1	CSIR	462
2	Dr Reddy's Laboratories Limited	34
3	Ranbaxy Laboratories Limited	26
4	Cipla Limited	16
5	Wockhardt Limited	16
6	Sasken Communication Technologies Limited	15
7	Indian Oil Corporation Limited	14
8	Lupin Limited	14
9	Orchid Chemicals & Pharmaceuticals Limited	14
10	Biocon Limited	13
11	Reliance Life Sciences Private Limited	12
12	Sun Pharmaceuticals Industries Limited	12
13	Ittiam Systems Private Limited	11
14	Tata Consultancy Services Limited	10
15	AurobindoPharma Limited	9
16	Ipca Laboratories Limited	8
17	Satyam Computer Services Limited	8
18	Dabur Research Foundation	7
19	Galaxy Surfactants Limited	7
20	Glemmark Pharmaceuticals SA	7
21	United Phosphorus Limited	7
22	Alembic Limited	6
23	Bharat Heavy Electricals Limited	6
24	Glemmark Pharmaceuticals Limited	6
25	Cadila Healthcare Limited	5
26	Dabur India Limited	5
27	Indian Institute of Technology	5
28	Jubilant Organosys Limited	5

Source: Compiled from the United States Patent and Trademark Office (USPTO)

sector, all of which are in the private sector. However, since 2006, six of India's leading private sector pharmaceutical companies have been taken over by foreign multi-national companies (MNCs) and as such ownership of the patents held by these companies is now very much in foreign hands. Only two of the PSEs are active in patenting in the United States, namely Indian Oil Corporation and BHEL. Both firms dominate in public sector enterprise R&D investments as well.

Patenting in India

Historically speaking, much of the patenting at the Indian Patent Office[6] (IPO) has been by MNCs. While this continues to be the case, a sort of shift has occurred since the mid-1990s although it must be added that the share of domestic inventors in Indian patenting has been fluctuating since this period and a very clear trend is not visible. Nevertheless, the increasing share of domestic inventors may be the effect of the impending TRIPS compliance of the Indian Patents Act, although this proposition requires careful empirical scrutiny before firm conclusions can be drawn. Table 1.7 summarizes the data on Indian applicants in the IPO. A few comments are in order before analyzing the data. First, the data available is for only one year, 2008–9, as the IPO was not publishing this level of disaggregation earlier. Second, it refers to applications and not grants as the IPO publishes data on applications only at the disaggregated level.

Once again, it confirms the picture that emerged from the analysis of the United States Patent and Trademark Office (USPTO) data contained in Table 1.6. Patenting at home and abroad is dominated by public sector entities although the share of PSEs is high only at the IPTO. Second, among manufacturing enterprises, with the exception of BHEL, the one sector or industry that dominates the patenting scene in India is the pharmaceutical sector.

Box 1.1 BHEL: the "most innovative company in India"

BHEL is one of the largest PSEs in India, with a turnover of US$ 9.6 billion. The company won the award for the most innovative company in India under the "high-technology corporates" category at the 2010 Thomson Reuters Innovation Awards. The award is based on three indicators: patent volumes, impact of patents, and efficiency and effectiveness of research.

Established in 1964, BHEL was charged with the explicit responsibility of designing and manufacturing heavy electrical equipment industry in the country. The products from the company cater to the core sectors of India's economy, namely power generation and transmission, transportation, and renewable energy. BHEL has been promoted as a success story of how a developing country can in a massive way design and build heavy electrical equipment to supply its needs and avoid technological dependency and foreign exchange loss (Ramamurti 1987; Surrey 1987). The enterprise manufactures 180 different types of products in 15 manufacturing divisions

Table 1.7 Patent applications by Indian inventors at the Indian Patent Office, 2008–9

Inventor	Number of applications
CSIR	165
Dr Reddy's Laboratories	147
BHEL	119
Ranbaxy Laboratories	101
IIT	91
Infosys technologies	81
Avesthagen	66
Tata Steel	65
Cadilla Healthcare	57
Matrix Laboratories	54
ICAR	35
Amity University	33
SAIL	31
Lupin Limited	30
Orchid Chemicals and Pharmaceuticals	22
AurobindoPharma	22
Jubilant Organosys	21
Indian Institute of Science	21
Ind-Swift Laboratories	19
Imylan Development Centre	17
Panacea Biotech	15
Tata Elxsi	14
Apex Labs	13
Rubicon Research	12
Central Institute of Research on Cotton	12
Tata Consultancy Services	11
ISRO	11
National Institute of Pharmaceutical Education and Research	8
National Institute of Immunology	7
University of Delhi	7
S N Bose National Centre	7
Thiagarajar College of Engineering	6
Rajendra Kumar Khare	5
Punjab Agricultural University	4
Total applications	1,329

Source: Controller General of Patents, Designs, Trade Marks and Geographical Indications (2010: 14–16)

spread across India, and also has a joint venture with two MNCs (GE and Siemens) to manufacture gas turbines and for effecting power plant improvements.

In 2012, about 74 percent of the electricity generated in India and about 80 percent of the nuclear power generated were through BHEL-designed and manufactured generation sets. With 1,438 patents to its credit, both domestically and abroad, BHEL has the distinction of being one of the most innovative companies in India. The company has also executed, success-fully, a number of power plant projects abroad and is considered to be one of the few MNCs from the PSE sector. The enterprise has one of the high-est research intensities among PSEs, of about 1.62 percent, over the last ten years or so. Also, for every Rs 1 crore that it has spent on R&D, it has managed to secure a sale of Rs 7 crores out of this R&D investment. Sales out of R&D contributed to about 18 percent of its sales during 2010–11 (see Table 1.8).

Table 1.8 Technological performance of BHEL

Year	Total R&D expenditure (Rs crores)	R&D expenditure as % of turnover	Sales credited through R&D (Rs crores)	Number of patents
2001–2	87	1.19	613	
2002–3	82	1.09	528	
2003–4	104	1.2	591	
2004–5	125	1.21	942	
2005–6	152	1.05	1,152	84
2006–7	253	1.35	2,720	
2007–8	464	2.17	2,982	175
2008–9	690	2.46	5,571	
2009–10	829	2.43	6,723	
2010–11	982	2.27	7,809	91

Note: 1 crore = 10 million.

Source: BHEL annual reports (various years), available at
www.bhel.com/financial_information/index.php (accessed March 8, 2013)

In 2010–11, BHEL filed 303 patents and copyrights, enhancing the company's intellectual capital to, as stated above, 1,438 patents and copy-rights filed, which are in productive use in the company's business. Currently, 532 patents and copyrights are in force. As of June 30, 2011, BHEL had cumulatively installed generating capacity of over MW 8,500 outside of India in 21 countries, including Malaysia, Iraq, UAE, Egypt, and New Zealand, and had approximately MW 5,200 in 19 countries under vari-ous stages of execution.

Some conclusions can now be drawn about domestic technology generation in India. Two indicators were used for measuring this activity, namely an input indi-cator such as R&D investments and an output indicator such as patents. After examining the trends in both these indicators, I am of the opinion that although private sector enterprises dominate in the performance of R&D, in terms of output the public sector is the one that dominates. This suggests that the productivity of R&D investments in the public sector is actually higher than in the private sector as one rupee of R&D investments in the public sector leads to more patents than an equivalent amount of R&D investments in the private sector.

Conclusion

This chapter analyzed policy changes with regard to PSEs in India as part of the government's desire to reduce its presence in industrial activities. This policy manifested itself in terms of paring down areas reserved exclusively for PSEs and in divesting the government's shareholding in a number of these enterprises and subjecting them to the discipline of the market mechanism. The PSEs appear to have come out very strongly in this process. For the group as a whole, both financial and technological performance have shown some significant improvements and the PSEs now rely considerably less on government sources for their investment and growth than they did about a decade ago. This robust performance has allowed them to withstand the negative effects of the recent global financial crisis.

While across the world the 2008 financial crisis has dented one's faith in the private sector, the remarkable performance of India's PSEs is a source of great solace to policy makers. However this rosy picture hides, to some extent, some of the weaknesses that the sector suffers from. One of these is in the area of technology and innovations. While PSEs such as BHEL are an outlier of sorts in terms of spearheading innovations, a large number of PSEs, especially those engaged in the distribution of services such as telecommunications, are much in need of having a clearer technological strategy. For instance, while the market for telecommunications equipment has increased significantly, the leading telecom equipment manufacturing enterprise is on the verge of closure. This is an area where public policy can still play an important role.

Acknowledgements

An earlier version of the chapter was presented at the international conference on "The State's Return to Business: Government-Linked Companies in the Post-Crisis Global Economy" at Siem Reap, Cambodia, February 9–10, 2012. I am grateful to the participants at this seminar, and especially to Terence Gomez, for helpful comments. However, the usual disclaimer holds good.

Notes

1   The public sector as a whole consists of (i) administration, (ii) departmental undertakings, and (iii) non-departmental commercial undertakings. It is the latter that I refer to as public sector enterprises. In the present study, I am confining myself to only public sector enterprises under the ownership of the central government.
2   See www.bsepsu.com/public-sector.asp (accessed 30 September 2013).
3   GERD is the overall investment in R&D in the country as a whole. Studies have shown that there is a positive correlation between GERD-to-GDP ratio and overall macroeconomic performance of a country as measured by rate of growth of GDP.

4   For China, the GERD-to-GDP ratio has actually increased to reach 1.42 percent by 2006. See Department of Science and Technology (2009).
5   Governmental R&D in India is primarily focused on the atomic energy, defense, space, health, and agricultural sectors. The spill-over of government research to civilian use is very much limited in the Indian context although in more recent times there has been a change following conscious efforts made by the government to produce results. This is especially so in the area of space research.
6   The official name of the Indian Patent Office is "Controller General of Patents, Designs and Trademarks, and Geographical Indications." Administratively it functions under the Department of Industrial Policy and Promotions, Ministry of Commerce and Industry.

References

Central Statistical Organization (2011) *National Accounts Statistics 2011*. Delhi: Ministry of Statistics and Programme Implementation.

Controller General of Patents, Designs, Trade Marks, and Geographical Indications (2010) *Annual Report 2008–9*. Available at http://ipindia.gov.in/cgpdtm/AnnualReport_English_2008_2009.pdf (accessed March 8, 2013).

Department of Science and Technology (2009) *R&D Statistics 2007–8*. Delhi: National Science and Technology Management Information System (NSTMIS), Government of India.

Mani, S. (2002) *Government, Innovation and Technology Policy: An International Comparative Analysis*. Cheltenham: Edward Elgar.

Mani, S. (2010) "Are Innovations on the Rise in India since the Onset of Reforms of 1991? Analysis of its Evidence and Some Disquieting Features." *International Journal of Technology and Globalization* 5(1–2): 5–42.

Nagaraj, R. (2006) "Public Sector Performance since 1950: A Fresh Look." *Economic and Political Weekly* (June 24): 2551–7.

Ramamurti, R. (1987) *State-Owned Enterprises in High Technology Industries: Studies in India and Brazil*. New York: Praeger.

Surrey, J. (1987) "Electric Power Plant in India: A Strategy of Self-Reliance." *Energy Policy* (December): 503–21.

2 The Chinese state, state enterprises, and the global crisis

Kee-Cheok Cheong, Li Ran, and Zhang Miao

Introduction: perceptions of the Chinese state

China's emergence as an economic power has brought increased scrutiny of the manner of its rise. That this rise has relied on state power and is at variance with the approach favored and followed by advanced countries has led to criticism of the state and its institutions over which it exercises authority through ownership or control.

Criticism leveled at the Chinese state takes two forms. The first is that its political order of authoritarian rule is unsustainable and will ultimately be overtaken by forces for democratization. Thus, Pei (2006) notes: "if current trends continue, China's political system is more likely to experience decay than democracy ... the very policies that the party adopted ... are compounding the political and social ills that threaten its long-term survival." The second is that authoritarianism cannot coexist with a true market economy. Hence, efforts to graft Western institutions onto an authoritarian structure also will not succeed. For instance, Chang (2010) concluded that: "China cannot make much progress toward (the rule of law), at least as long as the Communist Party is around." The second criticism, by extension, challenges the efficacy of China's numerous state enterprises, which have historically played a major role in the economy, and they need to be reformed through privatization or liquidation (see, for instance, Lall 2006).[1]

Yet China's experience to date has defied these predictions. It had achieved rapid economic growth for over three decades, through a model of growth that, though not quite approaching that of the developmental state, can nevertheless be described as state-led. State enterprises are at the heart of this model. But the onset of the global financial crisis has put this model to a severe test. What impact does this crisis have on state enterprises and how has their role changed?

We argue that this paradox of strong economic growth against a background of an extensive state role can only be explained by incorporating its historical and cultural context. This helps us to better assess the role of China's state enterprises, which have been subject to much experimentation and undergone extensive reforms. We examine these enterprises' ownership and governance structures, and then consider the impact of state enterprises on the Chinese economy. The implications of the global financial crisis for Chinese state enterprises are reviewed, followed by a brief case study of the state-owned bank, the Bank of China.

The Chinese state and society in historical context

The Chinese state predates by millennia the conceptualization and emergence of the now dominant nation state. Although bearing a close resemblance to a nation state, and despite transitions from imperial rule through republicanism, Leninism and to the "market socialism" of today, all within a century, the modern Chinese state is the outcome of centuries of evolution. Kuhn (2002: 1) argued that this state has been "shaped decisively by the flow of its internal history," although external models of governance have left their mark. Nevertheless, the Chinese state remains more the product of its own history than of foreign influences.

What are the salient characteristics of this indigenously evolved state? First, its prime objectives, as stated by Jacques (2011: 2), are defense of the realm and guardianship of its civilization, and its people, including economic moderniza-tion, and society transformation. These objectives, together with the need to modernize post-Qing dynasty China, give the state a far larger role than that of a nation state.[2] This role is reinforced by China's modern history, in which the chaos that reigned just after the establishment of the 1911 republic could only be solved by strong leadership backed by the apparatus of the state (Zhou Guanghui 2000). Second, the relationship between the state and Chinese society is much closer than in Western societies. Indeed, the state is at the apex of an orderly hier-archy in which layers of society make up the rest of the pyramid. Not only is there no mutual exclusivity between state and society, the state, a product of, and deriv-ing its strength from Confucian thinking for much of China's history, is very much part of society, deriving its authority from its missions above (Li 1997).

That the Chinese state, viewed in its historical context, is materially different from what the West believes to be the Weberian norm for a modern state should lead us, first, to question the belief that China's future depends on its convergence to Western norms of state and governance. The assimilation of new concepts of state governance is not necessarily a wholesale endorsement of these concepts but rather responses to adapt to a changing world, and consistent with what China has done throughout history. The Chinese state remains, to borrow from Kissinger (2012: 5) "singularly" Chinese, defined by its long history and cultural identity. Second, China's missions for its state imply a role that goes well beyond what is expected of a nation state.[3] Hence, from a historical perspective, neither the size of the state sector nor the Chinese model of state-led growth, also referred to as state capitalism, should surprise. These salient features must be borne in mind as we examine the magnitude and role of state enterprises.

From state-controlled to state-led: the changing role of state enterprises

China's state enterprises have undergone major transformation as the economy underwent economic transition from a command economy to one now described as market socialism. Before 1978, the State exercised centralized control over the entire economy, and all enterprises were state-owned. Dong and Putterman (2003:

112) estimated that state enterprises accounted for three-quarters of China's industrial output, employed two-thirds of all industrial employees, and were responsible for their welfare (e.g. pensions and housing). They also contributed 90 percent of all fiscal revenues during the period. Not surprisingly, lack of incentives left these enterprises performing poorly.

Hence, one of the first orders of business after 1978 was for the central government to enlarge state enterprises' management autonomy. Regulations by the State Council in 1984 separated the enterprise from the state, while the implementation of the contract responsibility system in 1987 granted state enterprises power to sell their output over and above assigned quotas and responsibility for their profits and losses (Wang 2004). Simultaneously, price reform gave state enterprises power to set prices above the planned price. Ownership reform saw equitization of state enterprises and the establishment of the Shanghai and Shenzhen stock exchanges in 1985 and 1987 respectively.

These reforms notwithstanding, managers lacked the autonomy to dismiss workers, so that large labor redundancies burdened already loss-making state enterprises with losses so large that the government had to take action (see, for instance, Mako and Zhang 2003).[4] This response took the form of State Council regulations in 1992 that gave state enterprises more rights in setting prices and wages, but more crucially of hiring and firing workers. A tax reform law passed in 1994 allowed state enterprises to retain a substantial proportion of their profits. In effect, these regulations gave SOEs more autonomy from the State (Wang 2004).

The reform strategy also shifted to retaining only the largest state enterprises while "releasing" the small ones (*zhua da, fang xiao*) through sale, privatization or closure.[5] To reduce their debt burden, state enterprises laid off an estimated 3.6 million workers between 1995 and 1997 (Zhou Haoming 2000: 2). Further, with corporatization and shareholding reform in 1999 that led to listing on international stock exchanges, a clean set of books without all the social costs was needed, together with retention of all income by the listed enterprise (Walter 2010: 96). In 2003, the State-Owned Asset Supervision and Administration Commission (SASAC) was established to represent the state as owner and to supervise the retained large state enterprises (*yangqi*). In 2005 non-tradable shares were converted into tradable shares that could be traded in the share markets to attract private capital.

As major institutions of state that are both instruments of policy and providers of funding to state and non-state enterprises, China's financial institutions also underwent reform. But reforms went beyond those discussed above to include those specific to the financial sector. Begun in 1984, when the People's Bank of China (PBC) spun off its commercial bank functions, financial reform saw, in 1994, the transformation of the Industrial and Commercial Bank of China, the Bank of China, the Agricultural Bank of China, and the China Construction Bank transformed into state-owned commercial banks; and three policy-related banks, the Agricultural Development Bank of China, the National Development Bank, and the China Import and Export Bank created. Until this occurred the only role of banks was to serve as windows for fiscal expenditure. Fiscal expenditure, not banks, financed development. Thus, bank lending to state enterprises were effectively state subsidies that ended up as bad loans in the banks' books.

Regulatory reform took the form of the establishment of the State Council Securities Commission (abolished in 1998) and China Securities Regulatory Commission (CSRC) in 1992, and the China Banking Regulatory Commission in 2003. However, important as effective regulation was, it could not deal with the large amounts of non-performing loans (NPLs) from state-directed lending to loss-making state enterprises which were not serviced. These NPLs, together with the Asian Financial Crisis, led China to recapitalize state-owned banks through four asset management companies in 2000.

The next phase of reforms saw the courting of foreign strategic investors through public listing in Hong Kong in 2005–6, and the setting up of foreign bank branches in China in December 2006, in line with China's stated commitment upon its accession to the World Trade Organization in 2001. The former required the adoption of international governance benchmarks (see the Bank of China discussion later in this chapter) while the latter was expected to entrench the application of these standards by bringing international competition to the banks' doorsteps. Although weaknesses remained (IMF 2011), these reforms have led to considerable strengthening of China's financial sector.

Table 2.1 summarizes the sequence and substance of the above reforms. The number of state enterprises corresponding to each reform measure is also shown. Throughout the reforms prior to 1995, the number of state enterprises (defined by ownership) had remained at around 100,000, reaching a peak 118,000 that year. This number fell sharply from 1995, with the adoption of the strategy of retaining only the large enterprises—by 1999, the number was fewer than half that four years earlier, and has continued to decline since.

Viewed in its entirety, state enterprise reform is more about corporatization than about ownership change. Indeed, the letting go of thousands of small state enterprises was part and parcel of a strategy to create national champions that will entrench the state sector as a driver of economic growth.

Chinese state enterprise today: ownership and governance and the non-state sector

Although far fewer in number (Table 2.1), state enterprises remain major players in the economy. They are not only the largest enterprises but also growing larger; while the number of state enterprises in 2009 has been reduced to just under one-eighth of that in 2000, their shares of output and employment have fallen to one-third and one-fifth respectively (Table 2.2). However, as shall be elaborated below, these numbers understate the size and reach of the state sector.

Ownership

The issue of state ownership has been complicated by reforms that produced a variety of corporate structures and types. Government ownership ranges from

Table 2.1 China's state enterprise and banking system reforms, 1978–2006

Year	State enterprise reform measure	No. of state enterprises	Banking system reform
1978	Enlargement of state enterprises' management autonomy	83,700	
1984	Implementation of the Contract Responsibility System	84,100	The People's Bank of China spun off its commercial bank functions
1990	Establishment of Shanghai and Shenzhen Stock Exchanges	104,400	
1992	State enterprises given more rights to set prices, wages, hire and fire workers	103,300	State Council Securities Commission and China Securities Regulatory Commission established
1994	Tax reform	102,200	4 state-owned commercial banks, 3 policy banks created
1995	Strategy to retain only the largest state enterprises while "releasing" the small ones	118,000	
1999	Corporatization and shareholding reform	50,700	
2000		53,500	State-owned banks recapitalized through four asset management companies
2003	State-Owned Asset Supervision and Administration Commission established	34,300	China Banking Regulatory Commission established
2005	Non-tradable shares converted into tradable shares in the share markets to attract private capital	27,500	Foreign strategic investors through public listing in Hong Kong
2006		25,000	Foreign bank branches allowed to operate in China under WTO rules

Source: State enterprise data from China Statistical Yearbook database (http://tongji.cnki.net/
overseas/engnavi/HomePage.aspx?id=N2011090108&name=YINFN&floor=1)

complete ownership of "strategic" enterprises through majority ownership to minority ownership which does not appear in government statistics. Cutting through the first two groups are "central enterprises" (*yangqi*) over which the state exercises control. These have also been referred to as the "national team" (Sutherland 2007) among state-owned "enterprise groups" (Mako and Zhang 2002: 1).

Further, state ownership is also exercised by about 100,000 sub-national enterprises belonging to provincial and local governments, although during reform, many local level state enterprises had been privatized, merged, or liquidated (Szamosszegi and Kyle 2011: 26). Quite autonomous, these enterprises do not always march in step with central government policy prescriptions (*ibid.*: 31).

Table 2.2 Selected statistics of Chinese state enterprises, 2000–2009

Year	No. of state enterprises as % of all enterprises	State enterprise output as % of total output	State enterprise employment as % of total employment
2000	32.8	47.3	53.9
2001	27.3	44.4	49.2
2002	22.6	40.8	43.9
2003	17.5	37.5	37.6
2004	12.9 (2.0)	35.2 (15.3)	29.8 (13.7)
2005	10.1	33.3	27.2
2006	8.3 (5.3)	31.2 (14.9)	24.5 (15.1)
2007	6.1 (3.4)	29.5 (13.7)	22.1 (12.9)
2008	5.0 (2.6)	28.4 (13.1)	20.3 (11.4)
2009	4.7 (2.5)	26.7 (12.5)	20.4 (11.1)

Note: This table includes only those state enterprises that are wholly or majority owned by the government. Enterprises in which the government has minority ownership are excluded. Data for 2004 include only state enterprises wholly owned by the government.

Source: China Statistical Yearbook database (http://tongji.cnki.net/overseas/engnavi/ HomePage.aspx?id=N2011090108&name=YINFN&floor=1)

There are also enterprises variously defined as quasi-state enterprises (see, for instance, Ma 2010: 86).

Finally, there are enterprises for which ownership is ambiguous. Some non-state enterprises have ownership structures that have been characterized as "unbelievably complex" (Knowledge@Wharton 2001: 1–2). Even officially defined private enterprises have received seed money and funding from the state at important junctures, a practice common in the IT sector (Economist 2012).[6] Urban collectives and local government-owned township, and village enterprises are also part of this sector.

This lack of a clear partition between public and private enterprises has produced apparent paradoxes that Western economic theories—agency, public choice, property rights, and organization among them—cannot explain. One is the coexistence of vibrant state and private sectors. Another is the growing financial muscle or global reach of state enterprises even as the state sector shrinks. A third is the competitiveness, management professionalism, and innovation capabilities of an increasing number of state enterprises, in contradiction of the Western perception of uncompetitive state enterprises. This distinctively Chinese system of industrial organization is only beginning to be understood by Western scholars viewing it through political economy lenses (Lin and Milhaupt 2011).

Governance

Despite improvement over time, governance indicators (Table 2.3) have confirmed the negative views of many commentators (for instance, Tan and

Table 2.3 China: selected governance indicators, 1996–2008

Year	Control of corruption	Government effectiveness	Political stability	Regulatory quality	Rule of law	Voice and accountability
1996	−0.20	0.04	−0.35	0.20	−0.20	−1.66
1998	−0.26	−0.33	−0.16	−0.26	−0.37	−1.38
2000	−0.22	−0.13	−0.22	−0.28	−0.44	−1.28
2002	−0.47	−0.05	−0.18	−0.49	−0.34	−1.57
2004	−0.61	−0.05	−0.21	−0.24	−0.35	−1.46
2006	−0.52	0.03	−0.46	−0.28	−0.52	−1.68
2009	−0.52	0.12	−0.44	−0.20	−0.35	−1.65

Note: Indicator values range from −2.0 (worst) to +2.0 (best).

Source: World Bank Governance Indicators (http://info.worldbank.org/governance/wgi/
   index.aspx#home)

Wang 2007). The weaknesses cited included ownership concentration, agency problems caused by strong managers and weak owners, lack of transparency and adequate disclosure, lack of judicial remedies for minority owners, and weak supervisory boards (*ibid.*: 159–66). This is despite the fact that the legal framework has been strengthened (Tsui 2010), putting the burden of blame squarely on poor enforcement.

One reason cited to explain this poor performance was that the concept and benchmarks of good corporate governance have been borrowed from the Anglo-American corporate model, and lacking any such experience, Chinese enterprises faced a steep learning curve (Tan and Wang 2007: 147). Some also argued that China's institutional experience, described as "control-based" (Liu 2005: 9) and "insider" governance (Tan and Wang 2007: 143), was not necessarily conducive to "market oriented" or "outsider" governance.[7] It is also plausible that measures to improve corporate governance simply could not keep pace with the changes taking place in the corporate sector, while regulatory institutions were still inexperienced. Further, given the uniqueness of the Chinese system described earlier, simply implementing Western rules and standards would not necessarily improve corporate governance (China Knowledge@Wharton 2010; Lin and Milhaupt 2011).

Still, there have been examples of good corporate practice. Baoshan Iron and Steel, China International Marine Containers Corporation, the Pearl River Piano Group, and Guangzhou Metro Corporation were said to be among the best-managed firms in China.[8] A plausible explanation is that management of these enterprises had incentives for performance, just like private sector enterprises (Kato and Long 2004). Also, international listing of large state enterprises not only subjects them to the discipline of the market but also forces them to compete for talent and link executive compensation to corporate performance, like any private enterprise. The global managerial labor market is also a strong determinant of Chinese state enterprises' CEO compensation.

Any discussion of Chinese governance would not be complete without reference to "*Guanxi* capitalism." Some argue it undermines governance (e.g. Gu *et al*. 2008) and that it was on the way out (e.g. Balfour and Einhorn 2002). Others have argued that *Guanxi* was helpful to governance by allowing transactions to occur without a proper system of legal contracts (Hsu 2005) and that it was more resilient to economic crisis than Western economic systems (Ruehle 2010). Indeed, McNally (2002) argued that it was this system that facilitated capitalist accumulation under authoritarian rule. Once again, the efficacy of Chinese governance must be understood in the larger context of social interaction, not just economic norms as is commonly understood.

State enterprises and the economy

Since state enterprises are key players in China's economy, they should have a material impact on growth and distribution. However, although numerous writers associated loss-making state enterprises with dampening China's economic growth (e.g. Rawski 2000), little empirical research exists that can make this direct link. Those that did (e.g. Chen and Yi 2000) used cross section provincial data which could not address the contribution of state enterprises to growth over time. As state enterprises were transformed by reform from loss-making to profitable enterprises, there was likewise little empirical work that linked economic performance (see, among others, Aivazian *et al*. 2005) to growth and almost none to social acceptance. Although by 2007, Madison (2007: 20–21) had concluded that, given their diminished importance, "this problem is no longer likely to be a significant obstacle to rapid economic growth," this is far from acknowledging their role in driving economic growth. However, Li and Putterman (2008: 376) noted that it was implausible that "China's economic growth could have progressed so rapidly if the country has been dragging along its state sector like an albatross round its neck for all of these years."

An increasing role for China's state enterprises as engines of growth is promoting innovation to facilitate technological catch-up. The 2006 Medium to Long-term Plan for the Development of Science and Technology (2005–20) aims to develop a national innovation system with "enterprises as the center, the market as guide, with commercialization and research interwoven" (Springut *et al*. 2011: 6). State enterprises would benefit from government incentives, including generous funding for research, subsidies, and assistance towards internationalization. By various quantitative measures, this effort is paying off (INNO-Policy Trendchart 2009: 3), although at firm level, the evidence has been mixed (see, for example, Zhang *et al*. 2009: xvi).

In terms of equity, reforms had freed state enterprises from their social burden, leaving a void in the social safety net that has not been filled even today. Social security experiments to take over this redistributive role, from the rehiring of some laid-off workers and compensation packages for those laid off to the establishment of the National Social Security Fund in 2001 helped relieve some of the hardships caused by the lay-offs but did not even come near to anything resembling a national social security system. Discussions about the creation of this system continued in the lead-up to China's 12th Five Year Plan.⁹ Thus, state enterprise reforms based partly on Western-style corporate restructuring had destroyed the traditional distributive role of Chinese state enterprises, leaving in its wake a vacuum that had to be filled through experimentation, often piecemeal, with social security.

Some idea of the distributional impact of state enterprise reform can be gleaned from data on layoffs and unemployment rates in urban areas (Table 2.4). Urban unemployment rose in the period covered by major reforms, spiking in 1993 and 2001. 1993 was a year after state enterprises were allowed to lay off staff, while 2001 saw state enterprise restructuring as China joined the WTO, and of financial sector restructuring after the Asian financial crisis. This unemployment rate has remained at 4 percent and above ever since. Of even greater significance is the far higher number of urban lay-offs. It is likely that the unemployment figures did not count migrant labor but layoff data did. If this was the case, many laid off might have returned to their places of origin. At the same time, China's vibrant economy must have seen a good number of those laid off rehired.

Spatial income distribution has also been affected by the shift in industrial production to the coastal regions. Figure 2.1 compares the location of industrial output between 1978, when China began its opening up, with 2010, three decades later. The areas where industrial output are concentrated (shaded darkest), fairly well dispersed geographically in 1978, have shifted to a narrow belt along China's eastern seaboard by 2010. The flow of migrant workers from the inland to the coastal provinces is the product of this pattern of development.

Table 2.4 Labor layoffs and urban unemployment in China, 1991–2003

Year	No. of urban unemployed (million)	Urban unemployment rate (%)	No. of urban workers laid off (million)
1991	3.52	2.3	—
1992	3.64	2.3	—
1993	4.20	2.6	3.00
1994	4.76	2.8	3.60
1995	5.20	2.9	5.64
1996	5.53	3.0	8.15
1997	5.70	3.1	11.52
1998	5.71	3.1	17.14
1999	5.75	3.1	22.78
2000	5.95	3.1	26.99
2001	6.81	3.6	28.11
2002	7.70	4.0	—
2003	8.00	4.3	—

Note: Dashes indicate data not available.

Source: China Statistical Yearbook database (http://tongji.cnki.net/overseas/engnavi/ HomePage.aspx?id=N2011090108&name=YINFN&floor=1)

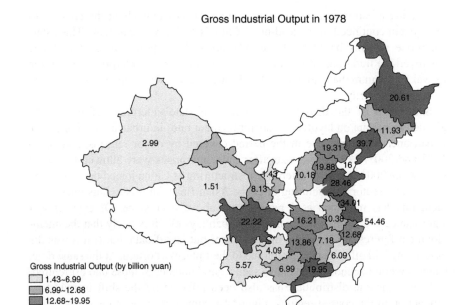

Gross Industrial Output in 1978

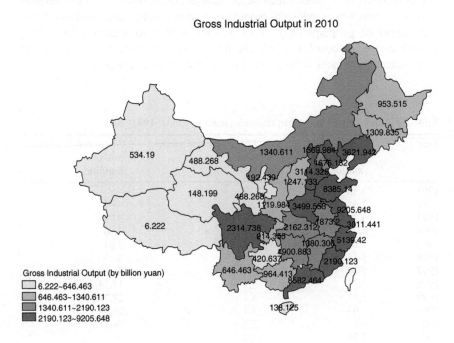

Gross Industrial Output in 2010

Figure 2.1 Comparing the location of industrial production in China, 1978 and 2010

Source: China Statistical Yearbook database (http://tongji.cnki.net/overseas/engnavi/
    HomePage.aspx?id=N2011090108&name=YINFN&floor=1)

Reform has also changed the enterprises' role in housing provision for their workers. As state enterprises shed this burden, workers were provided easy credit. With initially low prices and abundant loans, house prices began to climb. This brought speculators into the market, further escalating prices. Between 1997 and 2006, the average price of commercial and residential property increased 69 percent and 74 percent respectively (Table 2.5). State enterprises, owners of land, became housing developers to gain further revenue, often through speculation. According to SASAC, of the 129 central enterprises in 2009, 94 owned or controlled real estate development enterprises although real estate development was not their core business (Barboza 2010). In addition to bidding up the price of land,[10] helped by cheap credit from state-owned banks (see later), some state enterprise real-estate developers also started hoarding houses in anticipation of higher profits (Dreger and Zhang 2011).

The state as owner of state enterprises should be able to tap these profits to fund a comprehensive social safety net.[11] However, the successes of national champions and enterprises in strategic sectors have built powerful corporate interests able to resist pressures to distribute part of their earnings as dividends to government.[12] It is therefore no surprise that SASAC faced challenges to its authority, especially in its early years (Mattlin 2011). Thus, not only has state enterprise reform eroded the government's distributive role, the activities of post-reform state enterprises could have contributed to a worsening of disparities in access to social services.

The global crisis and state enterprises

Superimposed on these evolving developments is the global financial crisis (GFC) that, for China, began in 2008. Despite achieving the highest growth rate globally in 2009, China's response to the GFC has been roundly criticized for expanding the role of the state at the expense of the private sector (Economist

Table 2.5 Trends in demand for and supply of China's real estate, 1988–2009

Year	Floor space (m² million) commercial / residential	Sales value (RMB million) commercial / residential	Average sale price (RMB m⁻²) commercial / residential
1988	29.3 / 25.5	14.7 / —	— / —
1994	72.3 / 61.2	101.8 / 73.0	— / —
1997	90.1 / 78.6	179.9 / 140.8	1,997 / 1,790
2000	186.4 / 165.7	393.5 / 322.9	2,112 / 1,948
2003	337.2 / 297.8	795.6 / 654.3	2,359 / 2,197
2006	618.6 / 554.2	2,082.6 / 1,728.8	3,367 / 3,119
2009	947.6 / 861.8	4,435.5 / 3,843.3	4,681 / 4,459

Note: Dashes indicate data not available.

Source: China Statistical Yearbook database (http://tongji.cnki.net/overseas/engnavi/
HomePage.aspx?id=N2011090108&name=YINFN&floor=1)

2011). Forgotten in this criticism, however, is the US government's use of state money to rescue financial institutions at the heart of the GFC (e.g. AIG, Citigroup) and ailing companies (e.g. General Motors, Chrysler), and the UK government's nationalization of banks as responses to the crisis. Since the difference between these actions is only ownership of the enterprises involved, the real issue with these critics is ownership rather than the merit of the action itself.

The GFC arrived in China through the export sector; exports fell 16.3 percent, from US$ 1,418 billion to US$ 1,187 billion between 2008 and 2009. However, this exaggerates the impact on China, since only an estimated 60 percent of China's exports are made in China (Koopman *et al.* 2008). Pervasive process trade, estimated at over 50 percent of total exports (Van Assche and Ma 2009: 7) accounts for this, and for the equally sharp fall in imports over this period (Keidel 2009). China's exports, then, is not just about growth but perhaps even more about employment; large employment losses being a matter of concern to China's leaders.

However, Bottelier (2009: 5) noted several caveats to this employment impact. First, layoffs began in 2007,[13] well before the arrival of the GFC, as the government began to curtail investments in construction to cool an overheating economy and to prevent housing and stock market bubbles from developing. Second, the impact of this was felt in the construction sector, where many migrant workers were employed.[14] Employment loss was also from private sector small and medium-sized enterprises that supplied construction materials. Thus, employment losses from falling exports were estimated by Bottelier (*ibid.*: tab. 1) to be no more than a third of the total. Third, state enterprises, many with substantial retained profits and access to credit, were better insulated against employment losses than some private sector enterprises. Finally, the group most vulnerable to lay-offs was migrant workers, many with no social protection and few rights.[15] However, the rapid pace of recovery, thanks to the government's RMB 4 trillion stimulus, has resulted in a large proportion of the rural labor force rehired by the end of 2009.

The financial sector, much strengthened through reforms and not having purchased much of America's toxic assets, remained resilient to the GFC shocks. China was also not overly dependent on foreign capital for its development. Indeed, the troubles facing Western banks have catapulted Chinese banks to the forefront in global rankings.[16] Another impact has been that banks which have traditionally focused on large enterprises began to turn their attention to small and medium enterprises, especially after the government tightened credit in the aftermath of the stimulus package.[17] In its assessment report, the IMF concluded that China's financial sector "entered the global financial crisis from a position of relative strength" (IMF 2011: 7). However, it also outlined several risks, including the growth of "off-balance sheet exposures and of lending outside of the formal banking sector" that can reduce banks' loan portfolio quality (*ibid.*).

The adverse impact of the GFC on export-oriented enterprises and construction firms is a major source of the banks' greater vulnerability. Another was the large credit expansion that accompanied China's RMB 4 trillion stimulus package which threatened to reverse the hard-won successes in containing a potential real estate bubble and cooling an overheating economy just prior to the onset of the GFC. In the housing sector, already low borrowing costs encouraged over-investment in housing,[18] while local municipal governments have directed state enterprises to invest in housing or channel funds to real estate developers (Xu *et al.* 2009). Even those worried about the banks' heightened vulnerability, however, were undoubtedly mindful of the considerable resources the Chinese government could deploy to support these institutions (IMF 2011: 17).

One consequence of the GFC that may well have a more lasting impact is the likely slowdown of financial reforms of the kind advocated by the IMF. Whether this consequence is positive or otherwise remains to be seen. While the IMF and others lament this development, it should hardly be surprising if the GFC led the Chinese leadership to exercise greater caution moving this reform forward.[19] An important difference between the Asian Financial Crisis (AFC) and the GFC is that while during the AFC sizable NPLs signaled immediate danger to Chinese banks and thus spurred financial reforms, the weaknesses of banks during the GFC are nowhere as immediate. China's leadership clearly sees countering the continuing impact of the GFC as having a much higher priority than banking reforms. And, as the AFC clearly demonstrated, countering crisis impact is most effective under centralized decision-making followed by "unified action" (Yao and Wu 2011: 798).

Will financial reform continue, albeit with some delay or with greater caution? The answer will likely be yes. First, the lesson of the GFC is not so much that financial liberalization should be halted but that effective prudential regulation should have been enforced. The casualty is not financial liberalization but the neoliberal approach to liberalization. Second, the long-term costs to the Chinese economy of the weaknesses discussed above, in the form of distorting investment choices at the microeconomic level and of hampering the effective implementation of monetary policy at the macroeconomic level, are persuasive arguments for continued liberalization. These costs, not the accusation of Chinese culpability in the GFC in the form of adopting mercantilist policies (for example, by Wolf 2008), will provide the impetus for continued reform.[20] Indeed, China's 12th Five Year Plan speaks of reform to move towards market interest rates.[21] As history has shown, and given its abundant stock of foreign reserves, however, China will not be pressured by external voices but will manage this process at a pace it deems appropriate.

Case study: the Bank of China—a state enterprise under reform

The oldest bank in China and one of the "big four" state-owned commercial banks, the Bank of China (BoC) was established in 1912. It was the nation's central bank until this role was taken over by the Central Bank of China in 1928, but continued to issue currency notes under the Nationalist Government until 1942. Under the People's Republic of China, BoC functioned as a commercial bank, specializing in foreign exchange, and international trade. From 1978 to the mid-1990s, BoC, together with three other state-owned banks, assumed responsibility for financing of state enterprises from the fiscal budget. Because of extensive losses by state enterprises, BoC accumulated a portfolio of NPL that, had they been marked to market, might have rendered it insolvent (Bonin and Huang 2001: 3).

In 1994, the Chinese government, alarmed by the losses, began to deal with the state-owned banks' NPL problem by separating policy lending from commercial loans, as already described. BoC and the other state-owned banks were to undertake purely commercial lending (*ibid.*: 19). In 1996, the government began to set aside a large fund to write-off the bad debts accumulated by these banks. In 1999, an asset management company (AMC) was established to take over the bad debts of each of the state-owned banks. For BoC, it was Orient AMC which took over RMB 267 billion, some 20 percent of the bank's outstanding loans in 1999–2000 (Fung *et al.* 2004: tab. 1.1).

In August 2004, Bank of China Limited was officially incorporated as a shareholding bank. It was listed simultaneously on the Hong Kong and Shanghai stock Exchanges in 2006, the first Chinese commercial bank to go public in both domestic and foreign markets. Foreign shareholders, the Royal Bank of Scotland, UBS, Temasik and ADB invested US\$ 22.5 billion. Upon listing, the bank published its financial report that conformed to international accounting standards for the first time (Hope *et al.* 2008: 17).

Public listing, along with banking reforms, has had a salutary effect on BoC's balance sheet and performance by enhancing its capitalization and strengthening its capital adequacy. Assets and profits have been growing steadily even as NPLs fell, while the reserves cover to loss ratio rose.[22] Total assets grew 14.4 percent a year, deposits at 12.5 percent and loans by19.9 percent from 2006 to 2010 (Table 2.6). The share of non-performing loans fell from 4 percent to 1 percent while the

Table 2.6 Bank of China financial performance indicators, 2006–10

Indicator	2006	2007	2008	2009	2010	Annual change 2005–10	Change 2008–9
Total assets (Y billion)	5,332	5,996	6,956	8,751	10,460	14.4%	25.8%
Total deposits (Y billion)	4,182	4,480	5,173	6,685	7,539	12.5%	29.2%
Total loans (Y billion)	2,338	2,754	3,190	4,798	5,538	19.9%	50.4%
Net profit (Y billion)	48	62	65	85	110	18.05	29.4%
Reserve covering loss loan ration (%)	96%	108%	122%	151%	197%		
Capital adequacy ratio (%)	13.8%	13.8%	14.2%	16.5%	12.6%		
Non-performing loans (%)	4.0%	3.1%	2.6%	1.5%	1.1%		

Source: BoC Annual Reports, various years (www.boc.cn/en/investor/ir3)

reserve covering loss ratio more than doubled. Capital adequacy remained above 11 percent throughout the period.[23]

As part of the stimulus package to counter the GFC, BoC's lending increased 50 percent between 2008 and 2009 and by 15 percent the following year, raising the specter of loan portfolio deterioration. This credit expansion coincided with a sharp reduction of lending rates, which fell about a percentage point in November 2008. However, reserve coverage for loan losses continued to rise, while capital adequacy, which dipped slightly in 2009, remained robust. By 2010, NPLs made up only 1 percent of total loans. The stimulus package also brought about some reorientation of BoC's lending. In response to the central government's call to support affordable housing, to which 10 percent of the total stimulus package was allocated, BoC provided RMB 296.7 billion credit for this sector by the end of 2010.

Conclusion

The Chinese state and its institutions have evolved through adapting to new circumstances and absorbing external influences. Throughout this evolution, its role has remained more significant than that envisaged for the modern nation state. As key institutions, state enterprises are central to this role. They are distinguished from the stereotype in Western theories of public enterprises by the manner in which they are owned and controlled. This distinction leads to various aspects of performance—efficiency, profitability, management, and technological capabilities—and the environment they face, such as exposure to competition that set them apart. We also posit that some of the modern state conglomerates share a corporate structure that is arguably unique—neither state nor private, but possessing characteristics of both—with power derived less from state ownership than from how close its top management is with the political leadership.[24]

How did these state enterprises fare during the GFC? Although China's exports were impacted, this impact was felt more by the non-state than the state sector. Employment rather than net exports was the casualty, since imports also fell, thanks to process trade, leaving net exports positive even at the height of the GFC. Even here, the bulk of the impact was likely borne by migrant workers from the hinterland.

Holding few of the toxic assets, the major financial institutions, all state-owned, were minimally impacted by the GFC. They had benefited from financial reforms—recapitalization and transfer of NPL to asset management companies. Listing on stock exchanges mandated these banks to conform to international corporate governance benchmarks. Indeed, the GFC had propelled them up the global rankings. However, as part of the government's crisis response, they risked dilution of their asset quality and heightened vulnerability arising from existing systemic weaknesses. This risk should not be overstated, as the case study of the Bank of China showed. The US$ 3 trillion external reserves the state now commands provide insurance against these risks. The greatest impact of the GFC may well be to slow down the pace of China's financial liberalization. Memories of the AFC have undoubtedly been reinforced by events in the GFC in the minds of the Chinese leadership.

The performance of Chinese state enterprises, including banks, as they underwent reform and withstood the turbulence of the GFC has brought to the fore two paradoxes. One is how state enterprises were able to suffer limited impact from the GFC despite deficient governance. This likely applied more to non-bank enterprises. For the state-owned banks, listing and international competition had led to much improved governance. For the non-bank state sector, the existing governance indicators might have understated the actual standard of governance, especially since the employment of professional management by the large enterprises at least, combined with intense competition among state enterprises would have ensured acceptable governance standards. The much debated role of "Guanxi capitalism" as facilitating capitalist enterprise played an important governance role in the absence of institutional rules.

The second paradox is the apparent ability of state enterprises to perform in a system in which the state owns them and the banks that finance them, as well as controls the agencies that regulate them, a formula susceptible to serious abuse. This study provided a historical context for this lack of separation between state and society. At the same time, it is evident that there is *de facto* separation between ownership and control, with the former declining and the latter in the hands of professional management for the most important enterprises, producing in effect a system not very different from the Western model. Evidence of this separation comes from the need for the state to rein in state enterprises (e.g. in housing) and state banks (e.g. in dispensing credit).

Explaining these paradoxes obviously requires both historical and political economy perspectives. It is unfortunate that much of the analytical work on Chinese state enterprises in Western academic circles have been based on economics and/or on prevailing theories from just this discipline. These theories are also based on assumptions which, while generally valid in the context of Western societies, have limited applicability when transplanted to not just China but other East Asian countries (see Chapter 4 for the South Korean case).

Acknowledgments

We are grateful to François Bafoil and Edmund Terence Gomez for providing insightful comments on an earlier draft of this manuscript.

Notes

1   In Gordon Chang's book *The Coming Collapse of China* (2001), Chapter 3 was titled "State enterprises are Dying" and Chapter 7 "The State Attacks the Private Sector."
2   Jacques (2011) and Hsiung (2012) refer to China as a civilization state, wherein lies the entire civilization. Zhang (2012: 47–52) goes further to characterize the country as a "civilizational" state, which combines the essential qualities of a civilization state with features of the modern nation state.

3   Fairbank (1987: 17) noted the small size of the Chinese state in relation to its considerable mandate.

4   From May 1998, those who were retrenched were able to receive assistance through a re-employment service. The ILO (2002) reported that by the end of 1998, about 85 percent of those made redundant had registered.

5   This was announced in September 1995 at the Fifth Plenary Session of the Fourteenth National Congress of the Chinese People's Congress.

6   *The Economist* (2012) cited the example of Lenovo receiving seed money from the Chinese Academy of Sciences and government funds for the acquisition of IBM's personal computer business.

7   Tan and Wang (2007: 166–7) also proffered an explanation based on the Chinese tradition of Confucianism in which governance was based not on checks and balances but on the principle of *ren* (benevolence).

8   Meyer (Knowledge@Wharton 2001: 2) crediting them with "visionary leadership, creative marketing strategies, cohesive internal cultures, strong internal management controls, and a commitment to training employees and managers".

9   In the collection of papers that served as inputs into the Plan, two out of nine chapters and five out of twenty background papers were devoted to issues of social security and an additional paper to housing (Lim and Spence 2010).

10 Land records show that 82 percent of land auctions in Beijing in 2009 have been won by big state-owned companies outbidding private developers—up from 59 percent in 2008 (Barboza 2010).

11 State enterprise profits were estimated to be as much as 20 percent of the national budget in 2010 (Mattlin 2011: 3).

12 This is a consequence of the increasing autonomy enjoyed by state enterprise managers under reform. Greater autonomy also meant less information received by the central government as owners.

13 Keidel (2009: 5) also attributed employment losses in 2007 to the government's closure of small inefficient and heavily polluting export-oriented plants in southern China.

14 Bottelier (2009: 5) estimated total employment in the construction sector to be in the region of 55 million in 2007, and that 10 to 20 percent of these were laid off in 2008.

15 Cai and Chan (2009: 519, 523) estimated that unemployment among rural migrant workers was as high as 16 percent in 2009, compared to under 5 percent for the urban *houkou* registered workers.

16 As of July 2011, Chinese banks—the Industrial and Commercial Bank of China and the China Construction Bank—occupied the top two spots in terms of market capitalization.

17 See Zhang and Cheong (2011) and the references cited therein.

18 However, Huang (in Carnegie Endowment for International Peace 2011) provided an interesting justification for this financial repression. He argued that to the extent that the more wealthy lose more from this repression through an inflation tax, the government used this as a progressive form of taxation at a time when few Chinese citizens fell within the tax net.

19 The need for caution in financial liberalization is shared by other Asian countries. Khor and Tan (2010) noted that "backwardness" in financial innovation and cross-border financial intermediation, as well as underdeveloped capital markets, was what allowed Asia to limit contagion from the GFC; Asian leaders shared these views.

20 Huang Yiping *et al.* (2010) found evidence that financial liberalization was helpful to China's economic growth while financial repression inhibited it.

21 Okazaki *et al.* (2011: 37) drew lessons from the Japanese experience in financial liberalization to urge financial reform to facilitate internationalization of China's banks, in line with that for the RMB.

22 It is of course true that China's state-owned banks have benefited from being the only

avenue for the population to deposit their savings, for which meager interest payments were made to depositors. However, lending to state enterprises were also at "preferential" rates, so that such lending also yielded lower returns compared to normal commercial lending.
23   See Hope *et al.* (2008: 18) for data before 2006.
24   As an example, the president of the Bank of China, Li Li Hui, was once Vice Governor of Hainan and known to be well connected to the central leadership.

References

Aivazian, V. A., Ge Ying, and Qiu Jiaping (2005) "Can Corporatization Improve the Performance of State-owned enterprises Even Without Privatization?" *Journal of Corporate Finance* 11: 791–808.

Balfour, F., and Einhorn, B. (2002) "The End of Guanxi Capitalism?" *Bloomberg Businessweek* (February 3): www.businessweek.com/stories/2002-02-03/the-end-of-guanxi-capitalism (accessed April 8, 2013).

Barboza, D. (2010) "State-Owned Bidders Fuel China's Land Boom." *New York Times* (August 1): www.nytimes.com/2010/08/02/business/global/02chinareal.html (accessed January 3, 2011).

Bonin, J. P., and Huang, Y. (2001) "Dealing with the Bad Loans of Chinese Banks." Working Paper 357, William Davidson Institute, University of Michigan, January.

Bottelier, P. (2009) "China's Economic Downturn: Employment is the Critical Issue." *China Brief* 9(3): 4–7.

Cai, F., and Wing, C. K. (2009) "The Global Economic Crisis and Unemployment in China." *Eurasian Geography and Economics* 50(5): 513–31.

Carnegie Endowment for International Peace (2011) "Engineering China's Financial Reform." Panel Discussion transcript, Carnegie Endowment for International Peace, Washington DC, September 16.

Chang, G. (2001) *The Coming Collapse of China*. London: Arrow.

Chang, G. (2010) "China's Economy to Reach $123 trillion?" *Forbes* (January 8): www.forbes.com/2010/01/07/china-economy-robert-fogel-opinions-columnists-gordon-g-chang.html (accessed December 1, 2011).

Chen B., and Yi, F. (2000) "Determinants of Economic Growth in China: Private Enterprise, Education and Openness." *China Economic Review* 11: 1–15.

China Knowledge@Wharton (2010) "Corporate Governance in China: No Quick Fix, No Fixed Solution." *Knowledge@Wharton* (January 20): www.knowledgeatwharton.com.cn/index.cfm?fa=viewArticle&articleID=2162&languageid=1 (accessed January 15, 2012).

Dong X., and Putterman, L. (2003) "Soft Budget Constraints, Social Burdens and Labor Redundancy in China's State Industry." *Journal of Comparative Economics* 31(1): 110–33.

Dreger, C., and Yangqun, Z. (2011) "On the Chinese House-price Bubble." *VOX* (July 15): www.voxeu.org/index.php?q=node/6754 (accessed January 5, 2011).

Economist (2011) "The Long-arm of the State: The Government is Flexing its Muscle in Business." *Economist* (June 23): www.economist.com/node/18832034 (accessed January 2, 2012).

Economist (2012) "New Masters of the Universe: How State Enterprise is Spreading." *Economist* (January 21): www.economist.com/node/21542925 (accessed March 14, 2012).

Fairbank, J. K. (1987) "The Reunification of China." In R. Macfarquhar, and John K.

Fairbank (eds.), *The People's Republic, Part 1: The Emergence of Revolutionary China 1949–1965.* Cambridge History of China, vol 14. Cambridge: Cambridge University Press.

Fung, B., George, J., Hohl, S., and Guonan Ma (2004) *Public Asset Management Companies in East Asia—Case Studies.* October 7. Basel: Bank for International Settlements.

Gu, F.F., Hung, K. and Tse, D.K. (2008) "When Does Guanxi Matter? Issues of Capitalization and its Dark Sides." *Journal of Marketing* 72(4): 12–28.

Hope, N. C., Laurenceson, J and Qin, F. (2008) "The Impact of Direct Investment by Foreign Banks on China's Banking Industry." Working Paper 362, Stanford Center for International Development, Stanford University, April.

Hsiung, J. C. (2012) *China into its Second Rise: Myths, Puzzles, Paradoxes and Challenge to Theory.* Singapore: World Scientific Publishing.

Hsu, C. L. (2005) "Capitalism without Contracts versus Capitalists without Capitalism: Comparing the Influence of Chinese *Guanxi* and Russian *Blat* on Marketization." *Communist and Post-Communist Studies* 38(3): 309–327.

Huang Y., Xun, W., Bijun, W., and Nian, L. (2010) "Financial Reform in China: Progress and Challenges." Paper presented at the Conference on Financial Liberalization in China, Japan and Korea, Seoul, December 2–3.

ILO (2002) "Reemployment in Reform of State-Owned Enterprises: The Case of China." Geneva: International Labor Organization (May 31): www.ilo.org/public/english/dialogue/ifpdial/la/gp/china2.htm (accessed December 15, 2011).

IMF (2011) *People's Republic of China—Financial Syatem Stability Assessment.* June 24. Washington, DC: International Monetary Fund.

INNO-Policy Trendchart (2009) *Innovation Policy Progress Report—China 2009.* Brussels: European Commission.

Jacques, M. (2011) "How China will Change the Way we Think: the Case of the State." Transatlantic Academy Paper, German Marshall Fund, Washington DC, February.

Kato, T., and Long, C. (2004) "Executive Compensation, Firm Performance and State Ownership in China: Evidence from New Panel Data." Working Paper 690, William Davidson Institute, University of Michigan, May.

Keidel, A. (2009) "China and the Global Crisis: Recovery and Continued Reform?" XXI National Forum, Rio de Janeiro, May 18–21.

Khor H. E. and Song, T. K. (2010) "An Asian Response to International Financial Reforms." *East Asia Forum* (November 10): www.eastasiaforum.org/2010/11/10/an-asian-response-to-international-financial-reforms (accessed January 16, 2012).

Kissinger, H. (2012) *On China.* New York: Penguin.

Knowledge@Wharton (2001) "Think State-Owned Enterprises are Inefficient? Look at China." Knowledge@Wharton (August 15): http://knowledge.wharton.upenn.edu/article.cfm?articleid=415 (accessed November 30, 2011).

Koopman, R., Wang, Z. and Shang-Jin, W. (2008) "How Much of Chinese Exports is Really Made in China? Assessing Domestic Value-added When Process Trade is Pervasive." Working Paper No. 14109, National Bureau of Economic Research, June.

Kuhn, P. A. (2002) *The Origins of the Modern Chinese State.* Stanford, CA: Stanford University Press.

Lall, D. (2006) "A Proposal to Privatise Chinese enterprises and End Financial Repression." *Cato Journal* 26(2): 275–86.

Li C. (1997) "Confucian Value and Democratic Value." *The Journal of Value Inquiry* 31(2): 183–93.

Li, W., and Putterman, L. (2008) "Reforming China's SOEs: An Overview." *Comparative Economic Studies* 50(3): 353–80.

Lim, E., and Spence, M. (eds.) (2010) *Thoughts and Suggestions for China's 12th Five Year Plan from an International Perspective*. July. Beijing: Caincross Foundation.

Lin, L., and Milhaupt, C. J. (2011) "We are the (National) Champions: Understanding the Mechanisms of State Capitalism in China." Working Paper No. 409, Center for Law and Economic Studies, Columbia University, November 1.

Liu Q. (2005) "Corporate Governance in China: Current Practices, Economic Effects and Institutional Determinants." Working Paper 1125, Hong Kong Institute of Economics and Business Strategy, Hong Kong University.

Ma, S. Y. (2010) *Shareholding System Reform in China: Privatizing by Groping for Stones*. Cheltenham: Edward Elgar.

Maddison, A. (2007) *Chinese Economic Performance in the Long Run: 960 to 2030 AD*. Paris: OECD.

Mako, W. P., and Chunlin, Z. (2002) "Exercising Ownership Rights in State-owned enterprise Groups: What China can learn from International Experience." Working Paper 26878, World Bank, December 31.

Mako, W. P., and Chunlin, Z. (2003) *Management of China's State-Owned Enterprises: Portfolio Lessons from International Experience*. September. Beijing: World Bank.

Mattlin, M. (2011) *Chinese Strategic State-Owned Enterprises and State Control*. Asia Papers 4 (6). Brussels: Brussels Institute of Contemporary China Studies.

McNally, C. A. (2002) "China's State-owned Enterprises: Thriving or Crumbling?" *Asia Pacific Issues* 59: 1–8.

National Bureau of Statistics, China (2010) *China Statistical Yearbook on Science and Technology: 2009*. Beijing: China Statistics Press.

Okazaki, K., Hattori, M. and Takahashi, W. (2011) "The Challenges Confronting the Banking Sector Reform in China: An Analysis in Light of Japan's experience of Financial Liberalization." Discussion Paper 2011-E-6, Institute for Monetary and Economic Studies, Bank of Japan, March.

Pei M. (2006) "The Dark Side of China's Rise." *Foreign Policy* (March/April): www.foreignpolicy.com/articles/2006/02/17/the_dark_side_of_chinas_rise (accessed November 31, 2011).

Rawski, T. G. (2000) "Is China's State enterprise Problem Still Important?" Paper presented at the workshop on China's SOE Reform and Privatization, University of Tokyo, June 25.

Ruehle, S. (2010) "Guanxi as Competitive Advantage during Economic Crises: Evidence from China during the Recent Global Financial Crisis." Paper presented at the 21st CEA (UK) and 2nd CEA (Europe) Annual Conference, University of Oxford, Oxford, July 12–13.

Springut, M., Schlaikjer, S. and Chen, D. (2011) *China's Program for Science and Technology Modernization: Implications for American Competitiveness*. Report prepared for the US–China Economic and Security Review Commission. Arlington, VA: CENTRA Technology.

Sutherland, D. (2007) "China's 'National Team' of Enterprise Groups: How has it Performed?" Discussion Paper 23, China Policy Institute, University of Nottingham, July.

Szamosszegi, A., and Kyle, C. (2011) *An Analysis of State-Owned Enterprises and State Capitalism in China*. Report prepared for the US–China Economic and Security Review Commission, October 26. Arlington, VA: Capital Trade.

Tan L.-H., and Jiangyu, W. (2007) "Modeling an Effective Corporate Governance System for China's Listed State-owned Enterprises: Issues and Challenges in a Transitional Economy." *Journal of Corporate Law Studies* 7(1): 143–72.

Tsui, M. (2010) "Corporate Governance in China." *Corporate Governance e-Journal* (Bond University) 10(1): http://epublications.bond.edu.au/cgej/20 (accessed January 10, 2012).

Van Assche, A., and Ma, A. C. (2009) "When China Sneezes, Asia Catches a Cold: The Effects of China's Export Decline in the Realm of the Global Economic Crisis." Discussion Paper DT2009-01, Center for Interuniversity Research and Analysis on Organizations, Montreal.

Walter, C. E. (2010) "The Struggle over Ownership: How the Reform of State-Owned Enterprises Changed China." *The Copenhagen Journal of Asian Studies* 28(1): 83–108.

Wang, X. (2004) State-Owned Enterprise Reform and Corporate Governance of China." School of Management, Fudan University, mimeo. Available at http://coe21-policy.sfc.keio.ac.jp/ja/event/file/s1-6.pdf (accessed December 26, 2011).

Wolf, M. (2008) *Fixing Global Finance*. Baltimore, MD: Johns Hopkins University Press.

Xu, J., Yeh, A. and Fulong, W. (2009) "Land Commodification: New Land Development and Politics in China since the Late 1990s." *International Journal of Urban and Regional Research* 33(4): 890–913.

Yao X. and Xin, W. (2011) "Transition of China's Financial System After the Global Financial Crisis." *World Economy* 34(5): 792–804.

Zhang, W. (2012) *The China Wave: Rise of a Civilizational State*. Hackensack, NJ: World Centuiry Publishing.

Zhang, Z., and Cheong, K.-C. (2011) "China's SMEs and the Global Crisis: Challenges and Opportunities." Paper presented at the 8th SMEs in a Global Economy Conference, Nong Khai, Thailand, November 9–11.

Zhang C., Zeng, D. Z., Mako, W. P. and Seward, J. (2009) *Promoting Enterprise-Led Innovation in China*. Washington, DC: World Bank.

Zhou G. (2000) "In Search of a New China: State, Society and the Fate of Modern China." University of California at San Diego Modern Chinese History. Available at http://ucsdmodernchinesehistory.org/2010/03/27/841 (accessed December 12, 2011).

Zhou H. (2000) "The Challenges of China's Economic Reform: State Enterprise Reform and Financial Liberalization." Masters of Science Thesis, University of North Texas, Denton, TX, December.

3 The creative role of the state and entrepreneurship

The case of Taiwan

Michelle F. Hsieh

The dominant views in understanding postwar East Asian development have centered on the role of the state in facilitating economic development; they range from an earlier emphasis on the top-down approach of statism to the current emphasis on "embedded autonomy." The latter is about the type of state–society linkage conducive to the joint project of industrial transformation (Evans 1995). Of major concern are the "institutional innovations" that can lead to development and innovation (Block and Evans 2005: 515; Evans 2005; Block and Keller 2011). This chapter reassesses the issue by revisiting the role of the state in cultivating entrepreneurship through a historical analysis of the Taiwanese experience during the postwar period. Going beyond the conventional account of the East Asian developmental state, which comprises state control of finance and close ties between the state and the business elite, the chapter highlights the multiple linkages among the various Taiwanese state agencies and a series of small and medium-sized enterprises (SMEs) in enhancing the technical learning and export capacities of firms to succeed in the global market. Through an in-depth case study of the Taiwanese bicycle industry, a key export industry since the 1970s, this chapter reveals an unacknowledged model of state–industry relationship, one that goes beyond the well-understood model developed from the information technology (IT) industry.

Role of the state in industrial transformation of late developing countries

A prominent trend in understanding the role of the state in developing countries is the theory of late development. The latecomer thesis originated in the work of Gerschenkron (1962) on late-industrializing European countries in the nineteenth century, which then provided the basis for the contemporary version of the developmental state theory to explain the rise of postwar Japan and the East Asian Tigers: Taiwan and South Korea (Johnson 1982; Amsden 1989; Wade 1990). This theory focuses on the need for a specific state structure to create an export-based industrial system and induce industries to catch up technologically with those in advanced countries to compete internationally.

The conventional latecomer's catch-up model involves state control of finance whereby the state provides patient capital (which means large sums of capital for investment for a long period) to encourage the private sector to enter targeted industries, the so-called model of picking national champions. Empirically, East Asian states adopted industrial policies by urging private sectors to enter fields that they otherwise would not have been willing to enter or capable of entering, as epitomized in the success of the creation of world-class Korean large conglomerates (called *Chaebol*; Woo 1991; Amsden 1989). In the Taiwanese context, in the 1970s and 1980s, the state took on the role of direct producer in the way Wade terms "governing the market" (1990) by using state enterprises to engage in a big push in heavy industrialization in the upstream industries (such as steel and petrochemicals) to induce entry of the private sector into the downstream industries.

While it may be sufficient for the state to act as a direct producer or planner to bring about industrialization, this position argues that for development to be sustainable the state must have the capacity Evans calls "embedded autonomy", according to which the cohesive state incubates and nurtures new private firms by inducing them to invest in areas they would not otherwise undertake (midwifery) and then constantly pressures these firms to continually upgrade themselves (husbandry) in moving upward in the international hierarchy (Evans 1995). Local entrepreneurship is needed due to the rapidly changing nature of the high technology sectors in international competition. Prodding is needed because the natural inclination of business is toward short-term profits and may not take into account long-term developmental goals.

The linkages in the East Asian context focus on the state and large business nexus as a way for industrial transformation. The dense and tightly knit network between the Korean state and the *Chaebol*s was the showcase of the developmental state (Kim 1997; Woo-Cumings 1999). In this account, a cohesive state structure is required, often with a pilot agency for formulating sound industrial policies and forming dense policy/personal networks with the large business elite (Evans 1995; Chibber 2002). Emphasis is placed on a few large corporate businesses because when the state intervenes, it tends to reduce the number of players/producers in the industry, which makes monitoring, signaling, and sanctioning easier and thus cooperation between the state and private partners possible (Noble 1998; Okimoto 1989). State intervention tends to generate industrial concentration. There are also technical reasons to favor large industrialists, for they are considered capable of reaching economies of scale and of absorbing, improving and diffusing western technologies, and in turn, competing with advanced countries in the international market.

Taiwan as a puzzle

Yet, the Taiwan experience suggests a deviation from the above approach, for the state relied less on finance as an instrument to induce industrial development: it did not give out patient capital to firms. The émigré KMT regime and their aloof relationship with the local indigenous elite prevented the concentration of large businesses because the formation of a Taiwanese capitalist class would have been a major threat to the regime (Cheng 1990; Gold 1986). Consequently, the private sector's lack of access to long-term capital brought about a decentralized industrial structure with numerous SMEs. The conventional wisdom would imply that a decentralized industrial structure with numerous SMEs and a distant relationship between private capitalists and the state would be unfavorable for Taiwan's quest for rapid innovation-based industrialization.

At the same time, the statist model of creating national champions to compete internationally becomes ill-adapted, as can be seen in the recurrence of global financial crises in the past two decades. The Korean state-large *Chaebol* coalition, in which the state underwrote a system of business financing that led to large investment through massive debt-to-equity ratios via government guaranteed loans in the 1980s and international loans in the 1990s, was under siege when the impatient capital of the latter led to disastrous results in the 1997 Asian financial crisis. Moreover, the moral hazards created by these "too big to fall" corporations, together with the declining state power to discipline them, generated discontent within the society in a wave of democratization and cast doubt on the viability of the state-led model in the light of financial liberalization and increasing international mobile capital.

Taiwan's transition to high technology industrialization with an economy dominated by a system of SMEs and the fact that it has adapted to the globalized economy relatively unscathed by cyclical international financial crises have posed a puzzle to students of state and economic development. Are there alternative explanations? The success of the dynamic system of Taiwanese SMEs quickly lent support to the varieties of network and organizational theories in explaining economic outcomes associated with the literature on industrial districts and social capital (Powell and Smith-Doerr 1994; Woolcock 1998; Storper 2005).[1] This society-centered approach ranges from an emphasis on local linkages and networks among firms that facilitate trust and cooperation, and thus flexibility to the global production network (GPN) where integration into the GPN was the key to the drive behind high technology development. Empirically, the former suggests the importance of trust and cooperation derived from inter-firm networks independent of the state in contributing to Taiwan's economic success (Hamilton *et al.* 2000; Biggart and Guillen 1999). The latter emphasizes the role of multinational companies (MNCs) in connecting the Taiwanese suppliers to the world market, while the technological learning of the SMEs stemmed from doing original equipment manufacturing (Gereffi 2005; Henderson *et al.* 2002; Humphrey and Schmitz 2002; Chen 2009). Contrary to a state-led approach that emphasizes intervention in ramping up production, this position argues that the Taiwan experience has been a demand-propelled industrialization influenced by retailers in the United States and MNCs (Feenstra and Hamilton 2006; Hamilton *et al.* 2011; Hamilton 1999).

As important as the advantages that inter-firm linkages could bring about are, the society-centered approach lacks mechanisms to explain technological learning and upgrading. For example, the trust and cohesion emphasized by the network literature does not provide insights into the technological learning and capacity building of the SMEs. Moreover, the linkages to MNCs alone do not explain the variations in upward mobility among countries.

At the same time, studies by the proponents of the statecentric theories began to search for new forms of alliances between the state and industries that would be conducive to innovation in the globalized world; and analyses of the transformative state capacities that examine the evolving role of the state in responding to globalization have proliferated in the past decade. (Weiss 1998, 2003; O'Riain 2004; Evans 2005; Chu 2007; Block 2008; Breznitz 2007; Block and Keller 2011; Negoita and Block 2012). The literature some term "developmental network state" (DNS) focuses on the multiple linkages among the state, local firms and foreign capital in facilitating innovation and development in a globalized world. The focus is on a decentralized network structure of the state with multiple connections to various actors in coping with the changing reality where production and innovation have extended across national boundaries and involved complex collaborations in an era of liberalization with increasing foreign investment in various parts of the world (O'Riain 2004). The success of the Taiwanese IT industry has served as a prime example for the DNS literature. The embeddedness thesis in the Taiwanese context focuses on the role of state-funded research institutions, such as the Information Technology Research Institute (ITRI), and their collaboration with the private sectors in the development of the IT sector as a way of accounting for Taiwan's success in moving to high technology industrialization (Wang 2010; Mathews 2002; Amsden and Chu 2003; Mathews and Cho 2000; Mazzoleni and Nelson 2007; Breznitz 2005). Most of the narratives have agreed on the well-functioning division of labor between the state and the industry in contributing to the industrial ascent of the IT industry. The public research institutions focused on acquiring and absorbing new technologies and conducted most of the R&D up to the level of a working prototype. They then transferred and diffused the results to the private firms. The private firms, in turn, concentrated on final development and commercialization.

Despite the growing interest in public–private synergy, the actual working of these linkages remains underexplored; the existing studies tend to prescribe what the state ought to do and assume that the society will follow.[2] If Taiwan is considered as a case for the neo-developmental state theories, the actual working of these linkages between the state and society requires detailed scrutiny. This chapter joins the debate by addressing the following question: If succeeding in the world market has been an important element of Taiwan's postwar accomplishments, how do we explain the way in which Taiwan's SMEs connect to the world market as a distinctive feature of the country's postwar development? What happened in Taiwan went against the experience everywhere else. Traditionally, exports have mostly come from large firms because they can better meet the transaction costs of participation in the international market. If size and scale of economies are crucial to competing in the world market, how did a series of Taiwanese SMEs acquire the technical capacities needed for export and establish economies of trust with foreign buyers in the 1970s? If the various "embedded autonomy" theories are to have explanatory power, it has to be shown precisely how the state escorted the SMEs onto the world market.

Developing linkages with society: case study of the bicycle industry

This chapter explores the role of Taiwan's state agencies in assisting the SMEs in the export market through an in-depth case study of the bicycle industry, a key export industry in the 1970s, and investigates the mechanisms of the role of the state in the technological learning of the SMEs. This study focuses on an unacknowledged model embedded widely in Taiwan's practice that would account for the industrial upgrading based on the SMEs' networked learning and innovation. By revisiting the initial period of export-led development and its subsequent transformation, I intend to unpack the patterns of state–industry alliances that were conducive to development and to illustrate the processes involved.

Through in-depth case studies of the Metal Industries Research and Development Center (MIRDC) and, later, the Bicycle Industry Research and Development Center (BIRDC), and their specific patterns of interaction with SMEs, especially in the parts sector, I show the specific ways government-funded research institutions were able to enhance the export capacities and technological learning of the private sector. This case study provides insight into how and what kind of institutional arrangements can be made between the state and a series of SMEs in export-led development—an insight that goes beyond the conventional preference for the state–large firm nexus—and that is amenable for broad-based entrepreneurship to take root. The key argument is that the inherent nature of the groups created specific patterns with which the state developed linkages.

The bicycle industry is chosen because it is an industry dominated by SMEs in Taiwan and is typical of the export sector. It consists of an assembling sector and a parts sector with an organizational structure that exercises extensive subcontracting practices (as opposed to vertical integration); thus, it has overall similarities with the decentralized industrial structure of the Taiwanese economy. The industry is an export-oriented industry. It has been incorporated into global bicycle production since the 1970s, with over 90 percent of the bicycle production for export. Moreover, the industry has demonstrated an upgrading process, moving from being a Third World producer to becoming a key player in the global bicycle industry, despite losing advantages to cheap labor abroad. While there has been an increasing movement of production offshore, the bicycle industry continues to maintain its production in Taiwan and compete in the high-end segment of the bicycle trade. Bicycles exported from Taiwan reached 10 million in 1998, dropped to 4 million in 2003 and rose to five million in 2008. While the total volume of bicycle exports has declined, their total value has increased. For instance, the average price of an exported bicycle has risen from an average of US$ 95 to US$ 300 or more from 1998 to 2000. These figures suggest that upgrading has occurred. Therefore, this is an ideal case for assessing the hypothetical changing role of the state in the export and technical upgrading process.

In what follows, three points are made concerning the role of the Taiwanese state in enhancing the export capabilities and technological learning of SMEs, as seen in the bicycle industry, and the changing state–business linkages. First, I show how standards setting and the export inspection scheme were crucial in establishing learning and linkages between the state and the export-oriented private sector. The focus on quality improvement via standardization was important not only in building the technical capacities the SMEs needed for export, but also to establish economies of trust with foreign buyers, an important element in overcoming the disadvantages a decentralized structure could bring. This technological learning via standardization, an overlooked aspect in the existing literature, gave rise in turn to a vibrant parts sector and created the backward linkages and entrepreneurship needed for broad-based development.

Second, I demonstrate the limitations of the winner-picking policies upon which the East Asian developmental state literature draws when dealing with a decentralized industrial structure. The top down alliances of picking winners as illustrated in the case of the derailleur project and the Center-Satellite Factories Program actually created dissent within the industry.

Third, through the case study of the BIRDC, I show how the actual workings of the alliances between the state and a series of SMEs in the quest for innovation were carried out through capability building by providing external economies applicable to all firms. The state agencies played the role of information disseminators and orchestrators in bridging different networks and resources, which reduced the entry barrier for entrepreneurship and alleviated the R&D burden on individual SMEs.

Building export capacities via standardization

The export of bicycles skyrocketed in the early 1970s, and the main destination was the United States. For instance, a total of about 17,000 bicycles were exported in 1968, and 107,000 in 1970. By 1972 this figure had reached one million, and 1.3 million in 1973. This export pattern conforms to the general trend of export-led industrialization in the 1970s. It is striking that so many manufacturers mushroomed in exporting products, from about 250 firms (registered) in the 1970 to 447 (registered) by 1976. Moreover, over 80 percent of them had fewer than 30 employees, and over 90 percent had fewer than 100 employees. How did these SMEs gain the capacity to export so many bicycles, and sustain it? Entrepreneurs attributed this to their quick response to the market. Yet their quick response initially consisted of exporting shabby products, for many were recalled or returned at US Customs. Buyers' complaints were mounting. By 1973, many US stores refused to sell bicycles from Taiwan. In what follows, I will illustrate the intricate dynamics of the ties between the state agencies and firms in building export capacities by focusing on improving quality and technological learning via standardization.

In 1971, one of the first measures adopted by the Bureau of Foreign Trade (BFT) was to entrust the MIRDC with studying the bicycle industry and improving its technology.[3] The initial plan was to focus on improving processing and manufacturing methods, standardization, and quality control in order to teach firms how to do inspections and verify their components in mass production. A former engineer at MIRDC who was in charge of this Bicycle Assistance Project recalled the state of the industry and how he got involved with it:

> At that time [in 1970–71], BFD entrusted a case to us, asking, given the current problems we faced in the world market, how would we promote bicycle exports?...At that time, CETRA (China External Development Trade Council)[4] helped us collect bicycles worldwide, ranging from high-quality grade to cheap ones for us to study and do quality comparison and bench-marking... There were no standards or regulations on these parts at that time. There was the Chinese National Standards (CNS) established in 1947. But it was 1971 that we were talking about... So what we did was: first of all, visited all assembling factories, and through them we found all their parts suppliers and listed them all in the first year. We then surveyed all parts makers in the second year of the project and checked out their technology levels... Just assembling factories, there were over two to three hundred at least doing exports, ranging from small family [businesses] which had no modern equip-ment to some established factories. You can imagine all the possible problems.
>
> (Interview C0104)[5]

So the first step was to focus on improving quality. Standardization was the key because all the components should be interchangeable or fit when they were assembled together, since the same component could be produced by several suppliers in a decentralized SME network.[6] A key element for standardization was to set up the manufacturers' own industrial standards, which later became the new revised CNS. The former engineer who was involved in the project explained how this came about:

> For example, we were trying to understand where our standards should be. We looked at the Japanese Industrial Standards (JIS), the US Standards, German Industrial Standards, and integrated them and came up with our stan-dards. ... For instance, the JIS is very detailed. It tells you the exact tolerance and how you verify, sample, and inspect. The American requirement came later. The US standards did not care whether your nuts and bolts are inter-changeable. The European and American Standards are mostly consumer standards, based on performance and function. It does not give you the details of size and tolerance or individual parts specification unless there is a safety issue involved. But we [i.e., Taiwan] were not up to that level yet, so we opted for a very detailed one. For instance, our standards specification would tell you how surface treatment should be done, how one does electro-plating and heat treatment. We specified them individually. Our foundation was established based on JIS. At that time, the bulk of our efforts were devoted to standardization.
>
> (Interview C0208)[7]

Despite the emphasis being on standardization and quality control, it could be argued that the technical learning of these SMEs began in this way—learning about specs, learning about making the right blueprints, and learning how to verify one's own design and product. The engineer explained how they worked with firms on quality control:

> Then, the next question arises: one may then ask, how did one know if they had done it correctly [even] if they had followed the spec? We then showed them how to make gauges based on these standards and told them to follow this to verify and enhance precision before it went to production. It was about standardization. We spent a lot of time on this. The gauges that we developed at that time are still at MIDRC, at least when I visited in 1993. We also taught the assemblers how to do quality control and inspection of parts makers, and they would follow this standard. The problem at that moment was about standardization, not product development.
>
> (Interview C0208)

Here MIDRC was important in circulating and passing on information, such as JIS standards and the subsequent US Consumer Safety Commission's regulation on bicycles, to numerous parts makers. Technical learning via quality control and standardization meant that the manufacturers finally made the grade to become "qualified players" competing in the world market.

Establishing economies of trust: the development of an export quality inspection scheme

To build export capacities, the state enforced an export inspection scheme starting in 1976 as a way of establishing economies of trust between Taiwanese suppliers and foreign buyers. The MIDRC played a crucial role in realizing a workable export inspection scheme (in consultation with the export firms themselves) that did indeed improve the overall quality of the goods coming out of Taiwan.

When the export inspection scheme was first introduced in the 1970s for bicycles, export firms protested against the measure and treated it as government red tape. They held that the government did not know much about the export market and that the guidelines it had followed (the CNS from 1940s) were outdated (*United Daily News* March 28, 1971). MIDRC worked with the Bureau of Inspection and Quarantine Control in executing and evaluating the inspections of items like bicycles, as well as working with the Bureau of National Standards in coming up with the specs for export inspection based on their prior knowledge gained from working in the industry. Contrary to the image of a top-down process of implementation of state policies, the MIRDC acted as an instrumental intermediary between the state and the private sector. It helped collect information and assisted in the state-building process when Taiwan tried to strengthen its export trade promotion, as seen in the case of the export inspection scheme.

The existing literature credits the government's ability in elevating the reputation of products exported from Taiwan; and the inspection scheme boosted the national image in the 1970s, when complaints were piling up (Chu 1997; Wade 1990; Egan and Mody 1992). The case of bicycle exports was no exception. But what is often overlooked is the technical learning and the collective gains in terms of image boosting that accompanied this inspection scheme, and that they in turn lowered the entry barrier for exports for the SMEs. Moreover, the inspection scheme implies that the earlier efforts at standardization had become institutionalized and that information was able to reach all the firms that wished to undertake the venture.

Most entrepreneurs concurred that this export quality inspection scheme was important for enabling SMEs to reach out to the world market because it demonstrated their abilities to meet the spec and quality standards. "Standards and spec are very important!" exclaimed one industry veteran (Mr. Hsu). An assembler explained how they learned quality control:

> At that time, the inspection bureau and BFT offered seminars on quality control. They gave factories grades like ABCD based on their factories' capability in meeting quality requirements. There was incentive for making it to the top grade. That's say, if you were grade A, you paid 0.1 percent in export funds. ... This was how we started to learn about quality control and quality improvement.
>
> (Interview Senior Chou)

Another assembler credited the contribution of the quality control program:

> Thirty years ago, the problem was about quality. You know the story about the shops in the US that refused to repair bicycles made in Taiwan. So the government introduced a quality inspection scheme based on grades and entrusted the MIDRC to conduct the inspections. At that time, all exporters, except Giant, needed to bring their bicycles for inspection before export. I told the Vietnamese government that if they wanted to improve exports, they should adopt this inspection scheme by grades.
>
> (Interview Mr. Pai II)

This pattern of assistance by MIDRC to the bicycle export industry in the 1970s was actually part of a general trend in the state's efforts to respond to export problems. Several other industries had similar patterns and faced similar problems, starting with the sewing machine industry in the late 1960s and the machine tool industry and other machinery-related industries in the 1970s. As in the bicycle industry, technological learning in these firms also sprang from standardization and quality control measures that were applied to all firms (*MIDRC Report* 1973, 1983; interview info). This is in contrast to the conventional wisdom that focuses on the state's inducing entrepreneurship via finance, and which is used to support the idea of a developmental state (Woo 1991).

Moreover, reading through newspapers of the 1960s and 1970s (also confirmed by *MIDRC Report* 1973, 1983) reveals that the MIDRC organized many seminars on processing technologies (heat treatment, forging, die-casting, welding, etc.), skill training of primary labor forces, on-site training for production workers, maintenance of equipment, and management of modern factories, at a time when formal science and technical higher education was just taking off. The MIRDC thus served as the information arm of the government by surveying factories in different industries and by understanding the level of technological development and the problems of the different industries. In addition to setting the technical specs for different industries, the MIDRC provided a platform on which they could all improve their skills. This experience in the early 1970s vis-à-vis standardization and quality control became the basis of engineering skills formation, and the various supports provided a foundation for the bicycle parts sector.[8]

Creating backward linkages: the consolidation of a vibrant parts sector

The immediate consequences of this specific type of institutional arrangement in export strengthening and technological learning created backward linkages to the society by establishing a vibrant parts sector. By the early 1980s, Taiwan was the number one world exporter of bicycles and had gradually become a supplier of premium-quality bicycles. Existing studies attribute the success to learning by doing original equipment manufacturing; and thus the learning came (a) from foreign buyers such as Schwinn, and (b) from the leading bicycle assemblers like Giant, who in turn passed on knowledge to the parts makers (Cheng and Sato 1998). If one situates the question in a comparative context, however, it would be: How did Taiwan become the chosen one? For instance, the other outsourcing option would have been South Korea, which shared a similar level of development with Taiwan and had been actively engaged in exporting bicycles since the 1970s. It is plausible to argue that the earlier technical development of the parts sector, the one that focused on standardization and inspection, paid off and sowed the seeds for subsequent development. Without the presence of a dynamic parts sector and without the foundation for improvement in the quality of components, the Taiwanese firms would not have been able to win contracts with the more quality-focused bicycle buyers among the US independent bicycle dealers, like Schwinn, who made up the premium market segment.[9]

The presence and dynamism of the parts sector allowed the assemblers to negotiate with MNCs to increase local content by using local parts, instead of becoming the typical Third World factories that assembled imported parts in exchange for processing fees. The former vice president of Schwinn recalled the situation of sourcing in East Asia in the early 1980s, and how Schwinn came to use Taiwanese bicycle components (for higher-end bicycles) instead of Japanese ones:

> Schwinn was the first to move [referring to the first high-end bicycle manufacturer to outsource to Taiwan]. When Schwinn was in the process of

making that move, Giant [the Taiwanese bicycle assembler] rapidly expanded the supply base in Taiwan. It also came at the time when yen appreciated against the dollar rapidly, and that season we could no longer afford to purchase the componentry from Japan because of the yen parity in 1982 and 1983. ... Giant had just started this expansion in the supply base in Taiwan for several years. It was no longer financially viable for the Americans and Taiwanese to spec and buy the Japanese componentry. So this accelerated it. ... Giant said, "We [i.e. the Taiwanese parts suppliers] were just about to be ready. Let's go ahead right now this season and do this and push these new vendors. Let's take a year to make this conversion."

(Interview T0204)

The interviewee went on to compare the difference between Taiwan and Korea and explained why Schwinn did not choose Korea as the sourcing site:

We went to survey the Korean parts business. The component situation was well behind any kind of development Taiwan was doing. It was not developed and it was not going to get developed unless someone put the time and effort into it. There was not this vision and grain to develop Korea as a source of industry. ... I met with the components people in Korea, but the only viable item was the tires and tubes. That has been going on since the sixties.

(Interview T0204)

The owner of a Korean bicycle assembling firm articulated his dilemma from the time he started in the export business:

That company [a Japanese factory in the export-processing zone that he had taken over] was buying most of the components from Japan, because they were in the free export zone, like a bonded factory. They imported most components and started to import some components from Taiwan. They did not buy components from Korea. When I started this business, I had to import all components from Japan. By the late 1970s, the Taiwanese started to beat the Japanese and were becoming more and more competitive in the 1980s. So it was very difficult for us to compete with the Taiwanese assemblers with components from Japan in the US and Canadian markets. So from the start, my business was difficult.

(Interview KC0104)

Subsequently, the dynamic parts sector, together with the assemblers, consolidated Taiwan's position in the global bicycle trade from the 1980s.

The illustration and comparison with the Korean bicycle industry is not meant to discredit the postwar economic success of Korea, but simply to illustrate that the legacy of the Korean model of state-large firm nexus does not favor the development of an SME-based parts sector despite its relative success in its targeted industries (e.g. auto).

Picking winners? The limits of top-down alliances in a decentralized industrial structure

Not all state involvement in the industry works towards the industry's advantage. The decentralized nature of the industry made the winner-picking approach, the conventionally understood ingredient for success in East Asian industrial transformation, difficult to realize. The case of the bicycle industry is illustrative.

As an industry grows to be a successful export industry, the conventional account goes that the state plays an important role in its upgrading process through Center-Satellite Factories Programs and involvement in the R&D of key components. The Center-Satellite Factories Program in Taiwan was an attempt by the government in the 1980s to coordinate the SME networks by bringing the smaller suppliers into the orbit of the larger assemblers in various industries involving the parts sector. The assumption was that with stable demand, smaller suppliers would be more willing to invest in upgrading and improvement in technology, following the Japanese example. In the case of the bicycle industry, the Program focused on supply-chain management, quality assurance, cost reduction, etc. Yet my interviews with participant firms found mixed results. In part, the open overlapping network made this kind of systemization difficult to implement. The decentralized nature of the bicycle production network meant that the assemblers were not big enough to bind all the parts makers. What ended up happening was that there was overlapping of parts suppliers among the four major bicycle-assembling factories participating in the Program. Suppliers found it too much work to adjust to different interfaces (interviews Liao, Hsu; *IDB Report* 1993: 24). The spokesperson of the leading assembler articulated the problem:

> We did form a supplier network. But even so, there was overlap among the parts suppliers among different assemblers. This had become a problem. For instance, Maxxis [a tire manufacturer] supplied to all major assemblers, like Giant, Merida, Fairly, and Pacific, and so did other parts makers. Suppliers ended up participating in several systems. This was not sensible at all. This was how we [meaning the industry] then established the bicycle industry association (TBEA) so that everyone could discuss issues on the same platform.

> (Interview GH0204)

The decentralized nature of the industry caused it to push for an industry-wide association to address common needs, such as problems experienced in management, export promotion, and trade.

Starting in the mid-1980s, the Industrial Development Bureau (IDB) under Ministry of Economic Affairs began to support the crucial component project and entrusted ITRI with the research as a way to assist technological upgrading of the industry to cope with increasing competition from lower-wage countries. Existing studies see the programs of joint product development of the carbon-fiber bicycle frame between a leading assembler and the ITRI as well as the patented breakthrough in derailleur components and subsequent technology transfer to derailleur companies as successful initiatives of the state–industry alliance (*ITIS Report* 2000; Amsden and Chu 2003: 86). But closer examination with intervie-wees in the industry suggests mixed outcomes and a distant working relationship with the ITRI on these measures.[10] The interviewees questioned the feasibility of the commercialization of these products developed by the ITRI and felt that the SMEs were more in tune with the international market demand (interview info). This distance can be partly explained by the knowledge and communication gap between SME-based entrepreneurs and highly educated ITRI engineers.

The most controversial case was that of the crucial component project on derailleurs (bicycle gears). Even as Taiwan's bicycle industry became the number one exporter in the world, derailleurs continued to be controlled by Shimano, the Japanese component maker and world leader in the derailleur field. Thus, upgrad-ing involved R&D on a core component in order to bypass the Japanese supplier. The establishment of the BIRDC in 1992 was the Taiwanese government's general attempt to set up an industry-specific R&D center co-funded by the state and the private sector to promote the industrial upgrading of the bicycle industry. The initial goal focused on R&D for crucial components, and research went mainly into the development of derailleurs so as to decrease the industry's dependence on Japanese parts makers. Yet, the single focus on derailleurs led to complaints of unfair resource allocation and suspicion of collusion of collective means for private goods, whereas the firms expected the Center to fulfill the needs of the industry as a whole, especially since only a few firms were produc-ing derailleurs (*IDB Report* 1993: 116).

Firms that manufactured other parts claimed that R&D should focus on their areas because they were equally important in contributing to the export and performance of the industry. A leading handlebar maker explained:

> the R&D Center cannot just support the development of derailleurs; they need to work in other areas as well, right? Especially given that other components are growing while derailleurs are shrinking [in terms of quantities exported by Taiwan]. ... The truth is that the overall capacity of the R&D Center cannot even compete with Shimano [i.e., Shimano's R&D department].
>
> Interview HL0102)[11]

At the same time, the assembly firms protested that Taiwan's main strengths in bicycle development related to materials and frame, and therefore that the upgrading of frames should be the priority, not derailleurs (*IDB Report* 1993: 114). In short, the concerns were predominantly that over-concentration on the upgrading of derailleurs, along with neglecting other possibilities, might under-mine the competitiveness of the industry as a whole. Conflicting views on the priorities for R&D led to a halt in the operation of the Center, especially after the disclosure of a financial scandal involving executives of the Center who had had dealings with the major derailleur firm in the first year of the Center's operation (*United Daily News* August 17, 1993).

Coordinating networks: capability building by providing external economies applicable to all firms

The winner-picking approach experienced strong resistance from the industry.[12] As a response to the collective demand of the industry, the restructuring of the BIRDC sought to supply the various needs of the industry and service all its firms in areas where each individual SME could not deliver. These areas were related to technological development, including product development testing and certification, quality assurance, materials and manufacturing processing technologies, standards setting, R&D analysis and design simulations, and collection of marketing information (*United Daily News* June 25, 1994: §B09).[13] This approach of logistical support for product development that could benefit all was similar to what the MIRDC did in the 1970s.

One important means was the establishment of an independent professional R&D testing lab for the center. The BIRDC had collected almost all the industrial standards of the world and was able to perform tests and certification according to requirements (interviews C0104, H0108, W0103). One might wonder why testing and providing logistical support were important and how these means could possibly enhance the innovative capacities of the firms. Could they not be done by the firms on their own? I will use quotes from the former general manager of the Center to illustrate the relevance of an independent professional testing lab and its importance to R&D for SMEs. When asked how it would differ from firms' own testing facilities, he observed:

> It is a matter of credibility. Of course an individual firm is going to claim that their product is reliable and good. Judging from these firms' equipment, I wonder about the level of testing they could achieve. Of course, a few bigger ones have invested in testing equipment and do it relatively well. But most factories can't afford to spend that much money on testing equipment. Second, testing involves two dimensions. First of all, if it is just to verify and test whether or not my product meets the standards and is reliable; that is easy to do. Second, the testing becomes crucial when I am doing product development because I need to crosscheck and verify testing results at the R&D stage. Then this testing is more complicated. Let's take the suspension fork—put aside the suspension frame for now, that is even more difficult—as an example: you can probably verify whether it is safe or not. But the Center can tell you your damping ratio, and they would test for other, related technical issues, not just safety. Moreover, they can tell you how to improve the product, starting from the design aspects. You may be able tell whether a product is good or bad, but you don't know how to improve it. This is what professional testing can do. In my view, the R&D Center has done quite well in this area.
>
> (Interview C0204)

These collective services provided by the BIRDC, which may seem subtle, were effective in assisting SMEs, especially among the parts sector, in R&D and for export.[14] These services contributed to the strength and upgrading of the industry as a whole. Let's take R&D testing as an example. Testing and certification by an independent professional testing lab for the bicycle industry boosts the image of the export firms and establishes trust between the suppliers and foreign buyers. One important element for successful export is meeting the quality and industrial standards of the designated countries, and third-party testing and certification are usually required by the designated country. An engineer from the R&D Center shared anecdotes about how parts makers used the lab to demonstrate the technical capacities the firms possessed to potential buyers and noted:

> Our lab is the showroom. What I mean is that some firms would tell their buyers that we were their subunit and take them here to show off. We would have to explain to the buyer when they came to visit that the company had entrusted us to conduct R&D testing and quality testing services for them, and that we provided the services to all firms.
>
> (Interview H0108)

The testing became an especially important part of the R&D process after the rise in popularity of the mountain bike in the 1980s. The changes that accompanied it created new possibilities for bicycles with technological complexities. This meant that the standards and requirements relating to bicycle manufacturing became even more detailed, diverse, and complicated. Thus, having access to a testing center in central Taiwan, where most bicycle manufacturers were located, enabled the SMEs, especially parts makers, to tap into the external economies provided by the semi-public research agencies and to reduce the entry barriers for export and subsequent R&D.

Situating the question in a comparative perspective further illustrates the necessity for this type of overarching support for helping the parts sector to upgrade. In my comparative study with the Korean bicycle industry, when I inquired why parts makers did not export, I discovered that a key problem they encountered was the inability to meet the industrial standards of the export countries. Studies on Thailand's auto parts industry suggest that it has a weak indigenous parts sector despite the industry's being incorporated into the global production chains of automobiles. This industry consists of low-skill processing jobs and assembly activities using imported high-tech inputs. In other words, despite industrialization, backward linkages have not been created. A key problem challenging the local Thai parts makers is their inability to deliver parts of export-grade. Problems that firms have experienced include lack of an independent testing facility, lack of a broader effort to develop an automotive engineering program, and lack of technical and skill training.[15] Parts makers have had to pay hefty sums of money to send their products overseas for testing, usually to their assemblers in Japan. Without this testing, they are unlikely to win contracts from MNCs or to enter the international market (Doner 2009: 257). Put simply, they lack the kind of technological learning that is gained from learning quality control. The weak linkages between different levels of state bureaucracy and between state agencies and the parts makers make coordination and implementation impossible.

In addition to providing externalities for R&D testing and information dissemination, the state agencies have bridged resources and disseminated ideas between different networks in various industries and state research labs. For instance, the BIRDC assists in the upgrading bicycles by being a coordinator and integrating R&D resources from different publicly funded research institutes—resources and connections that are difficult for individual firms to obtain (interview Pai). The study of the application of new materials is a case in point. The center conducted a feasibility study for the use of magnesium in bicycle production and identified the bicycle components that might benefit from incorporating this new material. The application of a new material may in turn involve a new manufacturing method that the MIDRC could weigh in on. The Center would then coordinate between different public research labs and distribute the knowledge to firms, for example, by organizing seminars. In other words, rather than picking winners, the Center identifies common knowledge that is useful to firms. It is up to the firms to keep innovating and to apply that knowledge for their own purposes. It is plausible that this approach has contributed to alleviating the R&D burden on SMEs by shortening the learning curves of firms.

In other areas, the services provided by semi-public funded research labs such as the BIRDC and MIDRC have not only eased the R&D burden of SMEs and reduced undue risk-taking, but have also encouraged learning by inducing firms to become more creative in exploring ways to develop their products that they might not otherwise have undertaken.[16] For example, one interviewee reiterated the importance of working with MIDRC and the importance of inter-industry learning:

> Although MIDRC is not necessarily specialized in bicycles, they know a lot about materials. Moreover, they have worked with many different industries and they share with us their ideas from other industries. Of course, they cannot play favorites with individual firms, but we all have access to their facilities. It is imperative that we work with the R&D lab at the stage of product development because we can use their facilities for testing, so we don't have to invest in testing equipment up front for something that we don't even know is going to work.
>
> (Interview AL0208)

Evaluating the shifting roles of industry-specific R&D centers and the MIDRC in working with a series of SMEs suggests that embeddedness (linkages) can in fact be helpful when the focus is on problem-solving that benefits and seeds the development of an industry as a whole, especially when dealing with a decentralized network. The initial stage of these linkages in Taiwan was driven by meeting export demand. Standardization learning was a means for technical improvement, and it permitted the decentralized network to become qualified players in the world market. Subsequently, despite efforts from the state to pick winners, what proved to be a functional institutional arrangement for SMEs was when the state agencies provided capability building by supplying external economies for firms to tap into, and when the state agencies connected multiple networks to realize projects.

Conclusion

This research reveals an alternative development of SME-based entrepreneurship achieved by tapping into the external economies and resources provided by public research institutions. This interpretation is contrary to the conventional belief that the state is involved in the economy mainly by acting as a financier. In this analysis, the various state-funded research agencies have filled in the space that links the state and the society by coordinating and collecting information that feeds back to the state while disseminating and recombining resources among different networks (within state agencies, between the state and the private sector, and between different industries) that are conducive to technological upgrading in the private sector. This kind of diffused and decentralized linkage between state and society has assisted the network of SMEs by alleviating their R&D burden, averting risks, reducing entry barriers to export, cultivating entrepreneurship by information diffusion, and facilitating inter-industry exchanges.

Second, departing from the existing emphasis on the role of public higher-rank research institutions as the drivers in orchestrating R&D activities, the findings reveal the limitations of the top-down model of research alliances when dealing with a decentralized industrial structure. The stories conveyed here show that the linkages that are conducive to learning and catch-up are not based on the state and business elite forming cozy relationships leading to coherent industrial policies, but rest upon routinized interactions among lower-rank officials, engineers of semi-public funded labs, and series of SMEs where the networks are extensive and the actors are connected in multiple ways. The multiple and overlapping linkages—which tend to fly under the radar—are equally, if not more important than the higher-level formal ones. This diffusion of power also explains why embeddedness does not turn into crony capitalism. The linkages are conducive to broad-based development, as can be seen in the parts sector.

Third, this diffused model of linkages echoes the recent revival of interest in the "Developmental Network State" in facilitating innovation in industries that demand rapid changes in the transformation of higher-income countries (O'Riain 2004; Breznitz 2007; Block and Keller 2011). The historical account here suggests that such a pattern of collaboration worked at its best at the earlier stage of industrial development. It is not just the timing and stage of development that matter, but the patterns of state intervention needed to respond to the nature of the social groups the state intends to embed with.

Lastly, this pattern of institutional linkages with emphasis on the capability building of local entrepreneurship explains how the Taiwan SMEs were able to negotiate with MNCs, and how the economy was able to withstand the cyclical financial crises that have hit developing countries. The alliances between states and foreign capital in the past two decades, as witnessed in the establishment of numerous FDI export zones in developing countries and even in developed countries, are believed to drive economic growth in emergent economies. Yet the recent 2009 economic crisis reveals the limitations of this kind of FDI-driven model. The acclaimed success of the DNS, as in Ireland, has been largely fleeting (O'Riain 2011; Breznitz 2012). The Taiwanese experience reemphasizes the importance of indigenous entrepreneurship in responding to challenges in a globalized world. It is possible that without hefty patient capital from the state, SME-based entrepreneurship can thrive under certain institutional conditions. The process is not free from conflicts, but a successful outcome necessitates a state that is capable of adjusting and responding to changing conditions. It requires a bureaucracy not only capable of intervening in and initiating projects when needed, but capable of exiting and playing only a supporting role when those projects have matured.

Notes

1 This has been the dominant account within Taiwan in accessing the role of the SMEs in contributing to the Taiwan miracle (see Shieh 1992; Ka 1993).
2 See Moon and Prasad (1998) and Campbell (1998) for criticisms on the "embedded autonomy" approach to the developmental state.
3 MIRDC, established by the United Nations and Taiwan's Council for International Economic Cooperation and Development (CIECD) in 1963, aimed to promote the growth and technological development of the metal and metal-related industries. It became a state-funded research institution in 1967, entrusted by the Ministry of Economic Affairs to provide services and technological training to the manufacturing firms in Taiwan.
4 It was accomplished by the export-promoting organization established by the state in 1970. Aiming at trade promotion, the organization worked closely with export-oriented firms especially at the initial stage of export development in the 1970s. The funding came from the export promotion fund, whereby firms were levied 0.6 percent of their total export values by the state.
5 All quotes used here have been verified by various sources. Quotes are used extensively because they are crucial in reconstructing the context of how ideas came about.
6 This was a key problem at the initial technological development of this network-based organization for other industries. Similar problems occurred in the sewing machine industry in the 1960s. See *MIDRC Report* 1983: 26.
7 The Engineer's description is confirmed in *MIDRC Report* 1983: 28.
8 Interviewees also mentioned some individual entrepreneurs taking the initiative in disseminating information on JIS standards. Yet, judging from the evidence, I would suggest that the leading roles of individual entrepreneurs should not be overstated. Given the decentralized nature of the industry, it is unlikely that a firm at that scale would have been able to grow the whole parts sector. The key point here is that the MIDRC played a role in disseminating information across sectors, which accelerated the learning process.
9 Prior to the dealing with Schwinn, Taiwan's bicycles had been sold mostly in low-end mass merchandisers and discount chains such as Toys"R"Us, Walmart, and Sears.
10 Similar problems have been reported in studies on the machine tool industry (Gau 1999; Chen 2011).

11   The budget of over NT 200 million, an unprecedented amount of research funding allocated to the bicycle industry, was set for the derailleur project over five years starting in 1993. In contrast, the estimated R&D expenditure by Shimano, the leading Japanese derailleur maker, was about NT 300 million per year.

12   The IDB then moved the crucial component derailleur project from the BIRDC to the Mechanical Lab of the ITRI (United Daily News May 12, 1994). Even so, there was resistance from the industry to endorsing the derailleur project at ITRI (United Daily News June 1, 1994).

13   In fact, firms had been pressing for a professional testing center at several seminars and meetings with related government institutions when discussing the needs of the industry (e.g., *IDB Report* 1993; United Daily News June 25, 1994: §B13).

14   The importance of an R&D testing lab, and of collecting different national standards, has also been considered as important measures adopted by the R&D Center for machine tools in that industry's upgrading efforts since the 1990s.

15   For example, the proposal of creating an independent testing center for the industry gained little support among assemblers and government officials because assemblers had their own testing facilities and the government did not see the need for a separate testing center for parts makers (Doner 2009).

16   Matthews (2002), in his study on the ITRI research consortium, points out that a distinctive feature of the public research and development lab in Taiwan is its emphasis on learning and catching up, whereas research alliances in Europe and the United States are often about mutual risk reduction.

References

Amsden, A. H. (1989) *Asia's Next Giant: South Korea and Late Industrialization*. New York: Oxford University Press.

Amsden, A. H., and W. W. Chu (2003) *Beyond Late Development: Taiwan's Upgrading Policies*. Cambridge, MA: MIT Press.

Biggart, N. W., and M. F. Guillen (1999) "Developing Difference: Social Organization and the Rise of the Auto Industries of South Korea, Taiwan, Spain, and Argentina." *American Sociology Review* 64: 722–47.

Block, F. (2008) "Swimming against the Current: The Rise of a Hidden Developmental State in the United States." *Politics and Society* 36: 169–206.

Block, F., and P. Evans (2005) "The State and the Economy." In N. J. Smelser and R. Swedberg (eds.), *The Handbook of Economic Sociology*, pp. 505–26. Princeton, NJ: Princeton University Press.

Block, F., and M. R. Keller (eds.) (2011) *State of Innovation: The US Government's Role in Technology Development*. Boulder, CO: Paradigm.

Breznitz, D. (2005) "Development, Flexibility and R&D Performance in the Taiwanese IT Industry: Capability Creation and the Effects of State–Industry Coevolution." *Industrial and Corporate Change* 14: 153–87.

Breznitz, D. (2007) *Innovation and the State: Political Choice and Strategies for Growth in Israel, Taiwan, and Ireland*. New Haven, CT: Yale University Press.

Breznitz, D. (2012) "Ideas, Structure, State Action, and Economic Growth: Rethinking the Irish Miracle." *Review of International Political Economy* 19: 87–113.

Campbell, J. (1998) "Book Reviews on Evans Embedded Autonomy." *Theory and Society* 27: 103–46.

Chen, L. C. (2009) "Learning through Informal Local and Global Linkages: The Case of Taiwan's Machine Tool Industry." *Research Policy* 38: 527–35.

Chen, L. C. (2011) "The Evolving Roles of the State and Public Research Institutes in the Technological Upgrading Process of Industries: The Case of Taiwan's Machine Tool Industry." *Journal of Social Sciences and Philosophy* 24: 19–50 (in Chinese).

Cheng, T. J. (1990) "Political Regime and Development Strategies: South Korea and Taiwan." In G. Gereffi and D. L. Wyman (eds.), *Manufacturing Miracles: Paths of Industrialization in Latin America and East Asia*, 139–78. Princeton, NJ: Princeton University Press.

Cheng, L. L., and Y. Sato (1998) *The Bicycle Industries in Taiwan and Japan: A Preliminary Study toward Comparison between Taiwanese and Japanese Industrial Development*. Tokyo: Institute of Developing Economies.

Chibber, V. (2002) "Bureaucratic Rationality and the Developmental State." *The American Journal of Sociology* 107: 951–89.

Chu, W. W. (1997) "Causes of Growth: A Study of Taiwan's Bicycle Industry." *Cambridge Journal of Economics* 21: 55–72.

Chu, Y. H. (2007) "Re-engineering the Developmental State in an Age of Globalization: Taiwan in Defiance of Neoliberalism." In J. E. Woo (ed.), *Neoliberalism and Institutional Reform in East Asia: A Comparative* Study, pp. 91–121. New York: Palgrave Macmillan.

Doner, R. (2009) *The Politics of Uneven Development: Thailand's Economic Growth in Comparative Perspective*. New York: Cambridge University Press.

Egan, M. L., and A. Mody (1992) "Buyer–Seller Links in Export Development." *World Development* 20: 313–28.

Evans, P. (1995) *Embedded Autonomy: States and Industrial Transformation*. Princeton, NJ: Princeton University Press.

Evans, P. (2005) "The Challenges of the 'Institutional Turn': New Interdisciplinary Opportunities in Development Theory." In V. Nee and R. Swedberg (eds.), *The Economic Sociology of Capitalism*, pp. 90–116. Princeton, NJ: Princeton University Press.

Feenstra, R. C., and G. G. Hamilton (2006) *Emergent Economies, Divergent Paths: Economic Organization and International Trade in South Korea and Taiwan*. Cambridge: Cambridge University Press.

Gau, S. C. (1999) "Production Network and Learning Region: The Production Of Machine Tools in Taichung." Ph.D. dissertation, Tunghai University, Taichung.

Gereffi, G. (2005) "The Global Economy: Organization, Governance, and Development." In N. J. Smelser and R. Swedberg (eds.), *The Handbook of Economic Sociology*, pp. 160–82. Princeton, NJ: Princeton University Press.

Gerschenkron, A. (1962) *Economic Backwardness in Historical Perspective: A Book of Essays*. Cambridge, MA: Belknap Press of Harvard University Press.

Gold, T. B. (1986) *State and Society in the Taiwan Miracle*. Armonk, NY: M. E. Sharpe.

Hamilton, G. G. (1999) "Asian Business Networks in Transition: or, What Alan Greenspan Does Not Know about the Asian Business Crisis." In T. J. Pempel (ed.), *The Politics of the Asian Economic Crisis*, pp. 45–61. Ithaca, NY: Cornell University Press.

Hamilton, G. G., R. Feenstra, W. Choe, C. K. Kim, and E. M. Lim (2000) "Neither States nor Markets: The Role of Economic Organization in Asian Development." *International Sociology* 15: 288–305.

Hamilton, G. G., M. Petrovic, and B. Senauer (2011) *The Market Makers: How Retailers are Reshaping the Global Economy*. New York: Oxford University Press.

Henderson, J., P. Dicken, M. Hess, N. Coe, and H. W. C. Yeung (2002) "Global Production Networks and the Analysis of Economic Development." *Review of International Political Economy* 9: 436–64.

Humphrey, J., and H. Schmitz (2002) "How Does Insertion in Global Value Chains Affect Upgrading in Industrial Clusters?" *Regional Studies* 36: 1017–27.

Johnson, C. (1982) *MITI and the Japanese Miracle: The Growth of Industrial Policy, 1925–1975*. Stanford, CA: Stanford University Press.

Ka, C. M. (1993) *Market, Social Networks, and the Production Organization of Small-Scale Industry in Taiwan: The Garment Industries in Wufenpu*. Taipei: Institute of Ethnology, Academia Sinica (in Chinese).

Kim, E. M. (1997) *Big Business, Strong State: Collusion and Conflict in South Korean Development, 1960–1990*. Albany, NY: State University of New York Press.

Mathews, J. (2002) "The Origins and Dynamics of Taiwan's R&D Consortia." *Research Policy* 31: 631–51.

Mathews, J., and D. S. Cho (2000) *Tiger Technology: The Creation of a Semiconductor Industry in East Asia*. Cambridge: Cambridge University Press.

Mazzoleni, R., and R. R. Nelson (2007) "Public Research Institutions and Economic Catch-Up." *Research Policy* 36: 1512–28.

Moon, C. I., and R. Prasad (1998) "Networks, Politics, and Institutions." In S. Chan, C. Clark, and D. Lam (eds.), *Beyond the Developmental State: East Asia's Political Economies Reconsidered*, pp. 9–24. New York: St. Martin's Press.

Negoita, M., and F. Block (2012) "Networks and Public Policies in the Global South: The Chilean Case and the Future of the Developmental Network State." *Studies in Comparative International Development* 47(1): 1–22.

Noble, G. (1998) *Collective Action in East Asia: How Ruling Parties Shape Industrial Policy*. Ithaca, NY: Cornell University Press.

Okimoto, D. (1989) *Between MITI and the Market: Japanese Industrial Policy for High Technology*. Stanford, CA: Stanford University Press.

O'Riain, S. (2004) *The Politics of High Tech Growth: Developmental Network States in the Global Economy*. Cambridge: Cambridge University Press.

O'Riain, S. (2011) "From Developmental Network State to Market Managerialism in Ireland." In F. Block and M. R. Keller (eds.) *State of Innovation: The US Government's Role in Technology Development*, 196–216. Boulder, CO: Paradigm Publishers.

Powell, W. W., and L. Smith-Doerr (1994) *Networks and Economic Life: The Handbook of Economic Sociology* 368: 368–402.

Shieh, G. S. (1992) *"Boss" Island: The Subcontracting Network and Micro-Entrepreneurship in Taiwan's Development*. New York: Peter Lang.

Storper, M. (2005) "Society, Community, and Economic Development." *Studies in Comparative International Development* 39: 30–57.

Wade, R. (1990) *Governing the Market: Economic Theory and the Role of Government in East Asian Industrialization*. Princeton, NY: Princeton University Press.

Wang, J. H. (2010) *The Limits of Fast Follower: Taiwan's Economic Transition and Innovation*. Kaohsiung: Chuliu (in Chinese).

Weiss, L. (1998) *The Myth of the Powerless State*. Ithaca, NY: Cornell University Press.

Weiss, L. (2003) "Guiding Globalization in East Asia: New Roles for Old Developmental States." In L. Weiss (ed.), *States in the Global Economy: Bringing Domestic Institutions Back In*, pp. 245–70. Cambridge: Cambridge University Press.

Woo, J. E. (1991) *Race to the Swift: State and Finance in Korean Industrialization*. New York: Columbia University Press.

Woo-Cumings, M. (1999) *The Developmental State*. Ithaca, NY: Cornell University Press.

Woolcock M. (1998) "Social Capital and Economic Development: Toward a Theoretical Synthesis and Policy Framework." *Theory and Society* 27: 151–208.

Government documents (in Chinese)

IDB Report	*Research on the Development Strategy of Bicycles and Bicycle Parts Manufacturers*. Taipei: Industrial Development Bureau, Ministry of Economic Affairs, 1993.
ITIS Report	*An Analysis of Automobile, Motorcycle and Bicycles Industries in 2000*. Hsinchu: Industry & Technology Intelligence Service, 2000.
MIDRC Report	*The Development of Metal Industries Research and Development Center, 1963–1973*. Kaohsiung: Metal Industries Research and Development Center, 1973.
MIDRC Report	*The Development of the Metal Industries Research and Development Center, 1963–1983*. Kaohsiung: Metal Industries Research and Development Center, 1983.

Newspapers clippings (in Chinese)

United Daily News (March 28, 1971): §01.
United Daily News (August 17, 1993): §07.
United Daily News (May 12, 1994): §B12.
United Daily News (June 1, 1994): §13.
United Daily News (June 25, 1994): §B09, §B13.

4 South Korea

Government-linked companies as agents of economic development

Jong G. Back

Introduction

Government-linked companies (GLCs) have been the agents of economic development in South Korea, playing, in particular, a vital role in the various stages of the country's industrialization process.[1] The number of GLCs has been increasing despite the government's neoliberal drive involving privatization in the 1990s. Following the global financial crisis in 2008, public enterprises have acquired an even more prominent role, thereby placing the neoliberal-based Lee administration in a position of self-contradiction. The purpose of this study is to analyze the historical process of development of GLCs and to outline reforms to improve their performance.

Two perspectives have been proposed to explain why capitalist countries need public enterprises: a rational perspective and a historical perspective. In the rational perspective, public enterprises are necessary because of market failures such as monopolies, capital market failure, externalities, and equity problems (Chang 2007: 12; Jones 1982: 26). In the historical perspective, the emphasis is on the plan of development fashioned by the government involving, for example, attempts to deal with the issue of the shortage of private funds and the supremacy of the national goal of driving industrialization. The rational perspective is likely more appropriate for developed Western capitalist states that had established public enterprises to cope with market failure. The historical perspective is suitable for tracing the role of GLCs in less-developed economies that had an inadequate number of private enterprises to advance industrialization. The historical perspective is more appropriate for understanding the South Korean situation. This is because South Korea's arguably unique circumstances early in its nationhood—the end of Japanese colonial rule followed closely by the outbreak of a short but destructive Korean War—had a major impact on the country's institutions, both political and economic. Recognition of context is vital to understanding how these institutions developed.

An analysis of the ruling coalition is also helpful for a historical study of South Korean GLCs. The state was a coalition of forces that dominated society at a specific time and played a fundamental role in designing and implementing South Korea's development strategy (Back 2009: 71). The state created, changed, merged, liquidated, or privatized public enterprises that would emerge as a key agent for promoting development. The dynamics within the ruling coalition would decide the manner of evolution of the GLCs suggesting the need to understand where power was located as a means to understand public policies and economic outcomes.

This chapter consists of two parts. While the first part is a historical review of South Korean GLCs, the second is a discussion of GLC reforms. This historical review will deal with the three stages of evolution of the GLCs. The first stage is the period when the GLCs were established. From the 1960s, as South Korea's neo-mercantile ruling coalition promoted public enterprises as agents of industrialization, their number—and their importance—increased rapidly. The second stage, the age of privatization, occurred when neoliberal ideas were imported and became the dominant ideology of the ruling coalition. The third stage began with the 2008 global financial crisis. The responses of the Lee administration to this crisis indicate confusion and inconsistencies in policies involving GLCs, leading even to changes in the roles of these enterprises played. The second part of this study deals with possible reforms of these GLCs, in view of their changing role. The reforms of the GLCs include organizational changes, increasing competition, and establishing societal balance of power. This chapter scrutinizes the logic and facts of GLC reforms to ascertain whether they are able to persist playing a vital role in developing the South Korean economy.

The three stages of development of South Korean government-linked companies

Creation of government-linked companies as agents of neo-mercantile industrialization

Table 4.1 outlines the main phases of development of the GLCs, indicating that the number of public enterprises has been increasing. While there were only 14 GLCs before 1950, there were over 300 by the early 2010s. The number of GLCs increased rapidly after the 1960s when South Korea began to industrialize. Interestingly too, the number of public corporations continued to grow even during the period of privatization.

The South Korean GLCs have a legacy of Japanese colonial rule. After Korea's Independence in 1945, there existed huge "enemy properties." These enterprises could not be sold to private businesspeople even though the American Military Government of Korea imported and installed a capitalist system in the country. For instance, fledgling Korean capitalists could not buy the existing power-producing plants, railroad companies, and mining enterprises as they were too big and too important to be privatized. The Korean government had to transform these "enemy properties" into public enterprises such as the Korean Electric Power Corporation, Korean Express Corporation, Korean Coal Corporation, and Korea National Housing Corporation.

However, South Korea could not benefit much from this historical legacy. This

Table 4.1 Period of establishment and liquidation of Korean government-linked
         companies

Period	Number established	Number liquidated
Before 1950	14	—
1950–59	10	—
1960–69	20	12
1970–79	43	
1980–89	57	11
1990–99	69	27
2000–2010	80	15

Note: "Established" means the number of new companies. "Liquidated" includes the number of
      closed, merged, and privatized companies. A dash indicates data not available.

Source: compiled from various sources

is because of the Korean War and the consequent division of the country that
resulted in detaching the agricultural South from the more industrial North. In addition, the Korean War destroyed almost all industrial facilities in the two Koreas.
Therefore, South Korean industrialization in the south since the 1960s and the
GLCs had no roots in the legacy of Japanese colonial rule (Back 2009: 104–10).

Following the military coup of 1961 by General Park Chung Hee, the state
chose the neo-mercantilist industrialization strategy as the mechanism to rapidly
develop the economy and employed GLCs to help serve this agenda. That strategy exhibited six key traits:

- planned economic development;
- state-led economy;
- export substitution industrialization (ESI);
- import of foreign loans;
- maximization of latecomer advantage; and
- strong labor control (Back 2009: 169).

The GLCs would become a major pillar of that developmental strategy.

The need to employ GLCs was inevitable in South Korea because of the
absence of private enterprises that could undertake capitalist industrialization. As
a consequence of the Korean War, 1.5 million people had died, 85 percent of the
GNP had been destroyed, and any base of private enterprise had been eliminated
(Kim and Roemer 1979: 35). After the Korean War, the South Korean government and the American aid agencies began to encourage the growth of private
enterprises. However, in the 1960s only government-linked organizations were
able to run vital sectors of what was termed as social overhead capital (SOC), that
is railroads, expressways, and water and electricity supply. Table 4.2 clearly indicates the dominant role of the public sector in the economy, specifically in the
areas of transportation, infrastructure development, utilities, and, very importantly, finance.

Table 4.2 Share of the public enterprise sector in the value added of various industries

Industry	Share (%) in 1971–2
Agriculture	0.2%
Mining	32.6%
Manufacturing	16.4%
Electricity, water, etc.	71.7%
Construction	4.9%
Trade	1.2%
Transport and communication	30.8%
Finance	83.5%
Other	0.5%
Total	9.1%

Source: data taken from Jones (1975: 78)

Public financial institutions have played a major role in driving South Korea's rapid industrialization. Following the 1961 coup, the government obtained direct and indirect control of most major banks. As South Korea (hereafter referred to as "Korea") did not have enough private banks to fund industrialization, the government had to create public banks such as the Korea Development Bank (1954), Industrial Bank of Korea (1961), Kookmin Bank (1963), Housing & Commercial Bank (1967), Korea Exchange Bank (1967), and Export-Import Bank of Korea (1976). As a result, over 80 percent of the Korean financial sector came under government control.

The GLCs were created to ensure a competitive edge in product development and manage the entry of these Korean good into world markets (Rhee *et al.* 1984: 11). The strategy to nurture export promotion necessitated the presence of strong manufacturers supported by stable capital supply and advanced technology. Since Korea had few of such private enterprises in the 1960s, public enterprises were created to fill this gap in the industrialization process. The state developed three incentive systems for export promotion. The first was the granting of tariff-free access to imported intermediate goods for export production. The second involved providing the export sector with working capital through domestic bank loans and foreign loans. The third was the supply of intermediate materials, including land, water, steel, and electricity, at a low cost. To fine-tune the provision of these incentives, government-controlled banks were created to allocate funds at preferential interest rates and public corporations were incorporated to produce steel, oil, and electricity.

The GLCs were also a useful tool that the authoritarian government could employ to control Korean society. There were a number of reasons for the need to control society, including ensuring effectiveness of inputs and political stability to push through the industrialization process. The legitimacy of the military governments of Park and his successor, Chun Doo Hwan, depended on rapid economic growth and political stability. Under the system of selective incentives that had been created, a strike by businesspeople (who might be uncomfortable

with the coercive allocation of economic resources by the state) and that by workers could have made the government unstable. This could occur even though large
enterprises were potentially good partners of the ruling coalition. The state had
the power to let private businesses thrive or perish by controlling the input of
funds and intermediate materials through the GLCs. In fact, the state had tried to
control the manner of development of private enterprises to ensure they played a
role in achieving the developmental goals that had been outlined.

Many observers have concluded that the strategy of using the GLCs as instruments of economic development has been successful (Jones 1975; Song 2003;
Chang 2003). Per capita GNP had jumped from US$ 79 in 1961 to US$ 1,676 in
1979, and then to US$ 11,176 in 1997. The share of the GLCs in the GDP also
increased from 6.7 percent in 1960 to 10.4 percent in 1985, as shown in Table 4.3.
Song (2003: 1) notes that "Korean GLCs were dream trees of economic development … which bore dream fruits and made amazing contributions to economic
development."

Age of neoliberal privatization

In the early 1980s, theories of neoliberal development were imported into Korean
society. Aided by the Thatcher and Reagan governments and the Washington
Consensus, neoliberalism had achieved ideological hegemony in Western universities. Korea as a latecomer was accustomed to importing Western theories,
despite their different historical context and mode of governance. Privatization,
as a component of neoliberalism, became popular among members of the Korean
ruling coalition.

Arguments against the functioning of GLCs usually rely on the thesis that
public enterprises are far less efficient than private ones because of government
failure. One can encapsulate the thesis of government failure into three dimensions—the principal-agency problem, the free-rider problem, and soft budget
constraint (Chang 2007: 16). According to the proponents of privatization, the sub-

Table 4.3 Share of value added by Korean government-linked companies to the gross
domestic product (selected years)

Year	Value added (₩ billion)	Share
1960	31	6.7%
1964	42	6.1%
1970	221	9.2%
1975	738	8.3%
1980	3,600	9.1%
1985	3,337	10.4%
1990	18,000	9.4%
2005	39,500	4.6%
2008	35,600	3.5%

Sources: Sagong (1979); Ministry of Strategy and Finance (2011)

optimal performance of GLCs can be attributed to managers as they are not the owners of these enterprises. Managers of GLCs treat these enterprises as nobody's land and have no personal incentive in their sound development. Since GLCs are a component of the government, their managers tend to manage imprudently the risk of investment, expecting a bailout with public funds if their ventures fail.

However, contrary to the theoretical expectations of neoliberal scholars, some Korean GLCs were notably successful as agencies of economic development in the 1980s. For example, in that decade, the world's most efficient steel company was Pohang Steel Company (POSCO), a huge public enterprise (Chang 2003: 204). In 1986, POSCO produced 467 tons of crude steel per capita, while the average output of Japan's five biggest steel producers was 327 tons. POSCO charged Korean carmakers US$ 320 per ton of steel while American and Japanese steelmakers charged their customers US$ 540 and US$ 430 respectively. The supply of low-cost intermediate goods by a giant GLC had evidently contributed to the competitiveness of the Korean cars in the global market.

Another important role of the GLCs was to supply infant industries with funds. For example, the government created the Industrial Bank of Korea to aid the growth of medium and small businesses, while the Kookmin Bank provided households with financial support to increase consumption, the Housing & Commercial Bank financed the construction of houses, and the Korea Exchange Bank and Export-Import Bank of Korea supported the government's export-promotion drive among domestic enterprises. However, it was the Korea Development Bank (KDB) that played a crucial role in enterprise development, created as it was to supply long-term industrial aid, insure firms, and perform trust holding as the last resort for domestic firms. The KDB's share in the supply of long-term industrial funding has changed as Figure 4.1 indicates. Since the

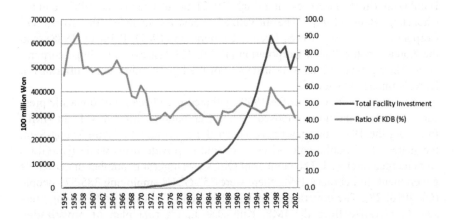

Figure 4.1 Role of Korea Development Bank in facilitating investments
Source: KDB (2004: 458–73)

early years of 1950s, its total ratio of funding has decreased from about 90 percent to 40 percent, while the amount of investment capital supplied continued to increase until the late 1990s.

As privatization became popular between 1980 and 2000, major newspapers and TV programs began publicizing scandals involving public enterprises. Businesspeople would openly deplore the backwardness of the GLCs. Neoliberal scholars appeared on TV programs criticizing the GLCs while politicians running for public posts promised the privatization of these enterprises. There was a gale of privatization, much of them without careful scrutiny.

Structural changes that had occurred within the Korean ruling coalition strongly contributed to the growing volume of privatization. From the 1980s, Korea's neo-mercantilist ruling coalition began to come under pressure to privatize from the *chaebols*, huge, well-diversified business groups that had been nurtured by the Park government to aid the industrialization process as well as develop export capacity (Back 2009: 279). These *chaebols* remained as junior partners to the ruling coalition under the military governments. Since the more successful export-promotion strategies were due to the performance of the *chaebols*, this allowed them to emerge as powerful institutions. Inevitably, as the latent power of the *chaebols* began to encroach on the actual power of the state, these enterprises no longer wanted to be seen as junior partners of the ruling coalition. The *chaebols* found the logic of privatization to be a convenient means of solving their problem. The privatization of GLCs would reduce the size and power of the government. Privatization of GLCs would also provide the *chaebols* with the opportunity to obtain control of highly profitable businesses as these public enterprises monopolized crucial sectors such as steel, finance, transportation, and water and power supply.

The wave of privatization in the 1980s began with the government's divestment of major banks and industries (Ok 2010). The privatized banks included the Hanil Bank (in 1981), Korea First Bank (1982), Seoul Trust Bank (1982), and the Choheung Bank (1983). The privatized industries included the Korea Oil Corporation (in 1980), Korea Dredge Corporation (1981), POSCO (1988), and the Korea Electric Power Corporation (1989). The last two were huge corporations. Their privatizations were instances of the largest public share offerings in Korea's financial history.

The privatization drive of the 1990s gathered pace because of domestic pressures and the conditions imposed by the International Monetary Fund (IMF) following the 1997 currency crisis. Under the government of Kim Young-Sam, the shares of 16 public enterprises were sold to private firms while five GLCs were merged or closed. The number of GLCs was highest in number under Kim's government. In February 1998, there were 552 GLCs employing 385,571 people (Ok 2010: 28). The government of Kim Dae Jung also came under strong pressure to privatize from the IMF. Kim Dae Jung's first plan of privatization concerned the 26 "mother companies" of the Korean GLCs. Five of them were to be completely privatized, six were to be privatized in stages, and 15 were not to be privatized. Kim's second plan of privatization concerned 82 major subsidiaries of these mother companies. In this plan, 33 were to be completely privatized, 28 were to be privatized in stages, 15 were not to be privatized, and six were to be merged.

In the late 1990s, Lee Myung-bak advocated a major privatization drive, calling it the "Policy of Advancing GLCs." Lee's privatization committee announced a plan to reorganize 92 of the 305 public enterprises; 24 of them would be sold, 36 merged to form 16 enterprises, five cleared, two transformed for competitiveness, and 20 reorganized to streamline their functions. The administration also announced a reduction in the number of civil servants by 22,000, from the existing 258,000. Finally, the plan to privatize the Korea Development Bank and the Industrial Bank of Korea, along with their five subsidiaries, brought to an end the era of developmental finance.

Privatization on trial

Effects of the 2008 global financial crisis

When Lee Myung-Bak won the presidential election in 2007, he declared Singapore as his developmental model. This meant that the drive to privatize would gather pace. Immediately after his inauguration, the Ministry of Strategy and Finance announced that 24 GLCs, including banks and industries, would be privatized. However, four years later, the record of privatization was very disappointing. Lee failed to fulfill his promise, only selling seven subsidiaries. *Chosunilbo*, a conservative newspaper that had long supported Lee's government, declared that "the door to privatization is closed."[2]

A Korean high-ranking official would argue that the international financial crisis of 2008 was the most important factor preventing Lee from rushing into privatization.[3] It was the worst financial crisis since the Great Depression of the late 1920s and was triggered by the complex interplay of factors within the financial system in the United States, designed to make the country competitive in the international money market. As the United States' Senate noted, "the crisis was not a natural disaster, but the result of high risk, complex financial products; undisclosed conflicts of interest; and the failure of regulators, the credit rating agencies, and the market itself to rein in the excesses of Wall Street" (US Senate 2011: 1). This crisis rapidly spread around the world.

Since deregulation and privatization were included as major factors that had contributed to the 2008 financial crisis, the privatization policy of the Korean government lost its ideological support. When the market fundamentalism of the Washington consensus came under heavy criticism around the world, the *Seoul Development Consensus* in the Seoul Summit of the Group of 20 in 2010 declared the end of the era of privatization. The British *Financial Times* concluded that this declaration did "little more than drive another nail into the coffin of a long-deceased Washington Consensus."[4]

Following the financial crisis, the Korean government was confronted with a number of dilemmas. The first dilemma was about the control of money supply.

In order to escape the economic recession, the state had to regain the control of money supply. The Korean government could not help by lending more money to public banks such as the Korea Development Bank and Industrial Bank of Korea even though there were plans to privatize them. There were also problems of collecting public funds from corporations such as Daewoo Shipbuilding & Marine Engineering, Daewoo Electronics, and Ssangyong Engineering & Construction. The government had poured a vast amount of public funds into these companies during the currency crisis of 1998 that had badly undermined the Korean economy. The government had failed to sell them because there were no buyers at the prices proposed. It was also impossible for the government to sell these enterprises at a lower price because of fear of a political backlash.

As a consequence of the financial crisis, the role of financial GLCs in particular rapidly expanded. The KDB had stopped foreign loans since 1993 in order to prepare for its privatization. However, it started offering new foreign loans amounting to ₩ 7.8 trillion[5] in 1997 in order to meet the urgent demand for funds. While the supply of foreign loans lasted for several years until the effects of financial crisis subsided, new industrial finance bonds issued by the KDB increased to ₩ 13 trillion annually. Major portions of new funds went to working capital loans and facility loans in order to stabilize the domestic market. Small- and Medium-scale Enterprises (SMEs) were especially weak during the financial crisis while large corporations were relatively stable. The KDB introduced its "Special Measures to Stabilize Management of SMEs," in November 2004, in order to provide working capital loans. In addition, from 2000 to 2005, the KDB provided ₩ 3 trillion to stimulate regional economies under the program of "Regional Economy Stimulation Fund," in cooperation with 25 regional government agencies (KDB 2005: 21; see Figure 4.2).

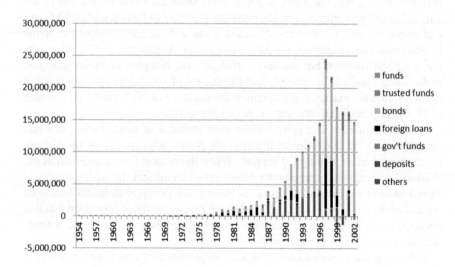

Figure 4.2 Annual new funds of Korea Development Bank

The second dilemma involved the issue of job creation. It is usual that the privatization of public corporations would result in the retrenchment of workers. Lee's government planned to retrench 19,000 GLC employees. However, because of the economic recession, the government had to encourage more job-creation than normal, even in private companies. Public enterprises had to be in the fore-front of job-creation. In view of these contradictions, Lee's government changed the name of the policy of privatization to the policy of advancement.

The third dilemma arose from the contradiction between the grand public investment programs and the privatization of public enterprises. The Lee admin-istration announced the grand *Four River Revitalization Project* in 2008, as a part of the *Green New Deal* strategy. This strategy was the Korean version of American *New Deal*, aimed at facilitating economic recovery through huge public investments. Lee declared that his government would invest ₩ 14 trillion (US$ 10.7 billion) in the project.[6] Not long later, Lee announced his intent to increase that budget up to ₩ 22.2 trillion (US$ 17.5 billion) and ordered the Korean Water Resources Corporation to invest ₩ 8 trillion in the project, although even inner circle members of the project committee were worried about the possi-bility of this enterprise's insolvency.[7] In short, implementing Lee's developmental strategy was not possible without the support of the GLCs. Table 4.4 indicates that the role of GLCs is still important with regard to not only the GDP but also employment.

Confusion in the neoliberal ruling coalition

While the proponents of privatization argue that the ineffectiveness of public enterprises harms economic development, in reality, such enterprises are neces-sary and effective tools to implement policies to drive growth. This issue led to the oscillation in the slogans about growth and distribution by Lee's government.

The ideological inclination toward neoliberalism appeared to be the funda-mental problem of the Lee administration. It should be noted that there is no theoretical support for preferring private enterprises over public enterprises. The Sappinton-Stiglitz Fundamental Privatization Theorem argues that "the perform-ance of private-sector firms is superior to that of SOEs only under stringent and often unrealistic conditions" (Chang 2007: 7).

The private partners of the Korean state were disappointed with the policy of "pension socialism" introduced by Lee. Kwag Seung-jun, the chairman of the Presidential Council for Future and Vision, declared that the National Pension Service (KPS) would participate in the management of its portfolio companies in order to promote development strategies such as the shared growth of large and small firms, the extension of the profit-sharing system, and restrictions on exces-sive M&A (mergers and acquisitions) activities of *chaebols*. The managerial intervention could extend to playing the role of a corporate watchdog as well as appointing CEOs of the firms in which the KPS owned a stake. This initiative by Lee therefore had serious implications for most major private firms. The national pension fund owned between 5 to 9 percent equity in the largest publicly-listed

Table 4.4 The three classes of Korean government-linked companies, 2010

Category	Total	Public enterprise			Quasi-governmental organization			Other public organizations
		Sub-total	Market	Quasi-market	Sub-total	Fund management	Trust administration	
Numbers	284	21	8	13	79	16	63	184
Budget (bill.)	464,271	181,460	88,557	92,903	173,866	98,376	75,490	108,944
GDP ratio (%)	43.7	17.0	8.3	8.7	16.0	9.3	7.1	10.2
Employees	247,793	75,442	27,459	47,983	66,940	18,696	48,244	105,411

Note: GDP ₩ 1,063 trillion, 2009.

Source: Ministry of Strategy and Finance (2011: 305).

firms, such as Samsung, Hyundai, LG, and SK. More significantly, the KPS remained the dominant holder of equity in then recently privatized corporations such as Korea Telecom and POSCO, a reason why these corporations denounced this effort as "a re-nationalization initiative."

Lee's government was responsible for contributing to the fastest income polarization in Korean history. Since the 1997 financial crisis, the proportion of non-regular workers had increased to 26 percent of the total workforce, double the OECD average. Old-age poverty was double the OECD average due to the weak presence of social safety nets. The nation's social spending stood at 7.5 percent, far below the OECD average of 20 percent. As a result, the GINI coefficient of income inequality reached 0.47 in 2007, the worst increase among the OECD countries. The situation had deteriorated because Lee had pursued the neoliberal policy of tax cuts for the rich and welfare reduction for the poor. Despite the emergence of these inequities, Lee's administration quickened its march toward neoliberal reforms involving deregulation and privatization. Korea had emerged as the "only significant" or the "only" neoliberal nation in this era when even the leading liberal countries of the world were declaring the end of neoliberalism.[8]

Changing roles of government-linked companies

The increasing number of GLCs in Korea has rendered ineffective the ideological emphasis on neoliberal privatization. While Table 4.1 indicates that the number of new corporations has been increasing continuously even during the period of privatization, it is important to pay attention to the changing role of GLCs.

The GLCs have increased their role in the economy to stabilize the market, more than ever before. In the first stage, due to the small number of private enterprises, the GLCs participated directly in the process of industrialization. In the second stage, the GLCs that directly participated in the market began to be privatized, influenced as the government was by neoliberal ideology and due to political pressure from the *chaebols* that had to compete with the GLCs. In the third stage, however, confusion prevailed over the neoliberal drive of privatization and the necessary changes that were required following the 2008 financial crisis that landed the Lee administration in a dilemma. A consensus among members of the ruling coalition drove the Korean government to give up its privatization agenda and renew the previous role of the GLCs.

Consequently, government intervention for market stabilization became more intensified and diversified. Table 4.5 indicates GLC creation in various spheres of the economy since the currency crisis of 1997. The Korean government created 105 GLCs—65 in the economic sphere, 14 in the cultural sector, 12 in education, 11 in welfare, and 3 in environment. The establishment of these GLCs was characterized by:

1   division rather than new creation; for example, the establishment of GLCs from seven subsidiaries of the Korean Power Corporation;

Table 4.5 New Korean government-linked companies since 1997

Social sphere		*Number*
Economy	Total	65
	Social Overhead Capital	29
	Technology	21
	Finance	9
	Labor	5
	Manufacturing	1
Culture		14
Education		12
Welfare		11
Environment		3
Total		105

2   creating support bases for the standardization of technology; for example, the Korea Ship Safety Technology Authority, the Korea Institute of Construction and Transportation, the Korea Institute of Marine Science and Technology Promotion, the Institute of Information Technology Advancement, and the Korea Technology and Information Promotion Agency for SMEs; and
3   diversification of the GLCs into areas such as labor, culture, education, welfare, and environment.

It is interesting that GLCs have been created in the spheres of labor and environment, hitherto neglected in favor of rapid economic growth. The ruling coalition had finally realized that upgrading to international standards in the spheres of technology, labor, and environment was directly connected to the promotion of the international competitiveness of Korean enterprises. Merely pouring a vast amount of money into industries was not enough to ensure international competitiveness.

Strategies toward effective government-linked companies

Organizational reforms

A historical assessment of the Korean GLCs would indicate that the most serious problem with privatization was its proponents' disregard of the different purposes of public and private enterprises. Even in a classic market economy, GLCs play a key role in managing market failures. Moreover, during market crises, GLCs are necessary for stabilizing the market. The purpose of public firms is to provide public goods while that of private enterprises is to ensure profit. In the Korean case, GLCs have served to overcome the shortcomings in the different stages—and sectors—of industrialization. Since their roles are different from private firms, privatization cannot solve the problem of ailing public corporations.

Another problem with privatization is that the productivity of public corporations is sometimes better than that of private firms. The Ministry of Strategy and Finance revealed that real labor productivity of public enterprises had been better than that of private companies during the period 2005–10. Table 4.6 presents the ratio of real labor productivity per person and per won of 24 public corporations to that of 47 private enterprises with similar average working capital.[9]

Another argument against the privatization of GLCs is that private companies often suffer from the same diseases as public enterprises, including corruption. Corruption in private corporations has been a longstanding problem. For example, Lee Kun-hee of Samsung had to launch an anti-corruption campaign against the executives of Samsung Techwin, a famous company of the Samsung group, because their executives had used corporate cards for private purposes and had received kickbacks from their subcontractors.[10] Many subcontractors were tempted to bribe procurement executives of leading companies in order to obtain new contracts.

Organizational reforms, as opposed to privatization, of public enterprises are desirable. Chang (2007: 22–3) suggests five organizational reforms. First, clearer and simpler job descriptions contribute to better performance. Second, transparency of management must be guaranteed to make monitoring easier and to lower costs. Third, a system of clear and effective incentives (material and non-material) is necessary to improve efficiency. Fourth, the establishment of a single competent agency for GLC supervision can contribute to better monitoring. Finally, reducing the number of GLCs, through liquidations, mergers, and even privatization of less essential public corporations, is necessary to improve monitoring.

The 1984 reform of the GLC evaluation system is widely seen as a successful case of improvement. The primary reasons for this reform were to ensure managerial autonomy, establish an evaluation system, increase transparency, and create a better incentive structure (Chang 2007: 23; Song 2003: 2–4). To increase managerial autonomy, the government minimized its control over the budget, procurement, and personnel management of GLCs. In order to reduce the burden of excessive inspections, the Board of Audit and Inspection was made the sole inspecting authority. In addition, the reform provided for a very sophisticated system of quantitative/non-quantitative indicators (distributed across four evaluation sectors) to decide on six tiers of material/non-material incentives (Sim 2004: 167–86).

This Korean Performance Evaluation System was promulgated in 1984 as the Basic Law for Managing Government-Invested Organizations in order to institute

Table 4.6 Real labor productivity ratio of public corporations to private corporations

	2005	2006	2007	2008	2009	2010
Real labor productivity per person	2.03	2.17	2.00	2.08	2.30	2.29
Real labor productivity per won	1.03	1.09	1.01	1.01	1.31	1.14

Source: Ministry of Strategy and Finance, press release, November 17, 2011

the organizational reforms of GLCs. This law was replaced by the Law of Management of Public Organizations in 2007. This included the small GLCs that the former had excluded. Other countries such as Pakistan, India, Venezuela, Brazil, and Mexico would adopt the Korean Performance Evaluation System. Mary Shirley of the World Bank and Anthony Bennett of the United Nations Development Program (UNDP) have endorsed the Korean system of evaluation, seeing it as a useful and successful endeavor (Song 2003: 8).

Increasing competition

Increasing competition can be a good method of improving the performance of the GLCs. Since public enterprises often function as monopolies, there is little chance of them benefiting from competition. Competition not only improves productivity but also provides an effective yardstick for comparing public enterprises with one another. The competitiveness of the GLCs might increase through exposure in three areas: international competition, competition with domestic private firms, and competition with domestic public firms.

The best way of increasing GLC competitiveness is to require public firms to export and compete internationally. International competition provides a good yardstick for evaluating productivity and promoting managerial efficacy of firms. In addition, a public firm, through its natural monopoly, could be in a good position to establish economies of scale and benefit from latecomer advantage. A public firm not enjoying a monopoly in the domestic market but facing competition in overseas markets would improve its competitiveness, contributing to improved balance of payments of the national economy. For example, POSCO was set up to advance the strategy of export promotion. If POSCO had enjoyed a monopoly in the domestic market, it would probably have grown to be a very ineffective organization. However, since it had to face international competition, POSCO was compelled to function more effectively, allowing it to emerge as the most efficient steel producer in the world.

Competition with private firms can be another good method to improve the productivity of public firms. Private businesspeople often complain of unfair competition from public firms. Therefore, it seems strange that they should harp on about the inefficiency of public firms as a reason for privatization. The competition between public and private firms would be particularly useful in key sectors of the economy. For example, construction companies have long complained of the dominance enjoyed by the Korea Land and Housing Corporation (KLHC) in the housing construction market. Nevertheless, the KLHC has provided most of the land, and at low prices, to all Korean housing construction firms and have assumed responsibility only for the construction of property in the lower tier of the housing market, that is for low-income households. This is a reason why the KLHC registered a huge debt of ₩ 107 trillion (US$ 93 billion) in 2009.[11] The KLHC proved to be the most effective agency for equitable development, achieving 100 percent housing supply for Koreans in 2008.

Competition between public firms can be a possible way of improving GLCs.

There are two ways to enhance competition between public firms (Chang 2007: 24). One is to set up another public firm in the same sector. The other is to establish a public firm that produces substitutable products or services. In 1991, the government set up a new telecommunications company specializing in international calls, DACOM, even though there already was a major public telephone company, Korea Telecom. Since then, this has contributed to the efficiency and service quality of both public companies.

Setting up societal balance of power

The supporters of public enterprises, as well as the proponents of privatization, warn that there are three major problems that the GLCs must deal with at the societal level: the spoils system, low quality of bureaucracy, and polarization. To escape these dangers, GLCs have to establish a balance-of-power, with the help of societal actors such as *chaebols* and civic organizations.

The spoils system is common in democracies. The party that wins in the presidential election tends to change the management of the GLCs, even though their tenures are guaranteed by law. After winning the election, a new government seeks to shape the policy machine in a manner that conforms with its agenda, in which the GLCs inevitably would have a very important role to play. In addition, having over 300 CEOs of public enterprises among its supporters is a good means to confirm political loyalty and ensure support for the new government. In this situation, the political appointment problem of "parachuters" and "revolving door" is common.

To avoid criticisms that senior managers in GLCs are political appointments, the Korean government has tried to institutionalize managerial autonomy along with a balanced recruitment system for public enterprises. The Korean government established the research committee for managers, which included non-government members such as the CEOs of private enterprises and representatives of civic organizations. Civic organizations play a particularly important role in this endeavor to guarantee managerial autonomy of public enterprises. A civic organization usually has a public purpose while the aim of public and private enterprises is the public good and profit maximization respectively. Bureaucrats seek to control corporations while private capitalists are willing to cooperate with the state to obtain access to state-generated concessions. Thus, only civic activists can be expected to pay attention to managerial autonomy, keeping in view the public role of corporations.

A high-quality bureaucracy is a prerequisite for the successful management of public enterprises. As long as bureaucrats run public enterprises, a low-quality bureaucracy constitutes an obstacle to the development of GLCs. One cannot expect to build a high quality bureaucracy overnight. However, with political will and adequate investment, it is possible to establish a high quality bureaucracy within a short time. The Korean case is an example of an excellent bureaucracy that was created within a generation, through administrative reforms and sound bureaucratic training. It is interesting that, somewhat counter-intuitively, a generalist training for the bureaucracy is more fruitful than training in economics (Chang 2007: 25). People of high caliber perform better in real management than specialists in economics.

The Higher Civil Service Examination (HCSE) has played a crucial role in ensuring the effective recruitment of generalists among high-ranking bureaucrats (Han 2007). The purpose of this examination is to recruit generalist bureaucrats, based on merit. The HCSE consists of two tiers. The first tier entails written examinations on subjects such as Korean history, the Korean Constitution, English, political science, public administration, economics, and international law. The second tier comprises examinations on topics such as administrative law, the Korean Constitution, and economics. People qualifying from the second tier are recruited as bureaucrats of class 7 to class 9 and they can apply for the first tier of the HCSE. People who pass the first tier are appointed as class 5 bureaucrats and they take charge of higher managerial positions. GLCs also recruit their employees from the second tier of HCSE examinations. These examinations contribute to creating an egalitarian and effective recruitment system not only for the bureaucracy but also for the GLCs.

While strengthening bureaucracy is important in its own right, not just to ensure efficient operation of GLCs, reforms of a related nature in other countries, notably China (see Chapter 2), have bypassed management by bureaucrats, opting instead to outsource management to professional managers. Adequately rewarded through performance-based incentives, these managers are also given complete autonomy in day-to-day operations, and hiring and firing of personnel. In the end, whatever the approach used, GLCs should be assessed by their performance.

While the GLCs have served as agents of economic development, there is a danger that these organizations can contribute to the polarization of Korean society. Since GLCs function as monopolies in the market, they tend to exploit monopolistic rents. Some managers of these corporations strive to derive exploitative benefits. Trade unions of these organizations usually collaborate with them and share the benefits. For example, even though the debt of public enterprises reached 20 percent of the GDP in 2010, some of the managers received excessive salaries, huge bonuses, preferential housing loans, luxurious condominiums, full subsidy for educational expenses, and so forth.[12] The growing debts of these corporations contributed to widening gap between haves and have-nots in society.

The Lee government subsequently began to emphasize the social responsibility of public enterprises to reduce polarization. The system of managerial evaluation was to be renewed to assess the performance of GLCs in the spheres of equal opportunity for the disabled and women, job creation, culture of sharing, reform of unfair trading practices, and fair compensation (Ministry of Strategy and Finance 2011: 299).[13] These initiatives reflect a contradiction in Lee's policies—seeking to privatize public enterprises on the one hand and proposing their social responsibility on the other. However, prodded by pressure from civil society to reduce polarization in society, Lee also promulgated "the Law of Social Enterprise" to expand employment and social services.[14]

Conclusion

This chapter has sought to employ the method of ruling coalition analysis to understand the evolution of the GLCs and propose possible reforms for them. There are three stages in the evolution of the Korean GLCs: creation, privatization, and response to global crisis. It is interesting that GLCs have been created even in the age of privatization. The GLCs were established to overcome the shortcomings of Korean industrialization since the neo-mercantile ruling coalition desperately needed capital, technology, and social overhead capital. These GLCs were established particularly to facilitate funding of economic activities, transfer technology, develop transportation, infrastructure, and telecommunications, and enhance the supply of intermediate goods for export promotion.

There is much evidence of the efficacy of the GLCs, debunking neoliberal arguments of the need to actively promote privatization. Consequently, the number of GLCs has been increasing rather than decreasing. However, the roles of GLCs have been changing. Under the neo-mercantile ruling coalition the government intervened directly in the market. Following several financial crises, the government began using the GLCs to stabilize the market. The role of the GLCs in market stabilization has become more intense and diverse. The neoliberal ruling coalition has also realized that upgrading to international standards in the spheres of labor, technology, and environment with the help of GLCs is directly linked to improving the latter's international competitiveness. Therefore, the Korean case indicates that the most important issue is not whether to privatize GLCs but how to make them effective organizations.

There is undoubtedly a need for reform of the GLCs, not their privatization, as a solution to their problems. This study proposes three modes of GLC reform: organizational improvements, increased exposure to competition, and ensuring societal balance of power. Organizational reforms include managerial autonomy and the establishment of an appropriate evaluation system. Increasing exposure to competition can improve the performance of GLCs, specifically by including other criteria for evaluating effective performance (i.e., capacity to compete in the international market, as well as with domestic private firms, and other public corporations). With a balanced recruitment system, high-quality bureaucracy, and social responsibility, GLCs can become effective organizations for socioeconomic development. These reforms would be easier to implement if the societal balance-of-power among the state, private enterprises (especially the *chaebols*), and civic organizations are established in Korea.

Notes

1   This chapter's reference to GLCs includes what is known in the literature as public enterprises, state firms, state-owned enterprises (SOEs), and government-owned corporations (GOCs). South Korean law classifies GLCs into five categories: public enterprise (market public enterprise and quasi-market public enterprise), quasi-governmental organization (fund management quasi-governmental organization and trust administered quasi-governmental organization), and other public organizations.

For details, see the Table 4.A1 in the appendix.
2 See http://news.chosun.com/site/data/html_dir/2011/08/18/2011081802500.html.
3 See http://news.mk.co.kr/newsRead.php?year=2011&no=404689.
4 See www.ft.com/intl/cms/s/0/8f33885e-ee90-11df-9db0-00144feab49a.html# axzz1iN2jJT1r.
5 The present exchange rate is US$ 1 = ₩ 0.0009.
6 The aim of the project was to build 16 dams, store up to 1.3 billion tons of fresh water, dredge 570 million tons of sand, create 190,000 new jobs, and increase economic activity worth some ₩ 23 trillion (Ministry of Land, Transport and Maritime Affairs 2009).
7 The Korea Water Resource Corporation was already under a heavy financial burden because it took charge of another new project of the Lee government—the Kyongin Canal Project. It had to borrow ₩ 1.8 trillion (75 percent of the total investment) and its debt ratio was anticipated to increase from 19.58 percent in 2008 to 94.0 percent in 2013. See http://newsmaker.khan.co.kr/khnm.html ?mode=view&code=114 & artid=200909101410441 &pt=nv
8 See www.koreatimes.co.kr/koreatime_admin/LT/common/nview.asp?idx=860& nmode=2.
9 In fact, Kang *et al.* (2008) later also showed that the performance of privatized public corporations was better than that of private conglomerate corporations.
10 See www.koreatimes.co.kr/www/news/opinon/2011/06/137_88712.html.
11 See http://cn.moneta.co.kr/Service/paxnet/ShellView.asp?ArticleID=2009 102010160801656.
12 See www.koreatimes.co.kr/www/news/include/print.asp?newsIdx=77540.
13 The Ministry refers not only to "social responsibility" but also to "corporate citizen." This emphasis on social responsibility of public enterprises might be inappropriate because their very purpose is to provide public goods.
14 While social enterprises can be subsidized by governments, they are legally bound to reinvest two-thirds of their profit.

References

Back, J. G. (2009) *Choice of Korean Capitalism*. Paju: Hangilsa (in Korean).
Chang, H.-J. (2003) *Globalisation, Economic Development and the Role of the State*. London: Zed Books.
Chang, H.-J. (2007) *State-Owned Enterprise Reform*. National Development Strategies Policy Notes. New York: UNDESA.
Han, S. Y. (2007) "A Historical Study on the Change of Bureaucrats-on High Civil Service Examination." *Korean Journal of Administration* 19(4): 1009–51 (in Korean).
Jones, L. P. (1975) *Public Enterprise and Economic Development*. Seoul: Korea Development Institute.
Jones, L. P. (ed.) 1982. *Public Enterprise in Less-Developed Countries*. Cambridge: Cambridge University Press.
Kang, C.-K., Choi, E-Y., and Lee, J. H. (2008) "Relationship between Business Conglomerates and Performances: Comparison between Privatized Public Enterprises and Chaebol Groups." *Study of Industrial Economics* 21(3) (June): 1011–40 (in Korean).
KDB (2004) *50 Years of KDB*. Seoul: Korea Development Bank.
KDB (2005) *Annual Report 2005*. Seoul: Korea Development Bank.
Kim, K.S., and Roemer, M. (1979) *Growth and Structural Transformation*. Cambridge, MA: Harvard University Press.

Ministry of Land, Transport and Maritime Affairs (2009) *Master Plan of Four River Revitalization Project*. June 8. Seoul: Ministry of Land Marine (in Korean).

Ministry of Strategy and Finance (2011) *2008–2010 White Book of Korean GLCs*. 2011.3. Seoul: Ministry of Strategy and Finance (in Korean).

Ok, D.-S. (2010) "Theory and Practice of the Management of Public Organizations–Conceptual Analysis based on Transaction Costs." *Study on Regulation* 19(1) (June): 3–37 (in Korean).

Rhee, Y. W., Ross-Larson, B., and Pursell, G. (1984) *Korea's Competitive Edge: Managing the Entry into World Markets*. Baltimore, MD: Johns Hopkins University Press.

Sagong, Il (1979) *Role of Public Enterprise on National Economy*. Seoul: KDI (in Korean).

Sim, J. K. (2004) *On Public Enterprise*. Seoul: Baeksan (in Korean).

Song, D. H. (2003) "Retrospect on the Evaluation System of Public Enterprises and Development." *Journal of Public Enterprise* 15(1) (December): 1–10 (in Korean).

US Senate (2011) *Wall Street and the Financial Crisis: Anatomy of a Financial Collapse*. April 13. Washington, DC: Permanent Subcommittee on Investigations, US Senate.

Appendix

Table 4.A1 Korean government-linked companies, 2010

Types	Name	
Public Enterprise (21)	Market Public Enterprise (8)	Korea Gas Corporation, Korea National Oil Corporation, Korea Electric Power Corporation, Korea District Heating Corporation, Incheon International Airport Corporation, Korea Airports Corporation, Busan Port \, Incheon Port Authority
	Quasi-Market Public Enterprise (13)	Korea Minting and Security Printing Corporation, Korea Tourism Organization, Korea Broadcasting Advertising Corporation, Korea Racing Authority, Korea Resources Corporation, Korea Coal Corporation, Korea Housing Guarantee Co., Ltd., Jeju Free International City Development Center, Korea Appraisal Board, Korea Highway Corporation, Korea Water Resources Corporation, Korea Land and Housing Corporation, Korea Railroad Corporation
Quasi-Governmental Organization (79)	Fund Management Quasi-Governmental Organization (16)	Korea Teachers Pension, Government Employees Pension Service, Korean Film Council, Korea Sports Promotion Foundation, Arts Council Korea, Korea Press Foundation, Korea Export Insurance Corporation, Korea Radioactive Waste Management Corporation, National Pension Service, Korea Workers' Compensation & Welfare Service, Korea Asset Management Corporation, Korea Technology Credit Guarantee Fund, Korea Credit Guarantee Fund, Korea Deposit Insurance Corporation, Korea Housing Finance Corporation, Small and medium Business Corporation

Table 4.A1 continued

Types	Name	
	Trust Administration Quasi-Governmental Organization (63)	Korea Education & Research Information Service, The Korea Foundation for the Advancement of Science and Creativity, National Research Foundation of Korea, Korea Institute of Nuclear Safety, Korea Student Aid Foundation, Korea Elevator Safety Institute, National Information Society Agency, Korea International Broadcasting Foundation, Korea Creative Contents Agency, Korea Agro-Fisheries Trade Corporation, Korea Institute for Animal Products Quality Evaluation, Korea Rural Community Corporation, Foundation of Agri. Tech. Commercialization & Transfer, Korea Institute of Petroleum Management, Korea Trade-Investment Promotion Agency, etc.
Other Public Organization (184)		Export-Import Bank of Korea, Korea Investment Corporation, Northeast Asian History Foundation, Institute for the Translation of Korean Classics, Seoul National University Hospital, Korea Foundation for the Promotion of Private School, The Academy of Korean Studies, Gwangju Institute of Science and Technology, Korea Research Council of Fundamental Science & Technology, Korea Institute of Science and Technology Information, Korea Basic Science Institute, Korea Research Institute of Bioscience and Biotechnology, Korea Institute of Nuclear Nonproliferation and Control, Korea Astronomy & Space Science Institute, etc.

Source : Ministry of Strategy and Finance (2011)

5   The state's business

Government-linked companies, the financial sector, and socioeconomic development in Malaysia

Edmund Terence Gomez, Elsa Satkunasingam, and Lee Hwok Aun

Introduction

The global financial crisis of 2008–9 dragged Malaysia's economy into recession that highlighted serious structural problems necessitating a major policy response. The Malaysian government proposed to resolve these problems by introducing a "new economic model."[1] During public debates that ensued about this "new model," there was much reference to the degree of government intervention in the economy and the need to review social policies such as affirmative action that involved distributing government-generated economic rents along ethnic lines to create a new domestic capitalist base. However, in government documents that were subsequently issued, including the *Tenth Malaysia Plan, 2011–2015* (Malaysia 2010a), which outlined how economic and social policies would be implemented, there was inadequate discussion about reform of government intervention to ensure efficiency, transparency, and accountability. There was, instead, extensive endorsement of neoliberal policies such as reducing the role of the government in the economy, promoting de-regulation and privatization, and endorsing the private sector as the primary engine of economic growth, even though the global financial crisis had exposed flaws in unregulated private markets, especially in finance. There was no discussion about institutional reforms to ensure checks and balances in the public sector.

The government's continued advocacy of neoliberalism is perplexing as Malaysia is an interesting case of a country where favorable outcomes were registered following the state's intervention in the economy to drive economic growth as well as redistribute wealth equitably. Government-linked companies (GLCs) have played a major part in the nation's economic development since the 1950s and still account for a large share of the corporate sector. GLCs, previously termed and constituted as public enterprises and trust agencies, have pursued various objectives, including industrial, agricultural, and commercial development, along with affirmative action in the form of nurturing Bumiputera[2] management and enterprise. The government also subscribed to active state intervention in the 1980s when it adopted developmental state-type policies in an attempt to replicate post-war Japan's economic growth, including employing government-controlled banks to finance domestic industrialization.

However, since the early 1980s, the government has persistently espoused neoliberalism, even though the outcomes of this policy initiative have not been commendable.[3] This neoliberal focus involved utilizing the stock market to rapidly create huge conglomerates, including through the privatization of major GLCs, before a wave of re-nationalization was instituted in the aftermath of the 1997 Asian currency crisis and widespread failure of privatized entities. The justification for this massive privatization exercise was that the GLCs had accumulated a checkered record, with a number of them reputedly performing below expectations.

What is clear is that government trust agencies, now called government-linked investment companies (GLICs), have exerted enormous state influence from the late 1970s by holding controlling interests in key economic sectors and, following the Asian crisis, have grown in scope and influence, including in the financial sector. The scale and scope of GLICs and GLCs are possibly greater at present than at any time previously, with widespread participation and influence in production, ownership, and policy, as well as a broad mandate to spearhead Bumiputera ownership of corporate enterprise.

Crucially too, following the global financial crisis, when policy reforms were publicly discussed, an interesting paradox emerged. On one hand, the government acknowledged the need to better utilize the GLCs to drive growth, yet paid inordinate attention to liberalization and further privatizations. On the other hand, liberalization has not appreciably increased domestic investments, including following its advocacy after the 1997 financial crisis. This is reflected in poor domestic investments since 2000. The paradox of the Malaysian case is that while government intervention in the economy is not well accepted or appreciated by domestic investors, liberalization as well as the promotion of the private sector as the key driver of growth has not inspired investor confidence, suggesting a problem with the form of governance of the corporate sector.

To obtain insights into this paradox, this study first appraises the outcomes of state intervention in the economy as well as the simultaneous implementation of neoliberalism and affirmative action, with a focus on the banking sector as the government tried to create a link between industrial and financial capital to nurture dynamic domestic entrepreneurs. An in-depth analysis is provided of ownership and control of GLCs in the financial sector, involving nurturing commercial banks that would compete in the private sector, though these same institutions would also be required to strive to attain the government's redistributive goals. This study also reviews the role—and under-utilization—of development financial institutions (DFIs), in pursuit of the government's developmental agenda, including fostering Bumiputera-owned small and medium-scale enterprises (SMEs) while also striving to alleviate poverty. The productive orientation of credit-based developmental schemes stands in contrast to how trust funds, privatization, and GLICs have functioned, involving the transfer of wealth, under the banner of Bumiputera capitalist development, to a select group of well-connected people. This practice of selective patronage has created considerable scope and tendency for non-productive acquisitive behavior. An evaluation will then be provided of the form of governance of the corporate sector, involving ownership and control of domestic enterprises. This chapter will conclude by drawing lessons from this corporate history to explain the Malaysian paradox.

History: public enterprises, privatization, and government-linked companies

State participation in commercial and developmental activities actively began before Independence in 1957. The incorporation of the Majlis Amanah Rakyat (MARA), formerly the Rural Industrial Development Authority (RIDA), in 1950 and the Federal Land Development Authority (FELDA) in 1956 signaled an intent to employ public institutions to spearhead Malaysian, particularly Malay, ownership and control of industrial and agricultural entities. FELDA and MARA stand out as public agencies that have significantly alleviated rural poverty. From the mid-1960s, State Economic Development Corporations (SEDCs) were established across Malaysia to foster industrial and commercial set-ups in all sectors of the economy (Puthucheary 2011). SEDC operations were manifestly political, with the state Chief Minister appointed as chair, and Bumiputera advancement a designated purpose.

Financial institutions played a complementary role in alleviating poverty and building rural and urban-based industries. In 1954, 11 "union banks" owned by cooperatives were merged to form government-controlled Bank Kerjasama Rakyat Malaysia Berhad (Bank Rakyat, or People's Bank), whose goals include improving the well-being of those involved in sectors such as agriculture, fishing, manufacturing, and transportation as well as promoting thrift. By the mid-2000s, Bank Rakyat had 1,200 cooperatives within its fold and 700,000 members (*Business Times*, February 9, 2006). It has, however, evolved from an institution that functions like a cooperative to a consumer bank with growing interest in Islamic financial services (Khaliq and Azhar 2011). Bank Rakyat is Malaysia's largest Islamic cooperative bank with 142 branches.

It was in the 1960s that active state intervention in financial services began, with the incorporation of the Malaysian Industrial Development Fund (MIDF) and Bank Bumiputra. Publicly listed MIDF was established in 1960 to assist manufacturing-based small firms to drive industrialization. Bank Bumiputra was established in 1965 to help expand Malay enterprise. But mired repeatedly in scandals and subjected to numerous bailouts, this bank was put through a few mergers and now functions as CIMB Bank. These banks' primary function was to accelerate Bumiputera participation in industrial and commercial activities.

Stark racial disparities formed the backdrop to the 1969 riots in Kuala Lumpur and the New Economic Policy (NEP) was formulated in 1970 to address the issue of economic inequality between Bumiputeras, Chinese, and Indians, the country's three main ethnic groups. The policy had two prongs: to eradicate poverty and to accelerate the restructuring of society to eliminate the identification of race with economic function. The second prong corresponds with affirmative action, and was meant to be phased out from 1990. Under the NEP, governance and policy frameworks shifted toward even stronger and more centralized state control and aggressive redistributive interventions to raise Malay participation in education, the public sector, equity ownership, and the corporate world. Public enterprises were created to establish industrial activities in new growth areas and to invest in other commercial ventures on behalf of the Bumiputeras. Perbadanan Nasional (PERNAS), the SEDCs, and MARA were tasked with increasing Bumiputera ownership of capital assets in modern sectors of the economy by taking up equity shares in joint ventures with the private sector which were to be transferred to individual Bumiputera ownership in the future. Petroliam Nasional (Petronas), incorporated in 1974 was vested with ownership of Malaysia's petroleum resources. Permodalan Nasional Berhad (PNB) was formed in 1978 as a unit trust fund for Bumiputera investors. Since the NEP stipulated that 30 percent of the shares of publicly listed firms be transferred to Bumiputeras to ensure more equitable distribution of corporate equity between ethnic groups, PNB was employed to acquire these shares at par value. PNB has a number of unit trust schemes, originally only for Bumiputeras, to aid in increasing individual Bumiputera equity ownership. PNB soon positioned itself as a major financial player, most forcefully demonstrated in its takeover of British plantation and mining interests, and is presently the second largest business group in Malaysia.[4] The number of public enterprises grew enormously after the NEP was introduced, from 22 in 1960 to 1,149 in 1992. These enterprises were spread across the manufacturing, services, agriculture, finance, and construction sectors (Gomez and Jomo 1999: 29–31). Table 5.1 provides a sample of the types of public enterprises that were incorporated by the government.

A large number of financial institutions known as Development Financial Institutions (DFIs) were established to fund Bumiputeras venturing into different sectors of the economy. The government defines DFIs as "specialised financial institutions" mandated to develop sectors seen as strategically important for "the overall socio-economic development objectives of the country. These strategic sectors include agriculture, small and medium enterprises (SMEs), infrastructure, maritime, export-oriented sector as well as capital-intensive and high-technology industries" (Bank Negara Malaysia undated). The Agrobank, formerly Bank Pertanian Malaysia Berhad, was established in September 1969 to fund agriculture-based activities, with a stress on supporting SMEs. Bank Pembangunan Malaysia Berhad (Development Bank), incorporated in 1973, was charged with encouraging and assisting Bumiputeras through each stage of enterprise development. In 2005, Bank Pembangunan and Bank Industri & Teknologi (Industry & Technology Bank) were consolidated to create Bank Perusahaan Kecil dan Sederhana, or SME Bank, to ease channeling financial aid to SMEs. In 1974, the functions of the Post Office Savings Bank, a DFI that had its roots in the Savings Banks that was established in the late 1800s, was launched as Bank Simpanan Nasional (National Savings Bank) to encourage and mobilize savings, particularly

Table 5.1 Malaysia: major public enterprises and trust agencies

Public enterprise	Year of incorporation
Federal Land Development Authority (FELDA)	1956
Selangor SEDC	1964
Penang SEDC	1965
Terengganu SEDC	1965
Bank Bumiputra (M) Bhd	1965
Johor SEDC	1966
Federal Land Consolidation and Rehabilitation Authority (FELCRA)	1966
Majlis Amanah Rakyat (MARA, Council of Trust for Indigenous People)	1966
South Kelantan Development Authority (KESEDAR)	1967
Kelantan SEDC	1967
Kedah SEDC	1967
Melaka SEDC	1967
Negeri Sembilan SEDC	1967
Perak SEDC	1967
Bank Pertanian Malaysia Bhd (Agricultural Bank of Malaysia)	1969
Pahang Investment & Industrial Company Ltd	1969
Perbadanan Nasional Bhd (Pernas, National Corporation)	1969
Perbadanan Nasional Berhad (PNS) (formerly known as PERNAS)	1969
Lembaga Padi dan Beras Negara (LPN, National Padi and Rice Authority)	1971
Pahang Agricultural Development Authority (PADA)	1971
Pahang Tenggara Development Authority (DARA)	1971
Urban Development Authority (UDA)	1971
Selangor Agricultural Development Authority (SEADA)	1972
Johor Tenggara Development Authority (KEJORA)	1972
Food Industries of Malaysia (FIMA)	1972
Credit Guarantee Corporation	1972
Perlis SEDC	1973
Pahang Trading Company (PTC)	1973
Johor Port Authority (JPA)	1973
Farmers' Organization Authority (FOA)	1973
Terengganu Tengah Regional Development Authority (KETENGAH)	1973
Rubber Industry Smallholders Development Authority (RISDA)	1973
Permodalan Nasional Bhd (PNB, National Equity Corporation)	1978
Heavy Industries Corporation of Malaysia Bhd (HICOM)	1980
Amanah Ikhtiar Malaysia (AIM)	1987
Tabung Ekonomi Kumpulan Usaha Niaga (TEKUN)	1988
Perbadanan Usahawan Nasional Berhad (PUNB)	1991
Multimedia Development Corporation (MDEC)	1996
Syarikat Prasarana Negara Berhad	1998
Malaysian Biotechnology Corporation (MBC)	2005
Pelaburan Hartanah Berhad (PHB)	2006
Malaysian Agriculture Food Corporation (MAFC)	2006
Ekuiti Nasional Berhad (EKUINAS)	2009

Source: Gomez and Jomo (1999: 30); Malaysia (2010a)

among the poor. The savings rate among Bumiputeras at that time was very low. Bank Simpanan Nasional would later be used to provide micro credit, involving uncollateralized loans, to SMEs (*Malaysian Business*, December 1, 2006). The Credit Guarantee Corporation was created in 1972 to ensure SMEs had access to credit facilities. The Export-Import (EXIM) Bank was incorporated in 1995 to support trade in goods and services with a focus on non-traditional markets. There are presently 19 DFIs of which six are banking institutions, that is Bank Pembangunan, SME Bank, EXIM Bank, Bank Simpanan Nasional, Agrobank, and Bank Rakyat (see Table 5.2).[5] In June 2011, the total volume of loans extended by the DFIs amounted to RM 52 billion (about US\$ 16.6 billion). The overall credit in the system was then about RM 800 billion, an indication of the under-utilization of these financial institutions. About 25 percent of these loans by DFIs were to small firms, of which 75 percent were Bumiputera-owned (*The Star*, September 2, 2011).

These DFIs targeted funding primarily at rural-based SMEs. However, the relevance of DFIs to the financial sector began to diminish appreciably from the early 1990s as the government's focus turned to the creation of conglomerates and corporate titans of scale and repute. State-owned commercial financial institutions were primarily responsible for facilitating the transfer of funds to well-connected businessmen, usually justified as positive discrimination in favor of Bumiputeras. Inevitably, NEP implementation fostered the emergence of a well-connected, large-scale Malay business elite through the distribution of government concessions, including the privatization of public enterprises.

Table 5.2 Development financial institutions in Malaysia

	Institutions	Date of incorporation	Objectives	Ownership and control
1	Bank Pembangunan	November 28, 1978	• Assist SMEs through various financing facilities, training and advisory services • Increase involvement of Bumiputeras in business • Provide medium to long term financing to capital-intensive industries, which include infrastructure projects, maritime and high technology sectors	MOF Inc.
2	Bank Perusahaan Kecil & Sederhana (SME Bank)	October 3, 2005	• Nurture and meet unique needs of SMEs by providing financing as well as financial and business advisory services • Contribute to growth of a more robust entrepreneurial community	MOF Inc.

Table 5.2 continued

	Institutions	Date of incorporation	Objectives	Ownership and control
3	Export-Import Bank of Malaysia (EXIM Bank)	August 29, 1995	• Provide credit facilities and insurance services to support exports and imports of goods, services, and overseas investments • Provide export credit insurance services, export financing insurance, overseas investment insurance, and guarantee facilities • Enable exporters to compete in overseas markets • Facilitate diversification and augmentation of the export basket of Malaysia with emphasis on export of capital goods • Promote Malaysia's international trade, particularly with emerging markets • To provide a vehicle for the implementation of the national policy of enhancement of international trade • Support firms to participate in reverse investment projects, particularly in non-traditional markets	MOF Inc.
4	Bank Rakyat	September 1954	• Provide financing, accept deposits, and produce satisfactory dividend returns for betterment of its members • Ensure satisfactory profit towards meeting dividend payments to members while charging reasonable profit rates that are not a burden to members	Ministry of Domestic Trade, Cooperatives and Consumerism
5	Bank Simpanan Nasional	December 1974	• Promote and mobilize savings, particularly from small savers • Inculcate habit of thrift and savings • Provide the means for savings by the general public • Utilize Bank's funds for investment including financing of economic development	MOF Inc.

Table 5.2 continued

	Institutions	Date of incorporation	Objectives	Ownership and control
6	Agrobank	September 1, 1969	• Provide financial and banking services focusing on agriculture sector • Upgrade and encourage agricultural financing • Serve as center of agricultural expertise • Provide credit rating for agriculture	MOF Inc.
7	Malaysian Industrial Development Berhad (MIDF)	March 30, 1960	• Promote development of the manufacturing sector • Provide medium and long term loans for financing new industrial ventures and expansion, modernization, diversification or relocation programs of existing firms • Manage and disburse funds under various special loan schemes targeting SMEs	PNB
8	Credit Guarantee Corporation (CGC)	July 5, 1972	• Assist SMEs, particularly those without collateral or with inadequate collateral to obtain credit facilities from financial institutions by providing guarantee cover on such facilities	Bank Negara Malaysia (76.4%), commercial banks (23.6%)
9	Johor Corporation (formerly Johor State Economic Development Corporation)	1968	• Contribute to economic growth through an efficient and effective business environment while upholding the community's interest • Upholding its position as a business that is competitive, profit-motivated, and recognized • Serve as a catalyst for sustainable business growth to fulfill its obligation as a state investment corporation • Contribute and add value to the community's well-being through its business as well as corporate social responsibility undertakings	Johor State Government

Table 5.2 continued

Institutions	Date of incorporation	Objectives	Ownership and control
10 Sabah Development Bank (SDB) (formerly Bank Pembangunan Sabah)	August 9, 1977	• Offer a wide range of financial and non-financial services to foster strong and healthy corporate participation in the growth of economy, both in Sabah and in Malaysia • To enhance entrepreneurial and corporate development to promote economic growth, particularly in Sabah • To act as financial intermediary for the state government of Sabah and its agencies, specifically the development of infrastructure and public projects	State Government of Sabah
11 Sabah Credit Corporation (SCC) (formerly North Borneo Credit Corporation)	June 15, 1955	• To contribute to socio-economy development of Sabah • To complement Sabah government's efforts by providing or facilitating financial credits to encourage private investment involving agriculture, light industry, development of rural and urban housing, and public utilities and amenities	State Government of Sabah
12 Borneo Development Corporation (Sarawak)*	1992	• Aid landowners who intend to develop their land, on joint venture basis for residential, commercial and industrial purposes • Involved in project-management, manufacture of building materials and builds schools, hostels, infrastructure, and recreational facilities	State Government of Sarawak
13 Borneo Development Corporation (Sabah)*	1992	• Provide financial assistance in the form of mortgage loans to the public to enable home ownership • Principal activities are property development and provision of loans to buyers of properties developed by the corporation	State Government of Sabah

Table 5.2 continued

	Institutions	Date of incorporation	Objectives	Ownership and control
14	Perbadanan Usahawan Nasional (PUNB)	July 17, 1991	• Integrated entrepreneur development packages in retail and SME sectors to help entrepreneurs develop business acumen, maintain a profitable venture, and shape their enterprise • Organizing training sessions on financial, general management, and marketing topics • Facilitate networking forums and group discussions among entrepreneurs • Organize mentor apprenticeship programs for new graduate entrepreneurs	Yayasan Pelaburan Bumiputera
15	Perbadanan Nasional Berhad (PNS) (formerly PERNAS)ʿ	November 29, 1969ʿ	• Develop the franchise industry while increasing the number of franchise entrepreneurs • Develop local products and market them abroad	Ministry of Domestic Trade Cooperatives and Consumcrism
16	Amanah Ikhtiar Malaysia (AIM)	September 17, 1987	• Reduce poverty among the poor by providing micro-credit financing to fund income-generating activities • Provide continuous financing facilities to Ikhtiar's entrepreneurs • Provide continuous guidance and training to poor households, the poorest, and Ikhtiar's entrepreneur	Managed by trustees from Prime Minister's Department, Ministry of Finance, and Ministry of Rural and Regional Development

Table 5.2 continued

Institutions	Date of incorporation	Objectives	Ownership and control

17 Cradle Fund Sendirian Berhad (CFSB)	July 18, 2003	• Non-profit government linked agency that manages the Cradle Investment Programme (CIP), wholly funded by MOF
		• Address the needs of technology entrepreneurs, in particular in obtaining pre-seed and seed funding
		• Provides funding to:
		  • Aspiring technopreneurs
		  • Researchers, lecturers, or students with ideas that come out of the academic or research arena
		  • Companies with technology-based ideas in order to attain commercialization
			Malaysian Venture Capital Management Berhad

18 Tekun Nasional	November 9, 1998	• Provide business and income generation opportunities • Financing of business capital • Provide guidance and support services • Provide a networking platform for all entrepreneurs	Ministry of Agriculture and Agro-Based Industry (MOA)
19 Majlis Amanah Rakyat (MARA)	March 1, 1966	• Encourage, guide, train, and assist Bumiputeras, particularly those in rural areas, to enable them to actively participate in commercial activities; • Aimed at creating a Bumiputera entrepreneurial community that is strong, professional, and resilient	Ministry of Rural and Regional Development

Notes: *Borneo Development Corporation (BDC) was established in 1958 and in 1975 it became a joint venture company owned by the state governments of Sabah and Sarawak. In 1992, BDC (Sarawak) Sendirian Berhad and BDC (Sabah) Sendirian Berhad were set up individually, ending the joint venture.
^In September 1996, PERNAS was privatized through a management buyout (MBO) when selected assets were taken over by Pernas International Holdings Berhad. As a result, a new acronym, PNS, was adopted.

The effectiveness of state intervention through public enterprises and the financing provided by DFIs to redistribute corporate equity between ethnic communities, particularly to increase Bumiputera stakes, was most evident in the first ten years of the NEP. Redistribution through the DFIs was possible because of the increase in volume of corporate assets owned by government agencies through the acquisition of foreign-owned firms. In 1970, Bumiputera ownership of corporate equity was a meager 1.5 percent; by 1980, it had increased appreciably by more than 10 percentage points to 12.5 percent. By 1990, when the targeted implementation of the 20-year NEP came to an end, corporate wealth attributable to Bumiputera individuals and trust agencies had risen to 19.2 percent, though way below the 30 percent targeted figure (see Table 5.3). During the subsequent 10 years, equity ownership owned by Bumiputeras and trust agencies rose to 20.6 percent in 1995, before falling marginally to 19.1 percent in 1999; by 2008, this share had risen to 21.9 percent. The most significant change in corporate ownership patterns since 1970 has been the appreciable decline in foreign ownership of Malaysian corporate equity—from 63.4 percent in 1970 to 30.1 percent in 1990, though it increased to 32.7 percent in 1999. By 2006, it had fallen marginally behind to 30.1 percent. These government figures on corporate ownership patterns along ethnic lines have been questioned, particularly after 1985, mainly because it was believed that the method used to tabulate corporate ownership was altered to allow for continued implementation of affirmative action.[6]

In the 1980s, the government spearheaded its heavy industrialization policy through state-owned enterprises. Inspired by Japanese and Korean industrialization through their developmental state model, Malaysia founded the Heavy Industries Corporation of Malaysia (HICOM) and forayed into automobiles, steel, and cement manufacturing. These large firms were to be government-owned and Bumiputera-managed, with financial and operational support from

Table 5.3 Ownership of share capital (at par value) of limited companies, 1969–2008 (percent)

Category	1969	1970	1975	1980	1985	1990	1995	1999	2004	2006	2008
Bumiputera individuals and trust agencies	1.5	2.4	9.2	12.5	19.1	19.2	20.6	19.1	18.9	19.4	21.9
Chinese	22.8	27.2	—	—	33.4	45.5	40.9	37.9	39.0	42.4	34.9
Indians	0.9	1.1	—	—	1.2	1.0	1.5	1.5	1.2	1.1	1.6
Other	—	—	—	—	—	—	—	0.9	0.4	0.4	0.1
Nominee companies	2.1	6.0	—	—	1.3	8.5	8.3	7.9	8.0	6.6	3.5
Locally controlled firms	10.1	—	—	—	7.2	0.3	1.0	—	—	—	—
Foreigners	62.1	63.4	53.3	42.9	26.0	25.4	27.7	32.7	32.5	30.1	37.9

Note: dashes indicate data not available.

Source: Malaysia (2010a)

Japan. The global recession of the mid-1980s hampered the launch of heavy industries, but their pre-maturity also showed up in the emergence of excess capacity, lack of competency, and severe under-performance, including because Chinese enterprises involved in these sectors had been bypassed during the implementation of these projects. Public enterprises suffered from a dearth of managerial experience and competency, and lack of policy direction in balancing efficiency and distributive objectives, exacerbated by poor auditing and governmental oversight, soft budget constraints, and malformed or perverse incentives. In 1981, available information on 260 firms under the purview of the Ministry of Public Enterprises showed that 94 were making losses and 21 had yet to operate (Jesudason 1989: 98–100). Between 40 and 45 percent of public enterprises were unprofitable throughout the 1980s (Jomo and Tan 2011: 335).

Notwithstanding the exceptional political motivations of these interventions and their racialized basis which severely undermined the performance of GLCs, Malaysia has generally adopted, largely without ideological current, conventional positions on the role of state and market in the provision of public goods and services. The ever pragmatist Mahathir Mohamad, Prime Minister between 1981 and 2003, mixed developmental measure such as government-driven heavy industrialization and privatization of key enterprises owned by the state. From the late 1980s, a sweeping privatization program was carried out. The recipients of state largesse, through preferential allocation of divested state assets, licenses, and contracts, had a dual role to play—be profit-oriented while also driving industrialization and developing Bumiputera enterprises. Privatization would facilitate Malay capital accumulation and nurture managerial experience and capability in the hands of Malay individuals (Tan 2008: 56–7). This hive of acquisitions and the rapid creation of Bumiputera capitalists peaked over 1991 to 1995.

There were weaknesses in the privatization program. First, in most projects the government retained shareholdings or secured effective control by issuing "golden share" rights. The Ministry of Finance retained majority ownership of key privatized companies including the two largest quoted corporations, utilities giants Telekom and TNB, the power producer. Second, many contracts were awarded without tender, among which were the North–South highway, national sewerage, and Bakun Dam projects. The beneficiaries had close ties to the government, chiefly to the United Malays National Organization (UMNO), the hegemonic party within the ruling alliance, the Barisan Nasional (National Front). Third, weak regulatory frameworks were institutionalized. Privatized projects were poorly monitored for compliance with performance, prudential, and social equity benchmarks and barely disciplined for corrupt or unproductive actions, especially for rent-seeking, sub-contracting, and profiteering off assets acquired at a discount.

Malaysia's privatization failed to cultivate Bumiputera industrialists and entrepreneurs as it intended; it both transferred and destroyed wealth enormously. The 1997 crisis hit many state-sponsored Malay capitalists and conglomerates the hardest. Well-connected firms were bailed out, largely by Malaysia's financially well-endowed oil corporation, Petronas, and renationalized, and national policy drastically reversed, with renewed emphasis on state ownership. This trend continues with GLCs approximating 37 percent of market capitalization on the Bursa Malaysia in 2010 (Malaysia 2010b).

The decade after the 1997 crisis experienced relatively sluggish economic growth, for the economy as a whole as well as the nationalized companies and GLCs. Corporate scandals continued to occur in spite of the introduction of corporate governance codes in the post-crisis period, while the performance of GLCs did not reflect that of a dynamic enterprise. In response to this problem, following a change of administration, when Abdullah Ahmad Badawi replaced Mahathir as prime minister in late 2003, the GLC Transformation Program was launched in May 2004. There are now seven GLICs: the Minister of Finance Incorporated (MoF), Khazanah Nasional Berhad, PNB, Employees' Provident Fund (EPF), Lembaga Tabung Angkatan Tentera (LTAT; Armed Forces Fund Board), Lembaga Tabung Haji (LTH; Pilgrims Fund Board), and the Kumpulan Wang Amanah Pencen (KWAP; Pension Fund Board). These GLICs have ownership and control of most of the GLCs (see Table 5.A1 in the appendix to this chapter).

GLICs can be distinguished by ownership and structure. One category comprises wholly government-owned entities that operate in a manner similar to equity funds, principally Khazanah Nasional, the most prominent GLIC. Khazanah, incorporated in 1993 to emulate the domestic and foreign corporate presence of the Singapore government's Temasek Holdings, is responsible for managing commercial assets and undertaking strategic investments. Another set of institutions operate as trust funds and pension funds, in which the government plays a statutory or guarantor role (PCG 2006: 29). Among these are the EPF, PNB, LTH, and LTAT. While Khazanah is the government's main investment holding arm, PNB, incorporated in 1978, was the primary NEP tool to acquire equity on behalf of Bumiputeras. EPF, a social security institution, provides retirement benefits for members through management of their savings. LTAT, established in 1972, is a superannuation scheme serving Armed Forces personnel. LTH, formed in 1969, is a special investment institution with an interest in diverse sectors, including plantation, property, banking, engineering, and construction. KWAP, set up in 1991, assists the government in funding its pension liability. The shareholdings of the GLICs are immense, although the role they play in implementing state policy is less directly under government oversight than Khazanah (see Table 5.A3 in the appendix).

Bank consolidation: an outcome of public policies

In Malaysia, government ownership in the banking sector commenced early, in the 1950s, and continued over the next two decades. By the mid-1970s, two Chinese-controlled banks, Malayan Banking (Maybank) and the United Malayan Banking Corporation (UMBC, later renamed the RHB Bank), had fallen under state control following runs on them. In 1990, of Malaysia's 58 financial institutions, the top three banks were controlled by the state.

In 1997, the currency crisis adversely affected firms owned by the well connected, who now held corporate stock worth far less than their acquired value, leaving them severely over-leveraged. Most non-performing loans (NPLs) held by domestic banks were by institutions owned by the government, that is RHB Bank (then known as Sime Bank), Bank Bumiputra (that evolved into CIMB following a merger), and Maybank. One key observation during the crisis is that DFIs were not adversely affected by the crisis. This suggested that government-owned enterprises, if left to professional management, could avoid financial crises.

In mid-1999, the government sought to merge Malaysia's 58 financial institutions, but not the DFIs, into six anchor banks. In this exercise, the most dynamic banks were brought under the government's direct control or indirect control of influential politicians. Following protests, particularly from the Chinese, the number of anchor banks was increased from six to ten. This consolidation exercise was an indication of the might of the strong state, a clear sign to private investors of their limited capacity to protect their corporate assets and property rights. By 2010 it was evident that Chinese influence had diminished in the banking sector while GLCs and Bumiputera individuals had increased ownership. It is noteworthy that since 2000, following this consolidation exercise, domestic investment rates in the economy, compared to the savings rate, have been paltry. From 2000 through to 2010, Malaysia registered a 40.6 percent domestic savings rate, considerably greater than the corresponding 21.4 percent gross investment and 10.4 percent private domestic investment. In contrast, over 1990 to 1997, domestic savings held a similar 39.7 percent, but gross investment burgeoned at 40.3 percent and private investment at 27.9 percent.[7] Table 5.4 indicates the present ownership structure of domestic commercial banks.

Table 5.4 Ownership structure of local commercial banks in Malaysia

	Name	Major shareholder	Status	GLIC ownership	%
1	Affin Bank Berhad	LTAT	GLC	LTAT	35.33
2	Alliance Bank Malaysia Berhad	Temasek	Non GLIC-owned	EPF	12
3	AmBank (M) Berhad	ANZ/Azman Hashim	Privately owned	EPF	11.1
4	CIMB Bank Berhad	Khazanah	GLC	Khazanah	28
5	Hong Leong Bank	Quek family Berhad	Privately owned	EPF	12.73
6	Malayan Banking Berhad	PNB	GLC	PNB	50.73
7	Public Bank Berhad	Teh Hong Piow	Privately owned	EPF	11.37
8	RHB Bank Berhad	EPF	GLC	EPF	46.03

Source: Bank Negara, October 5, 2011

In the first half of 2009, as Malaysia slipped into a recession, foreign investments plummeted, and domestic investors remained on the sidelines, the government was forced to review public policies involving ownership of corporate equity. Since investors, particularly domestic enterprises, were wary of the state, the government saw a need to review its regulatory processes. The government announced the liberalization of equity ownership regulation in key sectors, specifically services which had surpassed manufacturing as the leading contributor to GDP, including equity ownership in the financial sector. Under existing regulation, foreigners were allowed to own a maximum of 49 percent of equity in investment banks, Islamic banks, insurance companies, and *takaful* (or Islamic insurance) firms. This liberalization was an attempt to promote Malaysia as a hub for halal and Islamic services, including in banking, finance, and insurance. Foreign participation was expected to increase in these sectors, augmenting Malaysia's prospects to present itself as a center for Islamic financial services. However, the foreign equity limit for commercial banks was retained at the current 30 percent. There is little evidence that such reforms have helped to appreciably increase domestic investments in services indicating the need for a deeper analysis of the governance structure.

Governance in the Malaysian capital market

La Porta *et al.* (1996) contend, based on a study of 49 countries, that legal rules pertaining to the rights of investors and the quality of enforcement determine the level of financing and investment in the capital market of a country. They define legal rules as those that check ownership concentration, allow shareholders to exercise their voting rights, and as the protection offered to creditors and minority shareholders.

In this regard, the Malaysian capital market has adequate laws to protect investors. The banking industry is regulated by the Securities Commission and Bank Negara through the Companies Act, Capital Markets and Services Act 2007, Securities Industry Act 1983, Banking and Financial Institutions Act 1989, and Bursa Malaysia's listing rules. Apart from these laws, more measures were introduced to ensure corporate governance after the 1997 crisis (Mitton 2002) such as the Malaysian Code of Corporate Governance 2000 and the Guidelines for Corporate Governance for Licensed Institutions issued by the Central Bank (Bank Negara). The Companies Act was amended in 2007 to introduce statutory derivative action making it easier for minority shareholders to enforce their rights against directors who expropriate company property. In addition, the Minority Shareholder Watchdog Group (MSWG), established in 2000, effectively uses the media to publicize poor corporate governance and breaches of regulations. The Malaysian Code of Corporate Governance 2012 has initiated changes to corporate governance in line with global reforms. Bank Negara and the Securities Commission fall within the jurisdiction of the Ministry of Finance but these statutory bodies table their annual reports before Parliament which serves as a check and balance on the powers of the Ministry. It is clear that the Malaysian legislation and legal framework are adequate, but these laws are unable to address the concerns of investors due to the high ownership concentration by GLICs and families, as indicated in Table 5.5.

Within the banks, it is common for substantial shareholders, especially institutional shareholders, to nominate non-executive directors on the board of directors to protect their interests. The Chairman is tasked with leadership of the Board while the Chief Executive Officer leads management. The ideal position is for the Chairman to be independent of shareholders and management. However, Table 5.4 shows that the Chairmen and CEOs of GLIC-owned banks are linked to main shareholders or to other GLICs or GLCs. Investors' concerns about concentrated shareholding in banks and other companies are compounded when the Board and management reflect the influence of the substantial shareholder.

The study by La Porta *et al.* (2002) indicates that countries such as Malaysia, with concentrated shareholdings, have a negative correlation with the quality of investor protection. The capital controls, imposed by Prime Minister Mahathir during the 1997 Asian financial crisis to benefit firms associated with him and his close allies, heightened the perception of poor investor protection at the expense of crony companies (Johnson and Mitton 2003). The forced consolidation of the banks in 1999 that ended with greater government ownership and control over domestic banks raised serious concerns among investors as state-linked commercial banks had been actively employed to finance inefficient but politically desirable projects as well as the ventures of well-connected businessmen (La Porta *et al.* 2002). When politicians interfere in private banks, the perception of the negative effects of concentrated ownership on minority shareholders throughout the capital market is compounded (Dinc 2005). Laws alone will not change

Table 5.5 Links between chairmen, chief executive officers, and substantial shareholders of banks in 2012

	Substantial shareholder	Chairman	CEO
Affin Bank	Affin Holdings (owned by Lembaga Tabung Angkatan Tentera— 47.93%)	Retired general from the armed forces	Linked to Lembaga Tabung Angkatan Tentera (the substantial shareholder)
CIMB Bank	CIMB Group (owned by Khazanah Nasional— 28%)	Director and Chairman of Executive Committee at Khazanah Nasional	Brother of Prime Minister of Malaysia who is also Chairman of Khazanah Nasional
Malayan Banking	PNB held by Amanah Raya Trustees Berhad (50.73%) and EPF (10.90%)	Nominee of PNB	Panel member of Lembaga Tabung Haji
RHB Bank	RHB Capital Berhad (owned by EPF, 46.03%)	Former President and CEO in Pernas International Holdings	Former deputy chief executive officer of EPF

this perception when the executive is powerful and this is compounded by inadequate enforcement when compared to Asian nations such as Hong Kong, Singapore, and Thailand (Asian Corporate Governance Association 2012).

The government is not unaware of the impact of concentrated shareholding by GLICs. However, while liberalizing equity ownership in the services sector in acknowledgement of the problem and divesting some of Khazanah's assets in the capital market, GLICs have in some instances increased or shifted their shareholdings to other GLICs or GLCs, sending conflicting messages to investors. In 2011, PNB announced a takeover offer for shares in SP Setia, a well-established property developer, in which it was a substantial shareholder. SP Setia had 21 percent foreign ownership. The takeover offer was unattractive and was perceived as hostile but analysts believed that it would have been accepted as other GLICs held over 20 percent shares in the company. SP Setia's sound reputation was credited to its founder and chief executive officer's business acumen and PNB was forced to engage with him due to negative market sentiment. As PNB is primarily a trust fund for Bumiputera investors, the takeover offer was perceived at an attempt to increase Bumiputera ownership in the capital market.

Crucially too, Khazanah divested its shareholdings in GLCs such as Proton and Pos Malaysia to a private enterprise owned by a Bumiputera businessman perceived to be closely associated with UMNO. Although Khazanah sought bids from the capital market, it was implicit that the company taking over Proton should not only be capable of purchasing it but also continue its legacy as a GLC to promote Bumiputera rights.

The capital market also continues to be dogged by the perception of questionable enforcement, some of which is the result of a "spillover" effect from other enforcement bodies such as the Malaysian Anti-Corruption Commission and the Malaysian Competition Commission (MyCC). Although the Securities Commission and Bursa Malaysia have increased enforcement in recent years, the perception of selective enforcement and interference by politicians remains. There are unanswered questions about Malaysia Airlines' decision to enter into an out-of-court settlement with its former managing director in spite of a high court judgment to award the former substantial damages for mismanagement by the latter. There were also unanswered questions about the divestment of MV Agusta by Proton for the sum of one euro a year after it had been purchased for 70 million euros. Meanwhile, the Securities Commission's concluded that a major GLC, Sime Darby Berhad, had knowingly failed to make a mandatory general offer (MGO) under the Takeovers and Mergers Code 2010 to minority shareholders of E&O Berhad, a prominent hotel-based firm. There was evidence that Sime Darby would have obtained control of over 33 percent of E&O which would have triggered the MGO.[8] These cases which involve GLCs resulted in public perception that political influence over regulators had resulted in weak enforcement. These incidents indicate that although laws regulating the capital market and banking industry are adequate, their enforcement by the relevant institutions is subject to dictates of the office of the Prime Minister, who also serves as the Finance Minister, a practice that had emerged following the bank consolidation exercise.

Crucially too, the quality of enforcement is measured by the efficiency of the judicial system, rule of law, corruption, risk of appropriation, and contract repudiation by the government.[9] Investor concern over the hegemonic position of the executive in government is compounded by erosion of the independence of judiciary since 1988 when the Lord President and several judges were removed from office (Wu 1999). The judiciary continues to be plagued by accusations on improper judicial conduct resulting in one instance in a Royal Commission of Inquiry (Bhattacharjee 2009). The rule of law was threatened in the late 1980s onwards with repressive legislation which affected freedom of the press and freedom of assembly through statutes such as the Printing Presses and Publications Act 1987 and the Police Act 1967 (revised 1988). The combination of factors comprising concentrated ownership and weak enforcement against GLCs has resulted in weak investor protection.

The International Country Risk Guide (ICRG) indicates that Malaysia's investment profile decreased slightly in 2010 compared to previous years due to viability of contracts and payment delays. Malaysia's level of corruption in 2012 according to Transparency International is 4.9 out of 10 and it is ranked number 54 in the world out of 183 countries.

Conclusion: key lessons

This review of the GLCs, particularly financial institutions, indicates that specific historical circumstances have transformed the conduct of banking and their role in the economy. During the two decades from the late 1950s, the government employed the banks under its control as development-type agencies, specifically as DFIs which played a major role in cultivating domestic SMEs as well as alleviating poverty, although commercial banks were also employed to help nurture Bumiputera-owned SMEs.

However, the reason why banks, specifically the commercially run banks, have encountered numerous problems, including necessitating bailouts that involved subjecting them to mergers, can be associated with a number of factors. These factors include the active implementation of affirmative action, when the appointment of executives of public enterprises was based on race not merit, the introduction of neoliberal policies such as privatization which involved selective patronage, and the decline of checks and balances with the rise of a hegemonic ruling party, UMNO. The listing of GLCs and privatized firms on the stock exchange did not lead to any major productive outcomes in terms of creating large-scale enterprises known for the quality of their products or services. The banks that were most adversely affected by the 1997 crisis were not the DFIs or financial institutions owned by independent business people, such as Public Bank and Ambank, but government-owned commercial banks that had reputedly been abused to finance these now ailing companies. These banks were not subjected to stringent oversight, in terms of regulation, a core factor that shaped the way they evolved and how they did their banking. The private banks were bailed out by GLICs, an indication that government enterprises can perform well, a point noted when there is little evidence of the abuse of policy-related banks such as Bank Simpanan Nasional, Exim Bank, Agrobank, and the SME Bank over the past two decades.

This assessment of the banking sector draws attention to two crucial points. First, the key role that DFIs have been playing in funding economic development and alleviating poverty; second, the problems that government-owned banks encounter when having to deal with political interference, seen particularly after the 1997 crisis. DFIs can and have played an important role in driving industrial-ization as well as developing other key sectors of the economy, particularly agricultural and cottage industries in rural areas. This review of the DFIs indicates that an alternative banking system, where the state plays a crucial role in terms of forging a viable system to nurture domestic enterprises while also dealing with socioeconomic problems, can exist. The emergence of a burgeoning SME base also draws attention to the links between industrial and financial capital, involv-ing private and public institutions to drive industrialization. Unfortunately though, the government is clearly more intent on getting these DFIs to function as commercial enterprises no different from other banking institutions.

The role of regulatory institutions—including giving them greater autonomy—is evidently imperative since this history further indicates that the conduct of key actors within the hegemonic UMNO, primarily through the abuse of affirmative action, has impeded the rise of a dynamic domestic entrepreneurial community while also contributing to an abuse of state-controlled commercial banks. The development of GLICs and their ownership and control of banks draws attention to a related important point. Since the health of the banking sector is a reflection of the condition of the capital market, there is an urgent need for the devolution of power to regulatory agencies, such as the central bank, Bank Negara, that already have responsibility for closely monitoring the activities of the DFIs. Commercial banks should not be used to promote social policies as there are sufficient DFIs for this purpose, particularly since they are currently underuti-lized. DFIs should also be given autonomy in decision-making processes that involve the development of key economic sectors, particularly those that are rural-based where hardcore poverty continues to persist. As DFIs are not publicly listed or part of the capital market, concentrated ownership will not affect investor perceptions.

The need for such institutional reforms is imperative as recent government documents, including the Tenth Malaysia Plan, indicate the need to employ the banks to finance state-led strategies to develop new sectors of the economy as well as improve the quality and productivity of industries such as those in manu-facturing and agriculture that are in rapid decline due to poor investment in R&D to innovate or upgrade the quality of their products. These reforms, including the need to dispense with race-based business policies, are also important because SMEs constitute about 97 percent of all companies in the Malaysian corporate sector. The reluctance of owners of a large number of these SMEs to avail them-selves to the incentives and loans provided by DFIs, including the SME Bank, is due to fear of expropriation of their assets through policies such as affirmative action. These reforms should include more inclusive public policies as well as a more transparent and accountable form of governance in order to inspire investor confidence and help generate economic growth.

As for model of economic development, an important lesson from this assessment of the Malaysia's financial sector is the difference between the commercial banks and the DFIs. The state's attempt to drive industrial development by employing well-regulated DFIs, not subjected to neoliberal-type policies, has proven to be an effective mechanism to ensure a more sustainable and equitable pattern of economic growth. This indicates that while regulatory reforms are required to ensure a more transparent and accountable form of governance to ensure an equitable form of development, the institutional framework developed to manage DFIs as well as the GLICs and GLCs have to be well structured with sufficient autonomy to attain their development goals. What would be imperative here, given the ownership and control patterns of the DFIs, GLICs, and GLCs, are issues such as checks and balances as well as merit-based appointments of professional managers to ensure the quality of these public institutions are not undermined. With the reforms in place, the state can play a major role as a facilitator of domestic enterprises that have the entrepreneurial capacity to sustain economic growth.

Notes

1   The debates surrounding the reforms required within Malaysia were subsequently published in the government's document entitled the *New Economic Model, Part I* (Malaysia 2010b).
2   Bumiputera, which means "sons of the soil," is the term used in reference to ethnic Malays and other indigenous peoples. Of Malaysia's approximately 28 million population in 2012, Bumiputeras comprise 67.4 percent, Chinese 24.6 percent, Indians 7.3 percent, and others 0.7 percent.
3   See Gomez (2009) for a discussion on the simultaneous implementation of developmental state and neoliberal policies in Malaysia.
4   See Figure 5.A1 in the appendix for further insights into the ownership structure of such major government holding companies.
5   The Association of DFIs in Malaysia (ADFIM) states that it has 21 members, including Malaysia Building Society Berhad and Malaysian Technology Development Corporation. See: www.adfim.com.my/adfim_members.asp, and see Figure 5.A2 in the appendix for further details about DFIs.
6   See the report entitled *Overview of the 9th Malaysia Plan* by the Center for Public Policy Studies, available at www.cpps.org.my/Economic_Issues-@-9th_Malaysia_Plan.aspx.
7   Authors' calculations from Bank Negara data, various dates.
8   The Code indicates that if the acquirer acts in concert with a vendor to control more than 33 percent of the target company although the acquirer owns less than 33 percent shares, the MGO must be made to the rest of the shareholders. There was evidence that Sime Darby was acting in concert with the managing director and founder of E&O which would have resulted in Sime Darby controlling about 37 percent of the company. There were also allegations that the Chairman of the Board of E&O who was the husband of the Securities Commission's Chairman was involved in insider trading as he had purchased 450,000 shares prior to the takeover announcement. He is yet to be investigated by the Commission or Bursa Malaysia.

9   Efficiency of the judicial system is with reference to how it affects businesses from the investor's point of view while rule of law refers to adherence with law and order. Corruption is measured by whether government officials demand bribes in return for business licenses, while risk of appropriation refers to risk of forced nationalization, and contract repudiation refers to whether the government will postpone performance of its duties under a contract or attempt to scale it down if there is a change in economic or political conditions in the country.

References

Asian Corporate Governance Association (2012) *Corporate Governance Watch 2012: Market Rankings*. Hong Kong: Asian Corporate Governance Association.
Bank Negara Malaysia (undated) "Development Financial Institutions." Available at www.bnm.gov.my/index.php?ch=fs_mfs&pg=fs_mfs_dfi&lang=en (accessed January 6, 2013).
Bhattacharjee, R. (2009) "Reputation of Judiciary at Stake." *The Edge Financial Daily* (November 13).
Dinc, I. S. (2005) "Politicians and Banks: Political Influences on Government-owned Banks in Emerging Markets." *Journal of Financial Economics* 77: 453–79.
Gomez, E. T. (2009) "The Rise and Fall of Capital: Corporate Malaysia in Historical Perspective." *Journal of Contemporary Asia* 39(3): 345–81.
Gomez, E. T., and Jomo, K. S. (1999) *Malaysia's Political Economy: Power, Profits, Patronage*. Cambridge: Cambridge University Press.
Jesudason, J. (1989) *Ethnicity and the Economy: The State, Chinese Business and Multinationals in Malaysia*. Singapore: Oxford University Press.
Johnson, S. and Mitton, T. (2003) "Cronyism and Capital Controls: Evidence from Malaysia." *Journal of Financial Economics* 67: 351–82.
Jomo, K. S., and Tan, J. (2011) "Lessons from Privatization." In Mahani Zainal Abidin (ed.), *Malaysia: Policies and Issues in Economic* Development, 329–64. Kuala Lumpur: Institute of Strategic and International Studies.
Khaliq, A., and Kazmi, A. (2011) "Bank Rakyat Malaysia: Vision Remains while Mission is Revisited." *IIUM Journal of Case Studies in Management* 2(1): 41–8.
La Porta, R., Lopez-de-Silanes, F., Shleifer, A., and Vishny, R. W. (1996) "Law and Finance." NBER Working Paper 5661. Cambridge, MA: National Bureau of Economic Research.
La Porta, R., Lopez-de-Silanes, F., and Shleifer, A. (2002) "Government Ownership of Banks." *Journal of Finance* 57(1): 265–301.
Malaysia (2010a) *Tenth Malaysia Plan, 2011–2015*. Kuala Lumpur: Government Printer.
Malaysia (2010b) *New Economic Model, I and II*. Kuala Lumpur: Government Printer.
Mitton, T. (2002) "A Cross-firm Analysis of the Impact of Corporate Governance on the East Asian Financial Crisis." *Journal of Financial Economics* 64: 215–41.
Puthucheary, M. (2011) "State Economic Development Corporations." In Mahani Zainal Abidin (ed.), *Malaysia: Policies and Issues in Economic Development*, 577–96. Kuala Lumpur: Institute of Strategic and International Studies.
PCG (2006) Putrajaya Committee on GLC Transformation. Kuala Lumpur: Government Printer.
Tan, J. (2008) *Privatization in Malaysia: Regulation, Rent-seeking and Policy Failure*. London: Routledge.
Wu, M. A. (1999) "Judiciary at the Crossroads." In Wu Min Aun (ed.) *Public Law in Contemporary Malaysia*. Selangor: Addison Wesley Longman Malaysia.

Appendix

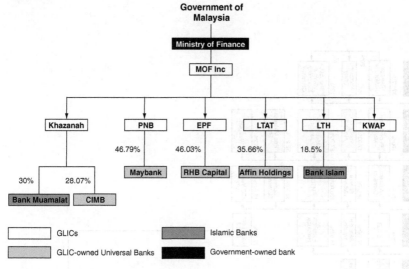

Figure 5.A1 Ownership structure of government-linked investment companies and government-linked companies

Source: company annual reports 2010; company official websites

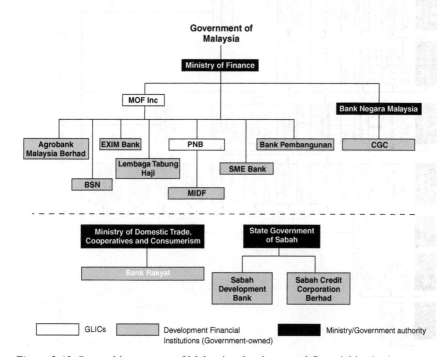

Figure 5.A2 Ownership structure of Malaysian developmental financial institutions

Source: company official websites

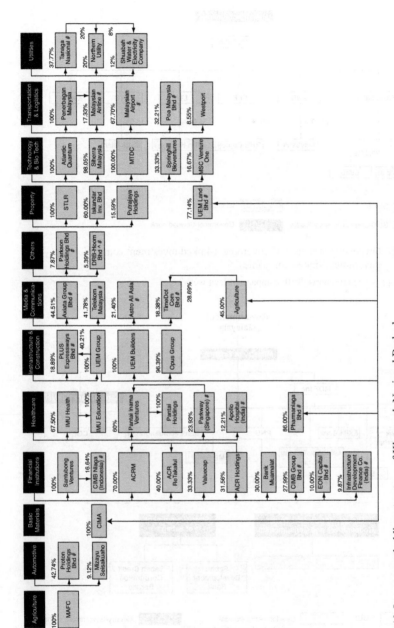

Figure 5.A3 Investment holding structure of Khazanah Nasional Berhad

Note: # = listed company; ^ = diversified.

Source: Khazanah Nasional Berhad, October 31, 2009

6 Poland

A systemic transforming process from state-planned to liberal economy

François Bafoil

After 1990, privatization became the decisive policy for the internal transformation of former Soviet-type economies throughout Central and Eastern Europe. It corresponded with the first post-communist decade (1990s) and provided a basis for the second transformation in the 2000s. This second transformation could be classified as being externally driven in that it took place as preparation for entry into the European Union (EU). These two periods are covered by the present chapter, which will focus on an analysis of the Polish case and the transformation of state-owned enterprises (SOEs). In the first part, the two main features of Soviet type centralised economies are recalled: the sectorial and territorial concentration of production units and the particular internal nature of their labor markets. These features had a strong on impact on subsequent events to the extent that they strongly influenced the decision to privatise at the beginning of the 1990s. The privatization policies adopted subsequently led to a profound deregulation of the labor market. The economic development that emerged in the 2000s, particularly in the Special Economic Zones (SEZs), was facilitated by pre-existing territorial structures. The final part of this chapter discusses the lessons learned about the role of the state, which played a pivotal role in the transformation process among foreign investors and the EU.

History: government–business linkages

One feature of Soviet-type economies is that all of them, without exception, were state-run and centrally planned. The centralising of decision-making took place under the control of the Communist Party whose constitution indicated that it had precedence over all other organisations either at state level or in society. Apart from agriculture which was not collectivised for particular historical reasons,[1] Poland was no exception to this rule. By the end of 1989, only 15 percent of agricultural holdings were collective (state farms and cooperatives) whereas industry was fully under state control. As in all other CEE countries, this corresponded to the obliteration of private activity which occurred when large industrial properties were expropriated immediately after the Second World War and all economic entities were placed under state control in the first post-war decade during the 1950s. At the end of the 1950s, Polish industry had the typical features of a Soviet type economy: a massive pre-dominance of heavy industry sectors (so-called "Sector A" heavy industries) to the detriment of light industry ("Sector B"); a very concerted territorial concentration with state companies becoming the main local and regional employers; a very dense centralisation of industrial activity within immense production units called *Combinats*. The so-called "noble" activities (research and training) oversaw a large number of production units without any autonomy of their own. Finally, the companies themselves were characterised by a centralised organisational structure. This was incarnated by the trio at the top composed of the Union leader, the company boss, and the Communist Party secretary who was the real head of the unit working in strict collusion with the regional political branch of which he was a member and who gave him his mandate in keeping with the principles of the nomenclature.

Mention should be made of two dimensions which had a considerable impact from the moment when the principles of a privatised economy became the rule of the new game after 1990. The first was the immense presence of public companies in the life of individual citizens and the very strong dependence of whole families on this type of enterprise. Public companies were much more than a public economic unit. They fulfilled an essential public role. They decided who got housing, spaces in holiday resorts, jobs, and they even managed the cemeteries and jails. This explains how difficult the very idea of privatization was for anyone who could thank a public enterprise for the lifetime job they and their families had. At that point, no alternative model was available: either in terms of an economic model, in terms of regional employment, in terms of stakcholders – private stakeholders simply did not exist – or in terms of employment as a result of territorial concentration. After 1990 the concept of path dependency was largely used to account for the continuity of processes initiated under Communism and notably in terms of different behaviour and costs linked to the adoption of new rules.[2]

Territorial concentration was the second dimension to have a profound impact on the post-1990 years in the sense that the SEZs created at that time are the direct result of this territorialisation of material and human resources. From this perspective, the success or failure of the industrial revival can be measured in terms of social capital. These two dimensions will be explored in the following parts of this chapter: firstly, the privatization policy and then the SEZs. A study of them reveals the legacies on one hand and the innovations on the other.

The role of the state in the privatization period

Prior to 1980, the whole of the private sector in Poland, apart from agriculture, was very small. Property was collective and the 8,400 public companies (3,177 of which were industrial) represented 80 percent of GDP and accounted for 88 percent of jobs. The 300 largest firms from among the 3,177 SOEs (or 10 percent of them) accounted for 59 percent of net Polish revenue. This explains the considerable impact of privatization, which took two decades to implement, on employment throughout the country. By 2011, the massive wave of privatizations was complete. Between 1990 and 2009, 7,516 companies were privatised of which 1,738 were commercialised and 2,191 were directly privatised. A further 1,933 were liquidated for economic reasons and the 1,654 existing state farms were also liquidated. Revenue generated from privatizations was slightly lower than expected but was nonetheless considerable during the period representing more than 10 billion zlotys[3] between 1999 and 2001 and over 25 billion in 2000. Again in 2009 and 2010, revenue exceeded 10 billion zlotys in spite of the crisis in 2008. In 2010, after a slow process over a period of two decades privatization was finally completed. Nonetheless, there are still several SOEs in existence which provides proof of their strategic importance. According to Blaszczyk, in 2005 the value of shares available to the state amounted to 33 billion euros and in 2006, according to EBRD data, SOEs were still producing 25 percent of GDP.[4]

These few facts provide information on the length of the process and by extension on the amount of resistance to the implementing of this policy. The level of resistance seems difficult to understand as privatization seemed to be the only real option at the beginning of the 1990s. Communism's economic disarray augured well for a speedy implementation of free market rules with privatization as the starting point. However, this is not how things happened. The object of this study is to account for initial divergences in decisions about how to go about privatization taking into account that, initially, social forces were hugely attached to the notion of "public property".[5] In this process of involving privatization by stages, conflict was limited to the major public companies. In order to achieve the process of privatization the main objective was to break the power of the former working class. Once this objective had been achieved, foreign firms were able to invest in Poland.

Privatization: sovereignty and technical issues

In Poland, on the eve of the 1990s, few social groups were in favour of rapid privatization.[6] On the contrary, privatization meant running the risk of becoming dependent on foreign capital. However, for former Soviet type countries and particularly for Poland, the end of Communism marked a victory for national sovereignty. This was accompanied by the strong conviction that nothing else could or should prevail over this one supreme fact.[7] The range of transformation programmes for property rights stemmed from this one essential idea.

One important group was made up of individuals who were hostile to any change that implied the liquidation of socialist benefits (relating mainly to employment).[8] They were massively present in the ranks of those who supported reformist Communists who had succeeded in a political metamorphosis by transforming the formerly dominant Communist Party into a democratic socialist party.[9] On the economic front, they supported the option which consisted in transforming property rights into Joint Stock Companies without the option of ulterior privatization. The aim was to commercialise companies (in other words, to register them as businesses) without any other change. This group was not successful in its attempts at economic transformation. The former economic *nomenklatura* found itself defeated in the middle of the 1990s when advocates of liberalism dependent on Western funds won the day. This is when new entrepreneurs without any links to the former ruling class emerged in the private sector.[10] This does not mean, however, that other options tended towards total privatization. Within the Solidarnosc camp, several different visions did battle with one another.

The first of these attempted to redistribute all socialist property to the Polish population of 38 million through mass privatization. The aim was to create a wide basis of small capitalists whose shares would subsequently be re-centred in restructuring funds. This mass privatization policy was hugely successful in Czechoslovakia (split in 1993 into the Czech Republic which carried on this policy, and Slovakia which stopped it opting for a more closed and protective policy without privatization) but not in Poland where it was implemented later and without the support of Polish citizens. In a similar perspective, another position defended the idea of Employee Ownership Plans as early as 1986. Under this plan, the transfer of shares to employees would be between 5 percent and 69 percent and would not give rise to any income during the first five years, following the example of cooperatives in the West though these remain marginal. This position obtained the support of the National Solidarity Commission. Another option was put forward by a group of economists from the Warsaw School of Economics (SGH). It postulated that that any SOE which employed more than 250 people should be transformed into a Joint Stock Company, with 20 percent of shares reserved for employees and the other 80 percent remaining the property of the state.

The radicals alone defended a position of full privatization. They were part of an active circle in Gdansk from the mid-1980s and were largely inspired by the lessons of Thatcherism and Reaganism for whom two imperatives prevailed: firstly, privatization was considered to be the only way to expel the Communists from key positions and to make economic behaviour effective; secondly, the general withdrawal of the state from all economic activity. For theoreticians, as early as 1988, it was necessary to "reject any form of 'enhancing' state property". Their aim was to succeed in a "genuine and radical transfer of ownership rights to the broad public".[11]

This profusion of positions on the way to proceed proves at least two things. On the one hand that Solidarnosc's political unity in their opposition to the Communist Party covered a number of divergent sensitivities; on the other hand that "the consensus of the round table talks was not pro-capitalist in character".[12] Technical issues relative to the nature itself of the companies to be privatised were added to this profusion of representations and political interest groups.

Sectorial inheritances

Certain sectors were barely if at all capable of privatization. This was the case for all industries which represented an immediate strategic interest: the ports, armaments and the railroads (public services). At the other end of the scale, certain sectors turned out to be easier to privatise if only because they were buoyed by strong social expectations and because in budgetary terms they did not cost anything as in the example of the service and housing sectors. The operation in itself was popular. This was not the case for the agricultural sector. The privatization of 20 percent of state farms and cooperatives was indeed popular but the procedure was made very difficult by the disappearance of property rights, changes in how land was allocated and transformations which had been put in operation over 40 years previously. In other words, former property owners found it difficult to justify their rights. Moreover, inequalities between small and large properties were huge as were those between engineers and qualified technicians on the one hand and the mass of unqualified farm laborers on the other. The sale of state farm assets exclusively favoured the former group (who were well aware of procedures within agricultural markets) and excluded farm laborers.

Finally, several sectors proved to be very difficult to privatise. This was the case for heavy industry sectors – the metalworking industry, machine tools, mines, and steelworks. There are two major reasons for this: firstly, the power of interest groups and, secondly, the inheritance of accumulated debt. Mass privatization was initially delayed because of the financial weakness of the companies involved. Half of those which were supposed to be included in the privatization programme had gone bankrupt and were therefore not suitable for privatization. In 1991, one third of all SOEs were running at a loss. In 1992, total debt accumulation by companies – US$ 24 billion – was the equivalent of the state budget.[13] Under these conditions, the state had no option but to hold on to its patrimony. It was forced to find temporary solutions in order to proceed subsequently to real privatization. The initial plan was to create public agencies or non-recapitalised banks to take on bad loans, even if it was obvious that such a solution ran the risk of making these structures permanent and turning them into "hospitals" for ailing companies. In 1996, a bank restructuring programme was created (the Bank Conciliation Procedure, BCP), whose aim was to force the bank to actively manage bad loans by involving it in the monitoring of the companies under its charge. However, the institutional conditions to implement such control did not exist. After this failure the bank privatizations took place and the major Western banks moved into Poland. Their arrival coincided with the repealing of the 1981 law and of the Foreign Direct Investments (FDI) law. This was valid for the whole of former Communist Europe.[14] Dependence on industrial and financial capital then became considerable. Whereas the share of FDI in the GDP of the EU15 countries was around 15 percent, it was over 70 percent in the East (see Table 6.1).[15]

Table 6.1 Share of foreign ownership in four strategic sectors

Country	Automotive	Manufacturing	Electronics	Banking
Czech Republic	93.1	52.6	74.8	85.8
Hungary	93.2	60.3	92.2	90.7
Poland	90.8	45.2	70.3	70.9
Slovak Republic	97.3	68.5	79.0	95.6

Source: J. Nölke and A. Vliegenthart, 2009, "Enlarging the varieties of capitalism: the emergence of dependent market economies in East Central Europe", *World Politics* 61(4) (October): 681.

The choices

Given what has been described above, it is easy to understand the variety of ways considered in Poland for the privatization of formerly collective or public companies. The first of these was "corporatisation". Using this approach, SOEs were transformed into a new separate legal entity – joint stock companies. This then made two options possible. First, "commercialisation without privatization", where it was intended that the joint stock company would make a profit and be subject to harsh budgetary constraints and market prices, but nonetheless remain under the control of the Public Treasury. The Treasury would continue to exercise control over the managers. In this case, 15 percent of the shares were given to the employees and 10 percent were allotted to social funds to cover social reform. The idea here was to allow these firms to escape privatization and to allow the state to remain the master of national strategy through the intermediary of the Treasury. Second, alongside this approach, the commercialisation procedure led the way to privatization. This happened in three different ways.

The first consisted of the handover of shares to employees through management buy-outs (MBOs) with several variants depending on employee status. This approach was widely used for the reasons mentioned above but it was also heavily criticised because of the absence of a distinction between "principal" and "agent". The first critics complained about the compromise whereby managers continued in their jobs in exchange for agreements established with employees on salary increases.[16] Others criticised the huge misappropriation which these handovers gave rise to with managers remaining unchecked and free to continue to meddle in the accounts.[17] Still others have pointed out the extent to which the processes of change within companies themselves led to corruption on a grand scale.[18]

The second approach was brought into being through mass privatization and involved 512 companies. It was initiated in 1996 and was extremely successful with 96.1 percent of the population favouring it and purchasing company bonds managed by 15 investment funds.[19] Within the company, 33 percent of shares were held by the first fund, 27 percent by the others, with employees receiving 15 percent of shares and the state 25 percent. In 1998, 42 percent of these shares certificates were converted and by 1999 almost all of them had been. However, this approach was very rapidly criticised for having been launched too late, on the basis of a small number of companies and without ascertaining long-term popular support as had been done in the Czech Republic.[20]

The third approach consisted of privatization to outsiders or in other terms foreign investors who had been held back over a long period of time by the type of governance inherited from the former regime.

Finally, during the first decade, the process towards the privatization of the Polish economy was very slow and the number of SOES remained large (see Table 6.2).

Table 6.2 The process of transformation in Poland during the first post-communist decade

Category	1989	1995	1997	1999
Public sector				
State-owned enterprises[a]	7,337	4,357	3,369	1,610
Municipal enterprises	0	481	265	
State treasury commercial companies[b]	1224	2,023	2,056	
(no. with 100 percent state shareholding)		(1,032)	(644)	
Commercial companies owned by state entities		4697	5,226	
(no. with 100 percent state shareholding)		(842)	(1,074)	
Commercial companies held by local authorities		1,219	1,594	
Private sector				
Domestic commercial companies	15,252	74,299	106,743	
Joint ventures	429	24,064	32,942	
Small and medium-sized foreign companies	841	548	518	
Individual entrepreneurs (1000)	813	1,693	2,090	
Cooperative and cooperative banks	16,691	19,822	19,775	

Notes: a. Governed by the 1981 law on state enterprises.

b. Governed by the commercial code. From 1992 onwards a different methodology was used.

Source: OECD, 1998, *Poland*, Paris: OECD, p. 47

Interest groups, limited conflict, and social demobilisation

What is striking in the slow movement towards the Polish privatization is the desire to expel the former leaders (directors and Workers' Councils) from the new companies. Once the working-class had been annihilated, privatization accelerated without any major social conflict. As Stuart Shields said: "One of the main tasks of the transition to capitalism has been to break the resistance of the working class".[21] Once this objective was achieved, the sale of firms to foreigners was speeded up.

Interest groups and insiders

In 1989, Poland presented two major original features within the landscape of Soviet-type economies. Alongside an agricultural sector, 81 percent of which had been privatised, it allowed a law that had been passed during the revolutionary period 1981–2 to continue: the law on company self-management. The law, which was legally adopted in 1981, shared power within the company between a Workers' Council and company management, known as self-management.[22] This "three Ss" law set up self-management, self-dependence, and self-financing in public companies with over 250 employees. Governance is a mixture of employee self-management and the type used in Joint Stock Companies. Three statutory bodies operate within a two-level system of governance. The basis is made up of the company's employees who elect the Company Council from among their members while the company director is appointed on the basis of a Council proposal which is then validated by an institutional organ (the relevant ministry or local authority). Company leadership is responsible for the management of company affairs in agreement with the Council. The Union deals with social affairs. This law which was adopted in 1981 as a result of social pressure has never been repealed, even after Solidarnosc was made illegal at the end of 1981 and disbanded in 1993. The law was not repealed simply because General Jaruzelski did not want to attack the working class openly as he desperately needed their support for his policy of measured openness.[23] This explains why self-management continued to function within the large companies where it represented pockets of resistance to Communist power. But this is also why it incurred the wrath of all those who had no intention of sharing any of their decision-making power. This included both the "hardcore" Communists before 1989 and the liberals after 1989. The former saw this new type of company governance as the main obstacle to political normalisation: the latter considered it to be a major obstacle to the modernisation of the economy.

The fight against the so-called self-management law was continuous throughout the 1990s. The different governments hoped to attract foreign investors and this latter group were waiting for the law to be repealed before investing. The irony is that this law which the first liberal governments had not managed to repeal was finally repealed under the authority of a social–democrat (formerly Communist) government.

The firm intention to limit the 1981 law was already part of the reform initiated by the then Minister for Finance Leszek Balcerowicz in 1990. The aim was to better define the role of the Treasury and the state enterprises and notably those in financial difficulty by means of a tax recovery commission. The law on bankruptcy which was announced in the plan very explicitly targeted the large insolvent companies which were due to be liquidated. The offensive was continued with the 1993 law which authorised company creditors (the banks) to transform 30 percent of the debts they held into shares without consulting the Workers' Councils. This was the beginning of the transformation of SOEs into JSCs. Again in 1993, under the authority of the new socio-democrat government (which came back into power in September 1993), another law was adopted which excluded a great number of companies from privatization.[24] In 1995, still under the authority of the social-democrats, parliament adopted a law postulating its agreement with any project concerning the privatization of the banks, telecommunications, and energy. President Walesa (right of centre) vetoed the law.

One year later when Walesa had been beaten in the election, parliament adopted the law but made two decisive changes to it. The agreement of the director and the Workers' Council was no longer necessary for corporatisation to take place. Added to this, corporatisation and commercialisation could take place without privatization. In other words, the authorities removed the constraint which the existence of these omnipotent councils entailed by excluding – at least provisionally – certain strategic sectors, the banks, and telecommunications from privatization. However, the respite was not to last. In 1997, the liberal government returned to this topic and announced its intention to accelerate the privatization of the remaining SOEs. At that time (1997), the private economy accounted for 61 percent of GDP. Four of the nine banks were privatised. Privatization was completed in the agricultural sector. In 1998, it was initiated for the two major sectors of energy and telecommunications. On 15 September 2000, a company code replacing the 1934 commercial code which governed the transformation of public companies was adopted. On the eve of the 2000s, the banking sector was put into foreign hands: 77 percent of the banks are currently in foreign hands as compared to 4 percent in Germany or 10 percent in Spain. The mining and transport sectors are still managed by the public sector. No major social conflict has hindered the process.

Weakness of collective action and transformations in labor relations

Given the ability of Solidarnosc to mobilise in the 1980s and its victory in the 1989 and 1990 elections, a vast social movement carried by 1990s unionism might have been expected to emerge. In reality, several factors prevented this from happening. The potential for conflict was undoubtedly significant at the beginning of the 1990s but as early as 1993 this weakened[25] (with the exception of the agricultural sector led by the union party Samoobrona). This disaffection with the unions, which certain observers have described as "passive tolerance" on the part of employees requires an explanation.[26]

The first explanation is perhaps that for the first time citizens were allowed to freely choose what organisations they wanted to belonged to. Before 1989, membership was mandatory and the unions did not defend the interests of the workers.[27] Moreover, the Communist unions played a substitutive role when market failure occurred, selling rare goods such as housing, cars, and so on. Once markets had been established they were no longer justified in doing so. Finally, once the market was in place it no longer needed the unions if only because employers did not want partners with whom they would have had to share their prerogatives. Furthermore, industrial companies were largely destroyed or had undergone profound restructuring. As a result of sectorial transformations, sectors imposing a strict individualisation of tasks emerged such as finance, insurance, and consulting. Largely non-integrated types of jobs were added to this following the example of self-employment.[28] This type of contract is based on private rather than social law. It is limited to the exchange of work for a salary and each party – the employee and the employer – reserves the right to terminate the contract if and when they see fit. Taken as an ensemble, these factors rapidly brought about a considerable reduction in union activity and even more so in labor-management negotiations in Poland and throughout Central Europe (see Table 6.3).[29,30]

The industrial branch level fell apart when faced with the decentralisation of negotiations within the company. Branch conventions only cover 30 percent of employees and when company agreements do exist they almost never deal with

Table 6.3 Level of organisation of social partners and rate of collective agreements
(% employees)

Country	Trade unions	Employers	Coverage of collective agreements	Firm council
Slovenia	42	50	98	Yes (broad)
Slovakia	35	50	48	Yes (weak)
Hungary	25	40	42	Yes (average)
Czech Republic	30	30	35	Exceptionally
Poland	18	19	30	Only in the SOEs
Latvia	19	30	20	Rare
Estonia	15	30	20	No
Lithuania	14	20	13	Planned

Source: Herbert Kohl, 2005, "Arbeitsbeziehungen in den neuen EU Mitgiedstländern und ihre Implikation für das europäische Sozialmodell" ["The working relations in the New EU member and their implications for the EU social model"], in Hrg von Timm Beichelt and Jan Wierlgohs (eds), *Perspektiven der ezuropäischen Integration nach der EU – Osterweiterung* [*Perspectives of European Integration after the EU Enlargement*], FIUT Viadrina, 51–71.

career advancement, salaries, training or information, all of which remain non-respected rights.[31] The paradox is that it is undoubtedly only in companies that are part of major foreign groups that social negotiation can be found. For these reasons, the market was the object of a plebiscite by *Solidarnosc* elites and intellectuals but not the working class. For some observers the success of economic liberalism in Poland can be explained by the ability of new liberal elites to have blocked the economic restructuring of the former Communist managerial class. These domestic elites are linked to foreign capital and supported by the World Bank and the IMF. They have managed to impose the domination of a neoliberal protectionist state through the intermediary of a vast policy of deregulation.

Deregulation and flexibility

Policies adopted to counter former public enterprise authorities were simultaneously accompanied by several measures in favour of FDI. First, in fiscal terms the rates were much more favourable to them than they were to insiders. As Shields points out:

> Compared to SOEs, foreign capital pays significantly lower levels of tax. The highest average rate of taxation, 40%, is for SOE firms with mixed state–domestic private capital, a 23% rate: but for foreign capital the average rate drops to 20%.[32]

Special Economic Zones accentuated this tendency. Revenue was the same everywhere in central and western Europe.[33] Collective installation costs were covered

and coupled with partial tax exemptions in order to obtain in exchange a commitment from the new investors to maintain employment over a certain period of
time. Criteria for defining a Special Economic Zone was initially based on the
presence of an unemployment rate that was over twice as high as the national
average. Certain regions supported by the state went as far as to offer tax exemptions on activity for a period of ten years in exchange for a promise to create
jobs.[34] Some of these zones gave rise to veritable pools of growth thanks to the
massive arrival of FDI whose implantation was facilitated by the establishment of
networks by public authorities. Moreover, the domination of foreign capital and
the withdrawal of social organisations allowed for the wide-scale deregulation of
work organisations to take place. This was based on the disqualification of former
employees and on massive social plans which were above all favourable to heavy
industry sectors and not at all to consumer companies. This contributed to aggra-
vating the gap between the sexes. Women were massively disadvantaged
compared to men who were targeted as a priority by public and private aid.
Finally, work methods which were often rejected in the West as being obsolete
were widespread in the East.

When taken as a whole these factors relative to the massive presence of foreign
financial and industrial capital have led several observers to use the term "dependent capital".[35] This is borne out by the fact that the headquarters remain in the
West as does R&D. Although there has been very clear progress in terms of building networks of firms, it nonetheless remains true that production units continue
to be very dependent on the West. Local suppliers are few in number even if the
networks themselves are significant. This is the case, for example, with the automobile industry[36] which in Poland experienced considerable growth.[37] This sector
has already been analysed many times.[38] However, a number of SEZs are of
particular interest in that they heralded original forms of economic development.

Case study: from Special Economic Zones to clusters

The SEZs were created in Eastern Europe in 1994–5 as a counter-measure for
structural unemployment as it is known (more than twice the national average),
which had hit certain regions hard. This was especially true for regions where old
industries such as mining, forges, and mechanical engineering were concentrated.
Copying the model which already existed in the West, these regions were aided
by the development at central level[39] of a whole series of fiscal incentives, and in
this case, profits were identical to those of former Soviet Europe.[40] Poland drew
up one of the most motivating sets of incentives as together with aid for training
and wages, the law on regional aid provided overhead exemptions for up to ten
years if the initial investment was of at least 10 million euros (or the equivalent)
or 500,000 euros if it was accompanied by the creation of at least 100 jobs for a
period of five years or twenty jobs for a year. There were further exemptions for
ecological investments and investments in technological parks.

Since 2008, 14 economic zones have existed in Poland (see Figure 6.1). Today,
they house 429 new companies, are spread out over 8,160 hectares, have invested

138   *Bafoil*

Figure 6.1 The fourteen Polish special economic zones
Source: PAIZ (Polish Information and Foreign Investment Agency)

over 12 billion euros and created over 160,000 jobs. After 2004, state aid granted
before this date was added to European aid and was increased with the agreement
of the European Commission because of the profound crisis which was undermining the said zones.[41]

The various industrial and agricultural redevelopment dynamics

The results below come from surveys carried out between 2007 and 2010 in
different intensely industrialised sectors before 1989.[42] Transformations undergone after this date gave birth either to Special Economic Zones, whose success
depended on the presence of numerous foreign investors, or to a wholes series of
small companies which were created from the ruins of major state enterprises.
Table 6.4 sorts the different cases into several categories. The first of these

Table 6.4 Special economic zones and clusters

Characteristics / SEZs		Lodz (textile/clothing)	Lublin (agriculture, farmers)	Walbrzych (mines)	Mielec (aeronautical)	Gdansk (Shipyards)
Legacies	Organisation before 1989	Mass organisation	Independent producers	Mass organisation	Hi-tech production	Mass production
	Social capital	Neighbourhood, weak unions, social tradition	Familial, neighbourhood, very weak unions	Weak?? Strong unions, social tradition	Strong aeronautical tradition	Strong unions, strong social tradition
	Employees	Little qualifications	Not qualified	Professional qualifications	Highly qualified	Professional qualifications
Actors	Domestic actors	Foreign trade No domestic investors	The local co-operative of producers	Very important for the development of the zone	Very important for the development of the zone	Important but without follow-up
	International actors (FDI)	Important (Italian)	No	Numerous and important (Toyota, etc.)	Important depending on local demand	Various and then abandoned
	Political actors	Lacking	Weak	Very involved, national, regional, and local	Very involved	Strong
	EU support	None	Weak/strong	Strong	Strong	Strong
Results 2011	Organisation in 2011	Small independent producers, tailor-made workshops	Small independent producers	A large amount of FDI, automobile cluster	High-tech, aeronautical cluster	Deep crisis
	Type of clusters in 2008	Marshallian district	Producer cooperatives	Hub and spoke clusters	Clusters of state companies	–

reflects legacies by stressing the notion of "social capital" which is linked to social and local traditions. The second concerns the actors whether these be employees, local/regional actors who managed to become intermediaries between former employees and new needs, foreign investors (FDI), and the EU. The final piece of criteria describes the situations encountered today according to the types of clusters identified by the OECD.[43]

First type: from mass production to small independent producers

The first type considers "social capital" (understood as experience, savoir faire, and qualifications) to be a basic factor. This notion of "social capital" characterises intermediary actors who play the role of brokers following the example of foreign investors. Public authorities have no decisive role to play here.

Lodz: from mass production to tailor-made workshops

The best example of this is the textile industry in Lodz. Lodz has a two-century-old industrial tradition and is often referred to as the Manchester of Eastern Europe. Considerable redevelopment of the city was carried out in an original manner which can be explained firstly by the state of industrial relations already existing there. Before 1989, these were not limited to forms of dependence on paternalistic bosses as was often the case elsewhere. On the contrary, relations here were based on networks for the exchange of services based on technical competence and interpersonal relations or in other words the exchange of self-help. Because of the dramatic collapse of former public employers (the SOEs) and therefore the drying up of orders, former employees were forced to draw on all the resources available to them, even organising the sale of their products in the street once the working day was over. This shows how they adapted to demand precariously during the transition years (1990–93) and subsequently in a more stable manner when demand took off again after 1995. At that point local products which customers no longer wanted when the Communist regime collapsed returned once more to favour. Workers then started buying shops and some organised themselves as cooperatives. At the same time others – most of whom were women – turned to the private sector to undertake different work and for the most part they used tools from their previous workshop. They maintained links with their former colleagues who were now shop owners and were thus able to use them as intermediaries to sell their produce.

The decisive element came into play when, at around the same time, between 1995 and 1997, people who had previously depended on the foreign trade units[44] and who were in direct contact with foreign buyers took on the role of intermediaries for small producers. As strategic intermediaries with foreign partners they were well able to negotiate their client portfolio after this date and position themselves as partners of those doing the ordering on the one hand and of the producers on the other hand. Before 1989 theses negotiators were located in Lodz where the textile *combinat* was also located. They therefore knew the companies very well

and also the state of the workshops, the cost of the machines, the cost of the products, their quality, the markets, in other the whole chain from production to
consumption. The costs involved in setting up as self-employed after 1989 were
very low: all they needed was a room and a telephone line given that they had taken
the clients' contact details with them. This did not only characterise the textile
industry but all large enterprises who had to negotiate with sectorial units which
depended on the Ministry for Foreign Trade. What distinguished the textile industry from others such as the cement plants[45] was the link with foreign partners. The
textile industry in Lodz consisted of the major Western and particularly Italian
textile and clothing factories. Thanks to the intermediaries they managed to impose
themselves as those who drew up the orders thus completely reshaping the sector's
profile in Lodz. In summary, the revival of the textile and clothing sector took place
on the basis of a complete renewal of the modes of organisation from the company
to the home and from mass production to fashion and indeed haute couture. This
was brought about by the use of former resources available to the different domestic actors (workers and intermediaries) and their links with external demand.

Lublin: from small-holding owners to producers cooperatives, and civil society

The second type is located in the Lublin region on the border with the Ukraine, in
the east of the country. This region has been classified as the one which is the most
"behind" of the 16 Polish regions.[46] A number of agricultural producers joined
together in an association in 2007and adopted the logo: "ecological agriculture
valley". They had three objectives: firstly to put a halt to the migration crisis which
was hitting the region hard (especially since 2004) thereby ensuring local employment; to promote products from the region which is known for its ecological
potential; and finally, to make a contribution to redefining regional identity. Since
then, the association has taken on marketing and export functions. It has also taken
on networking to the extent that it works, on the one hand with the university on
research projects, training, and certification and on the other with local shop
owners who provide an outlet for the products and a number of civil organisations.
Other groups defining themselves as clusters can be added to this list such as the
"Lublin region culture cluster" whose aim is to promote tourism. Others are even
more local, centring on a given district whose patrimony a group has decided to
promote. All are involved in carrying out coordinated activities for the promotion
of local produce. The EU has played a role at two different levels in the emergence
of a local civil society. The first of these has been at a financial level as it allowed
requests for finance to be lodged in the name of regional aid with university relations playing an important role in the setting up of projects. The second EU role
has been largely a symbolic one to the extent that the process involved in defining
the objectives and the action plans has borrowed extensively from the European
repertoire: "clusters", "good practice", "networks", are all categories widely used
in European discourse. They have the advantage of creating common references.
Although EU financial aid remains quite low, its impact on the types of organisation adopted nonetheless seems strong.

From mass production to high technology

In this second type of new private company which emerged after 1990, the central political actor was a decisive figure. And yet, the zones were not all successful. They can be divided into three different types reflecting a unique combination of different factors linked to historical resources, internal restructuring, external cooperation, and the human factor.

The Rzeszow Company: a driving force – historical tradition, a local area and high technologies

The first example is that of a company which managed to harness its industrial experience by reorganising local employment around its area of expertise and by building partnerships at international, national, and regional level. This company, Aviation Valley,[47] is heralded as exemplifying the success story of clusters in Poland. The company dates back to the period immediately preceding the Second World War when the Polish authorities decided to make what is now known as Galizia (located at the time just south of the centre of Polish territory) the industrial capital for the following 15 years. The valley was designed to be at the heart of a vast military defence plan at a time when the elites were convinced that war was inevitable with the country's two neighbours, Bolshevik Russia and Nazi Germany. The aviation sector was privileged for this very reason. Under Nazi occupation, the valley produced parts for Messerschmidt, the German aviation company. After 1945, the valley continued its specialisation in the military aero-nautical sector. During the communist period, the *combinat* produced helicopters which were well-reputed within the Soviet-type common market (the CAEM). Within this dynamic, a large university and a first-class aeronautical institution were set up in the town of Rzeszow. When the Soviet market fell apart at the beginning of the 1990s, the "valley" did not take long to re-adjust its industrial profile to the civil aeronautical sector, thanks to partnerships with both European and American aircraft manufacturers. They were aided in this by the central authorities when they created the first Special Economic Zone where the *combinat* had been located in Mielec in 1995.One of the particularities of this SEZ was that it was spread over two regions (*wojwodships* in Polish) who share different sections of aeronautical construction. This SEZ was considerably strengthened by European aid as the two *wojwodships* where it is located – Lower Carpathia and the Lublin region – granted it a considerable amount of the European aid they themselves receive. These funds were used to finance the rail and road infrastructure which service the zone and to put training programmes in place for companies likely to set up there. When the central operational programme devoted to encouraging innovation was created, it reserved the sum of 23.8 million euros for the valley as part of the project on "advanced material technology for aviation valley". Ten years later, in 2005, the sector became a shining example of a cluster which struc-tures regional and inter-regional sub-contracting, on the basis of public funding and the transfer of innovation through links set up with research. Finally, in the mid-2000s, the aviation company managed to enter into two decisive partnerships with two aviation giants: Airbus and Boeing. It supplies them with engine parts and has been remarkably successful in promoting the gains it has made through its association with the powerful image of both companies. There is no doubt that Aviation Valley provides a perfect illustration of the Porter approach which explains industrial success on the basis of cooperation between three actors: private companies, public authorities, and universities.[48]

Walbrzych: competitive wages, industrial capital, geographical dimensions and high technology

The second example of success is due to a different factor: the very competitive cost of labor. Competitive labor costs provided one of the main motivations for foreign investors. They were made all the more attractive as the amount of tax exemptions increased in direct proportion to the number of jobs created in the zone. Regional and inter-regional markets strengthened by nearby areas in full expansion provided another advantage. These areas are German Saxony and Czech Bohemia, both of which are also experiencing an economic renaissance.

Walbrzych in Lower Silesia provides a typical example of this successful conjunction of development factors. The region was formerly home to an outdated mining industry. It underwent a profound crisis in the 1990s and in the first decade of the 2000s it became one of the driving forces of Polish development. This SEZ was launched in 1996 and in less than ten years had managed to create 22,680 jobs and also to extend its boundaries. It initially measured 256 hectares, had increased to 473 by 2001 and to 1,422 by 2007. During this period the major firms settled here. In 1999, Toyota created 1,000 jobs producing 18,000 units per year. In the following three years, four Japanese sub-contracting firms set up AKS and Yagi Poland. The Italian producer Italmetal then arrived in 2003 followed in 2004 by Whirlpool (360,000 washing machines per year) and Electrolux. In 2005, Harris, Libra and others arrived and in 2006 KMPG. In total, 65 major international firms occupy 64 percent of available territory. There seems to be three determining factors for the arrival of foreign firms. Firstly, a labor force with a century-old tradition of industrial culture and a competitive wages structure: the gap between German salaries less than 150 kilometres away was around 1/10 when the zone was established in 1995. The second factor is the presence of public regional authorities who are strongly committed to supporting innovation and research carried out by reliable western partners. These authorities are made up of regional and municipal elites in Wroclaw which is the regional capital. They have great political clout in neighbouring districts. Most of them are elected without difficulty and developed an independent "local" political profile even if there have been clear affinities between them and the liberal coalition in power at central level since 2005. There are also private sector elites who have come together in a very dynamic chamber of commerce which works hand in hand with the team that manages the zone. Together, these elites, both public and private, set up a research firm in 2006 which is part of the European Institute of

Technology founded by the President of the European Commission. It has a budget of 120 million euros and brings together the major Higher Education Institutes of the region including the Wroclaw universities. Its aim is to promote innovation and make the results available to industry. Structural funds were used to develop an innovation programme thus allowing different public policies to be used conjointly. The third factor is geographical proximity. The Czech Republic is less than 20km away, Germany and the major Saxon research and technology pole is less than 150km away. In both cases, the transport infrastructure is vastly superior to the prevailing transport system throughout Poland generally. Unlike the other well-known "economic zones" in Poland, Gliwice in Upper Silesia which has been structured around the American investor General Motors to develop a powerful automobile cluster, the Walbrych "zone" is more diverse. It is also home to mechanical units, high tech communications, consumer products, etc.

In both cases, "successful" clusters are those which manage to put a solid structure in place for sub-contractors (and national sub-contractors also, particularly in the area of logistics) where the local area offers highly qualified employees considerable opportunities for promotion/mobility. Turnover rates are high among individual employees who experience little difficulty finding a new job in one of the various firms belonging to the cluster.

A declining zone: historical resources, dangerous restructuration, and pillaged resources

The final example concerns industrial areas in the western part of the country. Although regional motivation was strong, they did not manage to restart economic activity. The fate of the Gdansk shipyard is a perfect example of this. On the eve of the 1990s it seemed that, given its historical reputation, the investments made in it and the projects envisaged for the future, its success was ensured. However, fifteen years of transformation have put an end to the dream that this region would become the European cradle of the naval industry for several reasons, firstly because of competition from two different sources. The first of these sources was the German shipyards and particularly those in former East Germany located in Rostock and Warnemünde, all of which had been profoundly restructured over a period of fifteen years. Competition also came from the Baltic shipyards which specialised in markets that were more advantageous financially. Internal transformation was also slowed down by two major factors. On the one hand, the considerable strength which the trade unions had historically acquired and their initial hostility to any restructuring of the most symbolic location of the anti-Communist struggle; on the other hand, restructuring in this case was more like a plundering of the site's resources than a concerted plan where the privatization of certain activities was developed as part of a wider plan for the rebuilding of sub-contracting networks. In reality, under the guise of privatization a pure and simple pillaging of the *combinat* by budding SMEs took place. They took great advantage of it for a time but then once the orders had dried up were incapable of keeping ship-building activity going on any great scale. Private and somewhat farfetched redevelopment plans which characterised the 1990s were replaced by central planning with no clear vision of the kind of profile expected from the sector and in 2008 as European aid was piled on top of state aid the Commission ordered the Polish government to either restructure the site or to reimburse the aid received.

Conclusion: lessons learned

Several lessons can be drawn from these developments. One definitive lesson is that history and geography matter. The successful SEZs are in fact those where the political and economic actors have known how to rebuild the resources and notably human resources in function of the new issues in areas which were formerly well-developed or at the very least linked to regions experiencing growth. Having said that, it is clear that there is no spatial or temporal determinism at play. Growth peaks can be seen in areas surrounded by weak development and certain regions in the west remain in a state of deep crisis in spite of the fact that they formed an integral part of developed territories in Germany before 1945. The second lesson is that the state has remained the decisive actor for development and the driving force for all policies since 1990. The neoliberal ideology of the beginning of the 1990s that surfed on the wave of Reaganism and Thatcherism was accompanied by the restoration of the state, thus guaranteeing the coherence of public policies. Moreover, the privatization process was a key policy, not only because it transformed the whole economy into a new private one, but mainly because of democracy. Moreover, privatization was the first step in a longer process of adaptation to European and global laws which would result in the implementation of a coherent and more unified social system. Indeed, only a democratic state could secure FDI and only a full privatised economy could legitimise political elites by embedding the rule of law, even if corruption was present since the very beginning of the whole process. To this extent the central state played the major role, strongly linked to the private actors, domestic, and foreign ones.

In twenty years, the economic structure in Poland has been turned on its head. Whereas the Polish public sector (apart from agriculture) once accounted for about 88 percent of employment (72 percent including agriculture), it accounted for just 14 percent in 2004 while the private share constituted 74 percent. In the upheaval, SMEs largely prevailed leaving a very small share to the big companies which were often little open to restructuring. According to Adamski, 20 percent of non-qualified workers were retrenched by companies.[49] For many actors, the majority of these SOEs, which are in fact JSCs, have turned out not to be very competitive. Baltowski and Mickiewicz contend that the rapid pace of the privatization process has depended on sectoral productivity: "privatization should commence in those branches that guarantee the best results".[50] Finally, most observers consider that enterprises that remain under state rule are totally inefficient.[51] Others such as Konings,[52] however, consider that the SOEs are barely less competitive than other firms. Armess and Robert share this point of view when analysing cooperatives.[53] They stress the fact that cooperatives limit the risk of free riders. Furthermore, cooperative employees seem to have a greater level of attachment to the companies they work in which tend to show indicators of higher levels of productivity. The notion of subjective performance or in other words the level of satisfaction felt at work has been little analysed. It seems to be higher in cooperatives than in SOEs.

Finally, it is not easy to define the type of capitalism which emerged in Poland during the last few years. On one hand, we have seen that the arrival of FDI was strongly correlated with the repealing of the 1981 law in favour of the working class. "Managing by flexibility" was a slogan which has been widely shared by the new Polish and foreign managers. Productivity has greatly increased during the past two decades.[54] Some observers have concluded that "the capitalist spirit" that activates shareowners of private companies is one of early, ruthless, uncivilised capitalism. Aspects of the "Polish path of building capitalism", such as the elimination of the workforce's influence on the managerial influence deci-sion–making process, wider possibilities of the use of dismissal in case of ineffective performance and other negative sanctions, or the liquidation of many fringe benefits, suit top management very clearly.'[55] However, on the other hand a huge consensus has accompanied the whole historical transforming process. Not only was social support for FDI and globalisation never refused to the polit-ical elites, it was also one of the strongest among European societies. Moreover, policies in favour of the poorest regions (the eastern ones) were a constant of public policies implemented by parties both on the right and the left. Finally, the privatization process was the backbone of the social consensus which was massively in favour of privatization once it was understood that if this tough and difficult policy were not implemented the other steps of development would be halted. This social consensus was based on economic recovery supported by a massive inflow of FDI – 128 billion euros between 1990 and 2010 – and by considerable EU support through structural funds, more than 60 billion which was completed with more than 40 billion from the Common Agricultural Policy. Taken as a whole, all of these factors have clearly shown the definite importance of the state in the post-communist period.

Notes

1   In 1990, the agricultural share of GDP was about 15 percent. Private agriculture in Poland represented an exception within the Soviet-type economies since in the other countries there was no private agriculture, but only a very small part dedicated to private use (less than 1 percent depending on the periods). This exceptional Polish situation is due to the fact that in 1956, Gomulka was back in power after the revolu-tion of June and October 1956 after having forced Krutchev to accept two major changes in Poland related to Communist orthodoxy: freedom for the Catholic Church and the end of the collectivisation process of Polish agriculture. See Klaus Eugen Wädekin, 1977, "The place of agriculture in the European communist economies: a statistical essay", *Soviet Studies* XXIX, August.

2   Istvan Major, 1999, *Privatization and Economic Performance in Central and Eastern Europe: Lessons to be Learnt from Western Europe*, Cheltenham: Edward Elgar; David Stark, 1996, "Recombinant property in Eastern European capitalism", *American Journal of Sociology* 4: 993–1027; David Stark and Laszlo Bruszt, 1998, *Post-socialist Pathways: Transforming Politics and Property in East Central Europe*, Cambridge: Cambridge University Press; Francois Bafoil, 2009, *Central and Eastern Europe, Globalization and Social Change*, Basingstoke: Palgrave Macmillan.

3   4 zlotys = 1 euro, more or less.

4   Piotr Kozarzewski, 2007, "Corporate governance in state-controlled enterprises in Poland", Seventh International Conference on Enterprise in Transition, organised by the Faculty of Economics, Split, May 24–26.

5   One has to add that in 1989 nobody knew how to proceed. Everything was lacking: historical references, stock exchanges, skills and, above all, value within the firms to be privatised. Janos Kornai considered that this debate about the SOEs should not even have taken place because of the costs linked with the privatization process and the very meagre revenue drawn from selling off the firms. For the well-known Ungarian economist, it was much more useful to focus on the emergence of a new private sector, which he considered to be the only way forward for national economic recovery. It is a matter of fact that in Poland, since 1993, more than 1.7 million SMEs and 11,473 joint ventures have been registered (quoted in Denis A. Rondinelli and Jay Yurkiewicz, 1996, "Privatization and economic restructuring in Poland: an assessment of transition policies", *American Journal of Economics and Sociology* 55(2): 145–60, here 157).

6   Maciej Baltowki and Tomasz Mickiewicz, 2000, "Privatization in Poland: ten years after", in *Post Communist Economies* 12(4): 425–43.

7   It should be recalled that Poland as a country disappeared several times during the last couple of centuries: first, between 1795 and 1918, Poland no longer existed, having been partitioned between Russia, Prussia (becoming the German Empire in 1871) and the Habsburg Empire; it then became independent for 20 years, between 1919 and 1939, then disappeared under Nazi rule, and finally after 1945, the country was under Soviet rule. See Norman Davies, 1988, *God's Playground: A History of Poland*, New York: Columbia University Press.

8   Parliamentary debates, questions and interventions by MPs and senators or articles in the press revealed all too clearly that criticism of privatization was actually only a "cover for various private interests"; Baltowki and Mickiewicz, "Privatization in Poland: ten years after", 425–43.

9   Valerie Bunce, 1999, *Subversive Institutions: The Design and the Destruction of Socialism and the State*, Cambridge: Cambridge University Press.

10   Ivan Szelenyi and Szonja Szelenyi, 1995, "Circulation or reproduction of elites during the post-communist transformation of Eastern Europe", *Theory and Society* 24: 613–28.

11   Baltowki and Mickiewicz, "Privatization in Poland: ten years after", 427.

12   *Ibid.*, 429.

13   In Denis A. Rondinelli and Jay Yurkiewicz, 1996 "Privatization and economic restructuring in Poland: an assessment of transition policies", *American Journal of Economics and Sociology* 55(2): 145–60, here 154.

14   The Baltic States carried out the most rapid privatization, by selling all their banks to Northern partners, mainly to Swedish Banks. In Estonia at the end of the 1990s, no bank at all was national, all of them having been bought by Swedish Banks. Before the crisis in 2008, two major ones, Hansapank and SEB, controlled 74.6 percent of Estonian banks. See Zuzana Brixiova, Laura Vartia and Andreas Wörgötter, 2009, "Capital inflows, household debt and the boom–bust cycle in Estonian economics", Working Paper 700, Paris: OECD, available at www.oecd.org/officialdocuments/publicdisplaydocumentpdf/?doclanguage=en&cote=eco/wkp(2009)41. This situation

explained both factors of success during the 2000s and of deep crisis after 2008, when the Swedish Banks withdrew their support from the Baltic banks.

15 'Domestic bank lending, the second most important source of finance, is also clearly dominated by transnational companies. When compared with ownership relationships in Western Europe, the heavy penetration of the ECE banking sector by FDI is obvious. At the end of 2004 the market shares of foreign branches and subsidiaries in the Euro area amounted to a mere 15.5 percent; the figure was well over 70 percent in ECE economies'. Andreas Nölke Arjan Vliegenthart, 2009, "Enlarging the varieties of capitalism: the emergence of dependent market economies in East Central Europe", *World Politics* 61(4) (October): 681.

16 Kaufmann Daniel and Paul Siegelbaum, 1997, "Privatization and corruption in transition economies", *Journal of International Affairs* 50(2): 419–59.

17 Francois Bafoil, 1999, "From corruption to regulation. post-communist enterprises in Poland", in Béatrice Hibou (ed.), *Privatizing the State*, London: Hurst, 2004, pp. 48–76.

18 Roman Frydman, Kenneth Murphy and Andrzej Rapaczynski, 1998, *Capitalism worth a Comrade's Face: Studies in the Post-communist Transition*, Budapest: Central European University Press; R. Frydman, C. Gray, M. Hessel and R. Rapaczynski, 1999, "When does privatization work? The impact of private ownership on corporate performance in the transition economies", *Quarterly Journal of Economics* 114: 1153–91.

19 OECD, 2008, *Territorial Review: Poland*, Paris: OECD, p. 50.

20 Marie Lavigne, 1999, *The Economics of Transition: From Socialist Economy to Market Economy*, London: Macmillan; David Stark and Laszlo Bruszt, 1998, *Post-Socialist Pathways: Transforming Politics and Property in East Central Europe*, Cambridge: Cambridge University Press.

21 Stuart Shields, 2004, "Global restructuring and the Polish state: transition, transformation or internationalisation?", *Review of International Political Economy* 11(1) (February): 132–54, here 148.

22 In Polish: *samorzad*. The self-management vision is deeply anchored in Polish history: in 1945, Polish workers adopted a law on *samorzad* in the freed production units after the defeat of the Nazis. In 1956, *samorzad* became the flagship of the Revolutionary Autumn. In 1981, the first Congress of Solidarnosc adopted an important text regulating public and economic life, the "Self-Managed Republic". According to the conception of its authors, the new political system to be adopted should be based on two pillars. The first pillar was the "self-managed" public units (at that time nobody spoke of privatization), the second pillar was the "self-managed" local authorities. Two assemblies would be elected, and at the top, the popular "self-managed Assembly". This document was eliminated from public life on December 13 when General Jaruzelski imposed martial law. But, as noted above, it did not cancel the law on *samorzad* in the large SOEs.

23 To this extent, Jaruzelski preceded and inspired Gorbachev when he launched his policies based on *perestroika* (restructuring) and *glasnost* (clarity).

24 Law on the Ownership Transformation of Certain SOEs of Special Importance to the National Economy.

25 Georg Ekiert and Jan Kubik, 1998, "Contentious politics in new democracies: East Germany, Hungary, Poland and Slovakia, 1989–1993", *World Politics* 50 (July): 547–81.

26 Juliusz Gardawski, Jerzy Bartkowski and Jacek Czarzasrty Mecina, 2010, *Working Poles and the Crisis of Fordism*, Warsaw: Scholar. See also Juliusz Gardawski, Barbara Gaciarz, Andrzej Mokrzyszewski and Wlodzimierz Pankow, 1999, *Rospad bastionu? Zwiazki zawodowe w gospodarce priwatyzowanej [The Disintegration of the Bastions? The Trade Union in the Private Economy]*, Warsaw: Instytut Spraw Publicznych.

27 David Ost, 2002, "Imagining and creating the enemy: trade unions in the new Polish democracy", in Edmunta Mokrzyckiego, Andrzeja Rycharda, Andrzeja Zybertowizca (eds), *Utracona Dynamika? O niedojrzalosci Poklskiej demokracji* [*A Broken Dynamic? About the Immaturity of the Polish Democracy*], Wydawnicwo IFIUS Pan, 113–26.

28 Stéphane Portet, 2005, "Poland: circumventing the law or fully deregulating?", in Daniel Vaughan-Whitehead (ed.), *Working Employment Conditions in New Members States*, Geneva: ILO, 273–337; Daniel Vaughan-Whitehead, 2003, *EU Enlargment versus social Europe? The Uncertain Future of the European Social Model*, Cheltenham: Edward Elgar.

29 The share of workers in the trade unions did not diminish at the same rate that employees did. From 28 percent in 1991, this share dropped to 16 percent in 2008, according to the Opinion Office, CBOS. OPZZ, which is seen as the link and heir to the last Communist trade union before 1989, and is said to have included between 730,000 and three million members (see http://opzz.org.pl/o_nas/ogolnokrajowe_organizacje_czlonkowskie.htm); Solidarnosc, linked with right-wing parties, from 750,000 to 900,000 members (see www.solidarnosc.org.pl); and the Forum Trade Union, which was created in 2002, has 400,000 members.

30 See www.fzz.org.pl/index.php?option=com_content&view=article&id=9&Itemid=8.

31 Herbert Kohl, 2005, "Arbeitsbeziehungen in den neuen EU Mitgiedstländern und ihre Implikation für das europäische Sozialmodell" ["The working relations in the New EU member and their implications for the EU social model"], in Hrg von Timm Beichelt and Jan Wierlgohs (eds), *Perspektiven der ezuropäischen Integration nach der EU – Osterweiterung* [*Perspectives of European Integration after the EU Enlargement*], FIUT Viadrina, 51–71.

32 Shields, "Global restructuring and the Polish state", 148.

33 OECD, 2006, *Business Clusters: Promoting Enterprises in Central Europe*, LEED.

34 The total land area designated approximates 12,000 hectares with total invested capital amounting to over 80,000 million zlotys, as of 2008. Total direct jobs created by SEZs were approximately over 200,000 as of the end of 2008 (see OECD, *Territorial Review: Poland*, ch. 2).

35 Dorothee Bohle and Bela Greskovits, 2006, "Capitalism without compromise: strong business and weak labor in Eastern Europe's new transnational industries", *Studies in Comparative International Development* 41(1): 3–25; Dorothee Bohle and Bela Greskovits, 2007, "Neoliberalism, embedded neoliberalism and neocorporatism: towards transational capitalism in Central-Eastern Europe", in *West-European Politics* 30(3): 443–66.

36 In CEE countries, the car industry is considered the main industrial driver for regional integration. The main worldwide manufacturers and suppliers are present in several countries, from Poland to Romania and from Slovenia to Slovakia. Within this large "circle", which encompasses all the eastern producers and which represents the second biggest European location, a core circle has emerged. It delineates the four major CEE countries: Poland, the Czech Republic, Slovakia, and Hungary. All the car makers and all the suppliers are located in a pentagon which, in less than 300 km2, links the major cities of Wroclaw and Katowice in Poland, Prague in the Czech Republic, Bratislava in Slovakia and Györ in Hungary. See "Connected Central and Eastern Europe", *Financial Times* (December 14), esp. pp. 26–8.

37 The total value of FDI in the Polish motor vehicle industry exceeded US$ 10 billion between 1990 and 2005. Between 2002 and 2006, the automotive industry accounted for 6.2 percent of the total value of all FDI in Poland and equalled 2,619 million euros. About 90 percent of the cars produced in Poland are exported. The majority of exports go to the European Union, of which 32 percent go to Germany, 17 percent to Italy and 6.9 percent to France. The share of exports in the total production has been steadily increasing due to the lower growth of domestic demand and to a higher demand for

the models produced in Poland in Western European countries. However, cars manufactured in Poland are also popular in Central and Eastern Europe countries such as the Ukraine, where a large number of Daewoo's Lanos models produced by the FSO plant have been exported. More than 130,000 people are employed in the car sector.

38 Petr Pavlinek, 2006, "Restructuring of the Polish passenger car industry through foreign direct investment", *Euroasian Geography and Economics* 47(3): 353–77; Peter Pavlinek, Boleslaw Domanski and Robert Guzik, 2009, "Industrial upgrading through foreign direct investment in Central European automotive manufacturing", *European Urban and Regional Studies* 16(1): 43–62; Boleslaw Domanski and Krzysztof Gwosdz, 2009, "Toward a more embedded production system? Automotive supply networks and localized capabilities in Poland", *Growth and Change* 40(3) (September): 452–82.

39 At that time, the administrative level of the region did not exist.

40 OECD, 2007, *OECD Reviews of Regional Innovation, Competitive Regional Clusters: National Policy Approaches*, Paris: OECD.

41 Public aid is very tightly controlled by European regulation whose aim is to ensure that competition is not distorted. However, as a result of legacies from the Communist period and the profound crisis which had a negative impact on regional economic potential, the EU tolerated a certain bending of the rules. Public aid is therefore composed of aid granted in the name of structural funds to regions with a GDP below the threshold of 75 percent of the European average. This is the indicator used to designate regions which are "behind in development" and who can therefore benefit from the need for European convergence. Poland has been granted 60 billion euros from EU structural funds for the period 2007–13. This aid can be used to finance up to 80 percent of public investments and up to 50 percent of private investments. It also includes regional aid (sub-state), the amount of which is decided on centrally depending on regional parameters whose algorithm includes population, growth employment and unemployment factors.

42 The author has carried out several missions in Poland. In 2007 and 2008 he visited Poland in his capacity as Advisor to the OECD for the drafting of the Poland report which dealt with regional development and governance. This report, entitled *Territorial Review: Poland*, was published in October 2008. He returned to Poland in 2009 and 2010 when he headed a programme on research into clusters.

43 The OECD has identified four types of clusters which is defined in the following way: "A cluster is an agglomeration of vertically and/or horizontally linked firms operating in the same line of business in conjunction with supporting institutions", OECD, *OECD Reviews of Regional Innovation, Competitive Regional Clusters*, 29. The first type is known as a Marshall cluster. These are artisan SMEs specialised in high technology and services. "Hub and Spoke clusters" are dominated by one or several large firms supported by their sub-contractors and related activity. In this case, cooperation is based on the different advantages of proximity. The third type refers to companies dominated by services proper to the given branch but independent from each other. Finally, State Industry clusters are found in regions in which local business structures are dominated by a public or non-trading entity such as a military base, university or public institution.

44 Under the Communist regime, every *combinat* had an external foreign trade unit available to it which was the only department mandated to negotiate sales to foreign partners. This department had all the contact details of foreign clients whose foreign currency was much sought after.

45 François Bafoil, 2001, "The transformations of rules in post-communist firms in Poland", in E. Conte and M. Burowski (eds), *Poland: Social and Cultural Paradigms*, Fribourg: University of Fribourg, 323–39.

46 OECD, 2008, *Poland: Regional Development Report*, Paris: OECD.

47 In Polish, "Dolina Lotnicza", which in reality is a great marketing coup as it gave a

real identity to the whole region, whereas statistically it remains a rural region.

48 Michael Porter, 2003, "The economic performance of the regions", *Regional Studies* 37(6): 549–78.
49 Wladyslaw Adamski, Jan Buncak, Pavel Machonin and Dominique Martin, 1999, *System Change and Modernization*, Warsaw: IFIS Publishers.
50 Baltowki and Mickiewicz, "Privatization in Poland: ten years after", 443.
51 "Despite the creation of a market environment and rather hard budget constraints (with the exception of some sectors), the state controlled part of the enterprise sector in Poland is still much less competitive and efficient than the private sector of the economy. State controlled enterprises are still governed by internal actors and interest groups that had formed before the transformation began." Piotr Kozarzewski, 2007, "Corporate governance in state-controlled enterprises in Poland", Seventh International Conference on Enterprise in Transition, organised by the Faculty of Economics, Split, May 24–26, p. 2.
52 Jozef Konings, 1997, "Firms' growth and ownership in transition countries", *Economic Letters* 55: 413–18.
53 K. Amess and B. M. Roberts, 2007, "The productivity effects of privatization: The case of Polish cooperatives", *Internal Review of Financial Analysis* 16(4): 354–66.
54 As the former Prime Minister and now Central Bank governor Marek Belka said, "The fundamental thing about the Polish economy over the decade is a continuous reduction in unit labor costs. Poland has been even more successful than Germany, which is why our exporters are gaining market share even during a slowdown". Quoted in "Connected Central and Eastern Europe", *Financial Times* (December 14): 18.
55 Jacek Tittenbrun, 2011, "Divide and rule: privatization in Poland and the working class", *Critique* 39(1): 83–105.

7 Internationalization and a competitiveness agenda

State development finance agencies and the financial crisis in Brazil and Chile

Alvaro Artigas

Introduction

Brazilian president Dilma Rousseff (2010–) announced a massive and unprecedented influx of resources aimed at removing the infrastructure "bottlenecks" on August 15, 2010, in the capital city of Brasilia. What appeared to be a bold move in the direction of a new developmental track by Brazilian authorities has increasingly revealed a more subtle picture, where concerns from big corporations, business interests and the financial arm of the state—the Brazilian National Development Bank (BNDES)—have acquired unprecedented clout. The strengthening of state development financial agencies such as the BNDES is not circumscribed to Brazil and is a phenomenon widely spread these days in many emergent countries.[1] Even though this is by no means an exclusive developmental endeavor—European governments have recently hinted at a similar possibility[2]—regions such as South America shed remarkable light on these agencies' specialization and reform through a critical review of neoliberal policies adopted in the early 1980s and 1990s.

Empirical research on development banks and promotion agencies has not been matched by equally important theoretical arguments about state intervention in the economy which is telling of their implicitly controversial role in the economy. Current debates on the transformation of market economies and in particular on the stabilization of capitalist models, range from a strict neoclassical assumption, that these state institutions would distort the allocation of resources, to a more benevolent reading where interests and firms that gravitate around the state[3] contribute to development cycles and economic growth as well as provides for stability in capitalist systems.[4] The literature on these institutions has yet to account for the outcomes related to their interaction with the state in relation to the transformation of the institutional features of capitalism in emerging countries.[5] Where state development financial agencies (SDFAs) are indeed present and endowed with a clear mandate as well as sufficient resources, albeit not exclusively financial ones, they have successfully managed to compensate for the poor development of financial markets and strengthened the relation between political power and business interests.

Brazil and Chile's financial agencies, BNDES and the Chilean Economic

Development Agency (CORFO) respectively, provide two interesting contrasting approaches of SDFAs that underwent a radical transformation of their initial developmental[6] mandate in order to become key promoters of strategic industrial sectors and instrumental tools in the road to the optimization of administrative efficiency. In order to understand this transformation and its implications for national models of capitalist development and the interaction between government-linked corporations[7] (GLCs) and the state, it is imperative to understand how these developmental institutions were able to prevail in spite of having been dwarfed by the neoliberal tide of the 1980s and 1990s. Though having little if no place under the current economic paradigm, these agencies acquired sufficient autonomy vis-à-vis the new institutional framework and gathered sufficient organizational, financial, and symbolic resources to alter the nature of state–GLC interactions within development policies and during when responses were required to the 2008 crisis.

The great transformation of South American capitalisms in the last three decades will be my departing point, so as to elucidate how BNDES and CORFO navigated through capital reforms that would alter their historical role. We will then analyze how the 2008 financial crisis led to distinct strategies: while Brazil's privileged a narrow strategy with selective allocation of financial resources in order to cater to the strategic needs of a group of strategic GLCs (financing, infrastructure), the Chilean government favored a broad market-oriented strategy aimed at expanding markets capabilities both in terms of transversal firm competitiveness and access to finance. As much as these political choices comforted the authorities' agenda and demands raised by vocal business interests, they exacerbated preexistent inconsistencies related to markets' organization and growth strategies in the long run.

Developmental strategies in Brazil and Chile: development banks, ideological designs, and economic pragmatism

Developmental national goals and the creation and consolidation of development agencies transited throughout three distinct periods that range from the post-war period until the end of the 1970s, the beginning of the 1980s until the Asian–Russian crisis of 1998, and a final period from 2000 onwards. These periods marked both the transformations intervened in the national developmental project as well as the sequential change of organizational features within these organizations.

Both CORFO and the BNDES were governmental responses to a profound cognitive transformation, comparable to a paradigm shift[8] that was accelerated by economic ideas in response to the 1929 depression and the contraction of international markets after the Second World War. Critical theories emerged challenging growth models driven by natural resource's demand from international markets. The impact of dependency theory in the 1950s and new economic growth theory coming from the Economic Commission for Latin America and the Caribbean (ECLAC) headquarters in Santiago was paramount to this change and exerted a significant impact on policy makers. Led by strong executives and charismatic political leaders, these new views overcame existing resistances by national and international capital in the way of industrialization of these countries.

The first development programs led to the establishment of a set of public bodies, whose mission was to articulate the principles of an endogenous type of development. This initial task at hand—and this was a typical feature of the South American region—was to account for the vast natural resources available throughout the territory as well as to set up an industrial base that would add value to this primary sector. As much as development pathways were close enough in most South American countries at the same period,[9] the political goals of *industrialization* meant different realities in Brazil and Chile, hence industrialization programs experienced significant variations.[10]

Development banks against dependency: rise and fall of the Chilean developmental model

The creation of CORFO in 1939, as much as it was driven by basic industrialization needs, namely the necessity to improve energy production and set up a basic set of industries that would promote social development and allow for more complex industrial endeavors.[11] Nonetheless, the promotion of development relied heavily on the ability of planners to account for all the riches of the land and to promote a basic and viable industrial layout, those that would ensure rapid returns to the coffers of the Chilean state.

The heavily centralized institutional format adopted by CORFO matched Chile's administrative and political tradition: by virtue of that reality this public organization was subordinated to previously defined goals by the presidential administration and the economic ministries. CORFO laid down a sustainable and integrated set of public sectors that account for much of Chile's growth over the second half of the twentieth century such as ENAP (the National Petroleum Company) or CODELCO (the National Copper Corporation), to name a few. Yet its hierarchical subordination to the designs of the executive power and government agendas limited its operational autonomy.

From a developmental standpoint, the purpose of such an organization was to participate in the inception or development of economic sectors where private capital was not readily available. However, as much as it benefited from its ministerial status until 1998, CORFO did not have the capacity to set autonomous policies or to set policy goals of its own. Its contribution to the formulation of development policies was one based on the cumulative expertise it had gathered since its creation as well as its technical competence. Notwithstanding this, it remained a faithful executor of economic policies established by various ministries, such as Economy, Finance, Agriculture, Mining, and Transportation. Most major industrial endeavors that can be traced back to the 1939 to 1980 period were directly or indirectly related to CORFO undertakings, showing an extraordinary resilience and adaptability in terms of project undertakings in the economic area. Beyond more evident industrial development goals, this agency reduced the asymmetries existing between a strong developed center and poorer regions, especially in the southern section of the Chilean territory.

The military years (1973–89) drastically minimized the mission of CORFO and as a result of the stark ideological choice of that period; the new economic team in place jettisoned its historical developmental features. Among these were the coordination of the privatization of public firms and the concession of loans to public enterprises that were still under its supervision.[12] CORFO had to be adapted to a new institutional framework derived of an open free market capitalist model, as a result of the radical transformations brought by Pinochet's dictatorship and pursued after the return of democracy, which contemplated a limited capacity of State intervention. With the return of democracy in 1989 new financing lines were made available but directed to a set of different core missions that made impossible any reenactment of former developmental designs. CORFO did, in spite of it all, experience a substantial qualitative transformation that introduced some innovations into the optimization of productivity-related factors such as professional training, novel financial instruments and assistance protocols as to allow firms in need to access to state-funded credit lines.

With the return of democracy in 1989, CORFO was engaged in the formulation of policy instruments that would foster innovation through technological transfers, although at a limited initial capacity given the array of debts inherited from the military years and its much diminished capacity. This long process saw its culmination when the National Fund for Productive and Technological Development (FONTEC) and the Innovation and Development Fund (IDF), both subsidiaries of CORFO, set the existing guidelines regarding the allocation of public resources to the development of research activities and technology transfer, innovation and entrepreneurship. In March 2005 the two funds were merged and created INNOVA CHILE, CORFO's committee in charge of promoting and facilitating innovation in firms, as to encourage entrepreneurial development and to strengthen the national innovation system (see Figure 7.1).

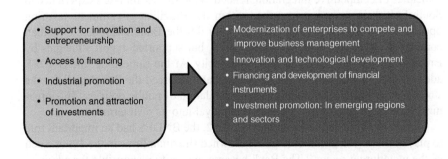

Figure 7.1 The Chilean Economic Development Agency's mandate for transformation

BNDES as a bulwark of Brazil's developmental and industrial ideals

The BNDES, very much like CORFO, provided a set of responses to the interrogations of the mode of industrialization in South American countries. What distinguishes the Brazilian path is the relative stability of the initial industrialization design that was the consequence of the development imperatives of such a large resource-rich country, striving for economic independence, and the incremental addition of new—sometimes contradictory—sets of tasks and goals.

The National Bank for Economic Development (BNDE), predecessor of the present institution, was created on June 20, 1952. The aim of this new federal agency was to become the national policy formulator and implementer of national economic development plans. Initially, the BNDE invested heavily in infrastructure, but the public firms created during these years funneled the Bank's investments to private enterprises and industries. As an example of this evolution the agricultural sector and small and medium businesses acquired credit lines from the BNDE in the 1960s. In 1964, the Bank decentralized its operations, opening regional offices in Sao Paulo, Recife, and Brasilia that acquired a network of accredited financial agents all over Brazil.

An important change in BNDE occurred at the beginning of the 1970s when it acquired the status of a public firm. The change allowed for greater flexibility in staffing, greater freedom in the operations of raising funds and lesser political interference, although under strict control throughout most of the military years (1964–85). The BNDE became a fundamental piece in the import-substitution industrialization (ISI) programs and as such it favored the capital goods and basic inputs sectors that received additional investment lines. The complexity of Brazil's industrial development at that time led to the creation of three subsidiaries in 1974 aimed at operating in the capital market in order to expand the capitalization channels of Brazilian companies.[13] The outcome of such ISI programs was not always successful yet they allowed Brazil to acquire an important and complex industrial tissue with no equal in the South American continent.

An important transformation occurred in 1982 with a transition of the Bank's missions and when it was given a new name, thus becoming the Banco Nacional de Desenvolvimento Economico e Social (BNDES). During most of the 1980s, principles of competitive integration, related to the successful NICs experience in South-East Asia gained momentum within the Brazilian government favoring openness to international markets. Not only did the Bank encourage Brazilian companies to compete with imported goods, but supported export strategies by Brazilian industrial firms in a modest capacity. At the same time, the BNDES adopted the practice of strategic planning that reinforced the Bank's call for the study, analysis and contribution to the formulation of public policies. This organizational cohesion ensured the Bank's survival into its own terms.

In spite of Fernando Color election in 1992, the BNDES had an important role to play in the privatization of large state-owned Brazilian firms in the 1990s, such as the metallurgic sector.[14] The Bank became the entity responsible for administrative, financial, and technical support of the National Privatization Program

(PND), initiated in 1991 without totally relinquishing to the hard core of its missions. Thus, the 1990s were particularly important in terms of a qualitative expansion of the Bank's tasks, such as the stimulation of regional decentralization, with increased investment in projects in the North and Northeast region, the adoption, for the first time, of environmental guidelines and an enhanced attention brought to the export capacity of firms beyond the big industrial holdings.

Another qualitative leap that benefited from unprecedented levels of macroeconomic stability took place during the two presidential mandates of Ignacio Lula da Silva (2003–9). The important social agenda brought by the center-left coalition required a rapid enhancement of social programs whose resources could not further be extracted through privatization of public equity. The expansion of the Brazilian economy demanded therefore to go beyond the strategy of the 1990s that relied on a massive influx of FDIs that also involved the integration of environmental sustainability, employment and welfare concerns, and the reduction of social and regional inequalities. The Accelerated Program of Growth (PAC) in 2007 was the culmination of these efforts in the path of securing steady growth levels with a strong component of social justice.[15] Let's finally add that BNDES's expansion and modernization, as much as it was the functional consequence of these new principles and related instruments, owed a great deal to a generational renewal of bank officials and technicians related to key networks of Brazil's present policy making machinery.[16] The BNDES has been reinforced as an organization with a widespread network of regional and international agencies,[17] improving competitive advantages in strategic areas (agriculture, industry, and energy) while at the same time adjusting the developmental project to the specificity of each sector.

The 2008 financial crisis and the use of incremental countercyclical instruments

In a context of continuous improvement of macroeconomic fundamentals and through a long process of trial and error of almost three decades, both the Brazilian and Chilean authorities were confronted with the 2008 financial crisis in unprecedented terms which allowed an equally unprecedented countercyclical response that mobilized time-tested and well-targeted instruments.[18] This was, no doubt, a radical turn for what had been traditional responses by South American countries during the previous 1981, 1994, and 1998–2001 financial crises.[19] The contraction of external demand, as much as it became a reality by 2010, was partly offset by the decade-long expansion of national markets and the spread of free-trade agreements, mostly directed towards Asia and the Pacific Rim. Development banks and promotion agencies were not only mobilized as valuable tools of this countercyclical response, but their strategic reach and financial capabilities were enhanced so as to improve both their reach and capillarity. A close examination shows nonetheless a significant variance in the responses of the Chilean and Brazilian governments, mostly due to the role played by development and promotion agencies and the strategy of support provided to public firms and GLCs.

Beyond concerns of a moderate deterioration of macroeconomic indicators, the coordinated response by state development bodies had to curb rising negative expectations among economic agents in order to ensure steady growth levels, precious for political and social stability to achieve short-term goals. There was a clear combination of short-term contingency plans, regarding monetary decisions in particular, but also mid-term growth plans to deal with the aftermath of the crisis. In this regard, enhanced liquidity and interest rates reductions practiced by central banks, as well as fiscal incentives, were important as they softened the impact of the crisis on the real economy and perceptions of problems in strategic industrial sectors at the national level, although both agencies also tried to reach to non-traditional sectors of the economy and to go beyond simple credit alloca-tion. In order to understand this evolution, it is extremely important to acknowledge the changing roles experienced by both public organizations and the attainment of greater levels of autonomy during the last decade. It is equally important to unveil how less visible goals managed to be enacted by governments within these organizations: the main emphasis in Brazil lay on strategic sector GLCs as engines of growth for the rest of the economy, whereas Chile stressed transversal financial and institutional market optimization.

A broad strategy: the optimization of Chile's financial market

The impact of the international economic crisis was rapid and deep, partly because of Chile's density of foreign trade and capital market integration,[20] trends that were actively pursued under the Bachelet government (2006–10). However, in the face of this event, the authorities implemented a series of fiscal and mone-tary policies that represented an interesting evolution departing from the previous choice of policy instruments that targeted speculative activities during the 1998 crisis. More importantly, Chile benefited from an outstanding macroeconomic status, as well as a long-consolidated domestic financial market. These two parameters explain in part the robust growth indicators during 2010 and 2011 and the quick recovery rates for the latter year.

The fiscal and monetary response decided by the administration determined the policy framework from where these agencies would be able to participate. The Chilean government announced a first set of decisions aimed at countering the crisis as soon as October 2008. Among them were measures intended to support small exporters and companies, small mining firms, and middle income families purchasing housing. The major announcement occurred on January 5, when the government launched a fiscal stimulus package of US$ 4 billion (2.8 percent of GDP and 14 percent of planned current fiscal expenditure). The plan was then complemented by a national agreement on labor market assistance, employment protection, and training stimulus, which was unanimously approved by the National Congress in May 2009. During that same year, the central bank reduced the interest rate by 775 base points and expanded the liquidity supply to CORFO that could thus provide financial institutions with additional credit lines at pref-erential rates.

These governmental orientations put SMEs as the highest priority on CORFO's agenda and led this organization to design specific instruments aimed at this particular level, which is tantamount of the subsidiarity principle implicit in this agency in relation to the state. Public relief programs had a visible dimension here, with specific export credit lines set down for small and medium export companies (EMT). The stress on international competition, a Chilean specificity given the size of its limited market, would nonetheless contribute, in the light of the discussions being held at that time, to the creation of employment and economic growth within the country. While both the Bachelet and Piñera government actively supported these programs, the decline of the international environment required addressing the situation of larger companies as well, both private and government-linked indiscriminately.

The promotion of Chilean exports profited from a more extensive coverage and flexibility by CORFO as shown by the program of Bank Loan Coverage to Exporters (COBEX), which backs up to 50 percent of loans granted to exporters by commercial banks. In order to increase the potential reach of this instrument, the government expanded the allocation of resources for COBEX to US$ 50 million, allowing for secured loans to increase to one billion dollars while at the same time reviewing the companies' selection criteria. Moreover, CORFO enhanced investment promotion funds by US$ 500 million investment credit lines issued through one of its operational funds. The Investment Guarantee Fund of CORFO (FOGAIN) provides long-term financing to small and medium enterprises to enable them carry out their investment projects, greatly expanding the resources available through the financial system while securing further reimbursements to the agency at acceptable social rates (see Table 7.1).

Table 7.1 Chilean counter-cyclical decisions associated with the 2008 financial crisis

Date	Decision	Specific adjustments
October 13, 2008	Extension of the Export Credit Insurance COBEX to US$ 50 million, totaling US$ 55 million	With a potential credit of US$ 1,100 million
October 13, 2008	Expansion of US$ 500 million in Credit CORFO Investment	Partial credit guarantee for SMEs to finance their long-term investments and favorable rates
January 5, 2009	Online partial guarantee for debt rescheduling SMEs with an initial contribution of US $50 million	
March 30, 2009	Online partial guarantee for debt rescheduling	Large companies with an initial contribution of US$ 50 million

Source: Chilean Economic Development Agency (CORFO), 2010

These two instruments count among the most visible tracks of intervention by CORFO for the period 2008–12, and confirm the complementarity with state designs when it comes to contingency responses to the crisis. They also confirm this agency's preference for a second-floor type of credit intervention as evidenced by CORFO's granting funds and guarantees for commercial banks as to ensure that non-traditional recipients such as smaller companies would effectively be financed. To refinance existing credit lines, companies were given the opportunity to approach a set of private banks that bid on these first funds:[21] This configuration is interesting as it shows the type of profitable public-private type of partnerships that have served as a guiding principle promoted by the Chilean government that we encounter in most of CORFO's different programs.[22] In order to overcome the consequences of a sluggish post-crisis scenario, private banks' participation into Chile's national recovery and development strategy has to be reinforced.

Stabilizing Brazil: reinforcing export-oriented sectors

Many observers thought the financial crisis in Brazil to be a crucial test for a growth strategy that had to come to terms with the principles of open regionalism and a recurrent temptation to enact former developmental schemes. Brazil had managed to show great resilience as a consequence of stronger macroeconomic foundations built over the previous three administrations (2002–12): both the reduction of fiscal deficits and the accumulation of important trade surpluses with Asia contributed to diminish the country's traditional vulnerability to external shocks, which allowed for considerable financial means to be channeled into countercyclical measures (i.e. credit accession first, followed by infrastructure works) that led to a rapid recovery after the 2008 crisis.[23] The commodity demand boom driven mostly by China reoriented Brazil's trade flows to the Asian continent and expanded the operational capabilities of EMNCs from the agro-industrial complex and the metallurgic sectors. This virtuous context allowed the Brazilian government to cope with the contagion effect of the crisis without requiring a loan from the IMF, which would have been indisputably accompanied with austerity and pro-cyclical policies, as had been the case in the 1980s.

Once the first consequences of the international financial crisis had been resolved, both the Finance ministry (Fazenda) and the Monetary Economic Council (CEM) decided to accelerate the adoption of countercyclical economic measures to reverse the recessive economic trends. The impressive growth rate of the Brazilian economy (7.5 percent in 2010)[24] shows that Brazil's reaction to the international financial crisis, although less encompassing and market-oriented as the one in Chile, succeeded in accomplishing its initial goals, through a combination of preexisting crisis programs, specifically the Growth Acceleration Program (PAC),[25] and economic expansionary policies implemented since 2008.

The role played by the BNDES in this two-stream government intervention plan proved to be extremely important. Not only did this organization become a centerpiece of President Rousseff's stabilization and growth program, but it participated in the formulation of several instruments aimed at modernizing the economy. In addition to supporting an ad hoc investment in infrastructure, machinery, and equipment, the BNDES expanded its export promotion activities, through significant technological and industrial investments that were equally important in promoting regional development, developing capital markets, and optimizing foreign trade balance through the strengthening of Brazilian companies abroad.

The BNDES was closely associated to the goals of strategic policies among which included the reinforcement of "national champions," and supporting the concentration of GLCs within huge sectoral and multi-sectoral conglomerates. This concentration had been called for by the BNDES as a consequence of the developmental syncretism introduced during the 1990s where traditional developmental designs coexisted with free markets principles. In this regard, the positive impact of larger companies managed to be progressively acknowledged when it came to financial, technological and managerial synergies that generated positive externalities for chain suppliers, distributors, and service providers. The BNDES has acted not only by helping to increase investments thresholds in these companies, as witnessed by the funding of their participation in foreign trade operations., The agency has increasingly expanded its credit lines to Brazilian foreign trade as well as their internal process of expansion and consolidation.

As previously indicated, this has also been particularly true for two important sectors where the Brazilian State has increased its participation share, although through different intervention schemes: mining (through Vale do Rio Doce) and oil (through Petrobras). Both companies have increasingly diversified the range of their activities while vertically integrating processing activities. As for Vale, even though the Brazilian State ceased to be one the shareholders in 1997, it decided to maintain a dominant position through different channels, among which included public funds facilitated by the BNDES which played a significant role in funding the firm's activities.[26] Yet the state's main participation in the company's capital base took place through Litel, a pension funds conglomerate led by Banco do Brasil that acquired control of the company's capital.[27] 49 percent of the shares in Valepar, which owns Vale, is in turn under the control of Litel, while 11.5 percent of the equity is held by BNDES. Put differently, the public funds block collectively owned 60.5 percent of Vale's equity, while the other major shareholders are Bradespar S.A. and the Japanese group Mitsui. Vale relies heavily on the Brazilian state, not only because of its ownership structure, but increasingly so because of the unprecedented volume of loans granted to this company by BNDES in a single operation (circa US$ 4 billion dollars).

In the case of Petrobras, the BNDES revised what had been its traditional stance during the first half of the decade from 2000 to 2010, in particular the reluctance to provide fresh money to a public firm, a strategy seemingly incompatible with 1990s privatization and internationalization designs of the Brazilian economy.[28] Here however, as in the case of CODELCO in Chile, the Brazilian government decided to enhance investment plans for this strategic firm in order that it remained under state control. This orientation was undoubtedly stimulated by the attainment of a temporary oil provision autonomy in 2006 and the prospects of massive reserves uncovered in 2007 in Tupi, near the bay of Santos. In 2009, the total amount of state contracts granted to the firm reached US$ 25 billion, funding not only the expansion of oil and gas in the Brazilian energy sector, but supporting petrochemical expansion, fuel transportation and storage, and handling of natural gas. In addition to direct financing, the equity arm of the BNDES (BNDESPar) has also since 2010 increased its stakes in Petrobras, as previously seen in the case of Vale, with a total participation volume of 47 percent of the total resources of that institution.[29]

Other than the immediate impact of BNDES programs on employment— 290,000 direct jobs for 2009–10—this agency greatly contributed to the reinforcement of internationally viable economic sectors expanding industrial equipment supply chains and supporting offshore services. For instance, Petrobras alone benefited from more than 70 projects in prospecting and refining in existing oil fields in the country, which will transform this GLC into one of the five largest integrated energy companies in the world.[30] The BNDES granted Petrobas unprecedented investments for the 2009/2013 period, amounting to a total US$ 174.4 billion thanks to an unprecedented government bond issue (US$ 12.5 billion).

Both SDFAs have acquired unprecedented international clout that is the result of a balanced developmental state design, involving three fundamental variables: the positive reinforcement of existing terms of trade for exportable commodities; the waning of international trade regulations; and an enhanced governance capacity by executive powers in both countries, whether through interactive relations with regional organizations (CAF in Latin America), direct internationalization (such as BNDES in the UK and Uruguay and soon in Shanghai) or better coordination of these organizations with other public agencies already operating abroad (such as ProChile). GLCs or big public consortiums, most notably CODELCO and PETROBRAS, but also EMNCs or Multilatinas, have been the main recipients from this expansion abroad and contributed to reinforce the most dynamic corporations in both countries.

Conclusion: stabilization or convergence of development strategies?

Development agencies in Chile and Brazil have shown extraordinary resilience in spite of important economic policy shifts, beefing up their institutional resources and adapting them into viable models of intervention in the economy. Their institutional legitimacy has been very much dependent on the credibility of state developmental plans but also on their own capacity to become an effective lever in directing major local businesses actors to key economic sectors that they wish to develop. Free markets and open regionalism principles were an irreversible transformation of these countries' economic programs, backtracking from traditional forms of public ownership towards a more technical, diffuse type of interventions. The nature of national development projects varied and as a consequence of this so did the intermediate goals and the choice of financial instruments, hinting that beyond any general constraints derived from the 2008 crisis, the explanation had to be found in the interactions between the state, SDFAs and relevant economic players at the national level.

CORFO accomplished an important qualitative leap forward when it improved the reach of public investments into neglected areas of economic activity, through specific credit allocation or promotion programs. It is, however, in its capacity to formulate innovative instruments to enhance its reach and promote institutional complementarity within preexisting programs, such as Prochile, that CORFO has shown the full length of its operational autonomy. In Brazil, the BNDES benefited instead from a quantitative expansion that allowed this organization to aggressively engage in the promotion and sophistication of industrial value chains in strategic sectors. Instead of disrupting preexisting pathways, the crisis contributed to accomplishing these new goals through the allocation of new funds while developing new financing schemes on an ad hoc basis. A close scrutiny of these long term institutional features and conjuncture choices reveal two distinct—and to a certain extent antagonistic—strategies of development that have been replicated in part by other South American countries and regional projects.[31] These two distinct pathways are not, however, devoid of inner contradictions which reflect some of the inconsistencies of existing developmental projects, both in terms of sustainability and means to accomplish their respective ambitions. A key limitation of Brazil's development strategy is that it is too narrowly conceived, in the sense it has concentrated its operational capacity to a limited set of agencies and GLCs under the hierarchical command of the Presidential office. In what follows, I will assess how the broad strategy pursued by the Chilean government has relied on a rather horizontal steering of governmental agencies, financial institutions and corporations improving the institutional and legal framework for GLCs but not necessarily targeting them.

Brazil's narrow strategy: financial crowding-out and other perils

Brazil's strategy has so far consisted of channeling existing and potential financial resources to a select group of firms where the government has a property stake or a strategic interest.[32] I classified such a strategy as narrow in the sense it directed most of the agencies efforts (i.e. technical know-how, expertise, resources, and credit lines) to enhance the competitive advantage of a set of predetermined recipients in international markets. Another equally important feature of the narrow strategy lies in the ability of the BNDES to intervene and nationalize private firms through capital expansion.

Due to this strategy, the BNDES has become a central piece of the Brazilian development plan over the past decade and this is partly the result of an increased interaction with the state and the all-powerful Brazilian presidency.[33] The Brazilian agency consistently improved its financial stability and reach during the 2000–2010 period, due to successful counter-cyclical interventions and again throughout the worst episodes of the current financial crisis. On the other hand, the BNDES has become a precious instrument in the hands of the Brazilian government, in the sense it allowed for swift, yet indirect, state intervention in several vital sectors of the economy. Both GLCs and public firms have clearly benefited from the transformation of BNDES's instruments, given the fact that the main priority to date has been the expansion of productive capacities of Brazil's untapped natural resources. The exploitation of the Pre-sal reserves and the importance this will have for budget stability and the overall economic status of Brazil in international markets is considered to be a top priority by the Brazilian authorities and a core agenda of the new multi-annual development plan called Brasil Maior.[34]

As much as there is a competitive agenda aimed at improving the remaining hurdles in the road to development, a close scrutiny of competitiveness-bound initiatives reveal that many of the plans financed by the BNDES are production driven, involving mostly big GLCs, and not necessarily dealing with an optimization of these corporations' trade operations. An example of this lies in the much delayed decision to deal with the much delayed reforms of what is known as the "Custo Brasil": there is a lack of modern infrastructure and the persistence of bottlenecks to development to this day, in the form of insufficient connectivity networks and poor port facilities. As much as port reform has long been pointed out as an endemic problem in the road to development of modern Brazil,[35] it is one of the many problems faced by industrialists who wish to expand their operations abroad, but far from being the only one in this respect.

Two other important shortcomings related to BNDES's operations cast a shadow of doubt on the capacity of this public organization to significantly contribute to enhancing competitiveness levels of very much protected GLCs. The modest development of financial markets remains in Brazil a major issue in this regard and so far BNDES has not addressed this issue, resorting instead to direct or indirect financial assistance to those GLCs concerned on an ad hoc basis. The second shortcoming lies in the viability and sustainability of internationalization plans in Asia and Africa that are still unclear in terms of what they intend to achieve, and how.[36]

There is another potential troublesome feature of Brazil's narrow strategy that is very much related to the unprecedented financial means at hand and the intervention capacity that the BNDES has cumulated after the 2008 crisis. The fact that the BNDES actions are guided towards a specific set of economic sectors is not without its perils when it comes to the capacity to address transversal issues that are vital for most areas of the economy—among which include subcontractors of GLCs—and the difficulty other economic interests will have in making their demands heard at an executive level.[37]

Market outcomes of Chile's broad strategic choices

The broad dimension of CORFO's activities lies in the specific features of the Chilean economy that remained mostly unchanged by the financial crisis. As such, the strategy pursued by the Chilean state is an development policy mix, whose main goal is to expand markets operational capabilities in terms of competitiveness, both internal and external, and provide firms with access to finance.

The pursuit of this strategy has mostly relied on the capacity by the Chilean state to consolidate its role of shaping the development of the economy, through a regulatory dimension that is quite dissimilar from the one pursued by Brazil. The very composition of the Chilean market, with GLCs that compete with strong multinational groups (e.g. Anglo American and Mitsui, to name just two) has led to a limited diversification of existing natural resource extraction activities (other than copper and lithium): the mining sector remains to this day the main industrial sector of activity. As such, the efforts of CORFO have been mostly diverted to the backing of a vibrant service sector, consisting mostly of SMEs, among which many are subcontractors of the mining industry, and the creation of new sectors (ICTs) resulting in attempts to facilitate the operating conditions of all firms.

Lastly, regulatory standards serve as a useful measure of the broad strategy reach as adopted by Chile's development agency. The expansion of activities abroad and attraction of foreign investments through an extended set of related agencies (Pro Chile, Innova Chile) are very much in agreement with CORFO's service-oriented approach, mostly aimed at regulating market's inefficiencies through an inclusive legal and institutional framework, but not necessarily as a way of steering the market or promoting specific sectors over others. Moreover, and in visible contrast to Brazil's narrow model of development, CORFO and the Chilean state have fewer leverages of assistance for ailing GLCs, due to CORFO's relative autonomy and post-2008 orientation towards credit facilitation.

As in the case of Brazil, the Chilean strategy is not exempt from inherent risks. CORFO relies on its own financing capacity as well as on credit lines that have to be approved when voting the annual national budget; this is in contrast to BNDES's use of tax payer's money and treasury bills to finance schemes. In spite of the presence of a relatively conservative and autonomous management who have oversight of the organization's resources—this has led to an administrative autonomy as well—there is always a risk of an alteration of its intervention capacity due to credit restrictions, unprofitable investments or a swing of policy preferences related to development orientations.

Is Chile's broad strategy sustainable? CORFO has proven, after 2008, to be extremely proactive in reacting accordingly, in terms of optimization of market opportunities and creation of policy instrument designs in spite of its limited resources; it has also contributed to helping modernize firm-related services and financial markets. Yet this model relies on an adaptive strategy that differs greatly from the Brazilian view on industrialization, and might jeopardize the emergence of new strategic industrial sectors such as the one of the lithium industry in the Atacama Desert, where the Chilean state is endowed with the largest available possession of this resource.[38] Moreover, the sometimes excessive obedience of Chile to the present free market paradigm (a neutral role for the state regarding sectoral developments) limits any change in relation to CORFO's role that would not be of an incremental nature. Out of this model, however, and the extended but restrained missions of Chile's promotion agency, the country might not be able to emulate other emerging countries' development and diversification of the national economy's sectors.

As it has been argued in here, the study of SDFAs reveals much of the nature of the state's relationship with GLCs. Whether important sectors have privileged access to development designs or transversal class associations to articulate their demands of market liberalization, the fact is that in dynamic emergent countries SDFAs have managed to enhance their pivotal role. The success of national strategies in both case studies, in their capacity to reinforce existing agencies and public bodies such as CORFO and the BNDES, is due to their ability to act as intermediaries that would ensure an interventionist capacity in the economic process without necessarily leading to adverse reactions by investors and key social actors, or the reiteration of previous statist-driven models of development. If relative autonomy is preserved, these agencies can carry out, and even amplify, the reach of governmental decisions, through a creative array of ad hoc instruments that have proven their effectiveness after 2008.

Notes

1   Recent initiatives include the project launched in 2011 by Indonesian authorities to reestablish the defunct Bank Pembangunan Indonesia. See www.thejakartaglobe.com/home/finance-ministry-supports-proposal-to-establish-national-development-bank/433581.

2   This was also outlined in the political program of the Socialist candidate and new French president François Hollande, who voiced these views during the presidential campaign in 2012. See www.parti-socialiste.fr/dossier/le-projet-de-francois-hollande.

3   More recently, the literature has pointed to the role of development banks and agencies in developing countries going beyond addressing market failure to addressing development failure. See Vusi Gumede, 2008, "Social Protection in Latin America and Africa," Africa Notes (Summer) (published by the Institute for African Development, Cornell University, Ithaca, NY), and Vusi Gumede, 2011, "The Role of Public Policies and Policy Makers in Africa: Responding to the Global Economic Recession," in M. Ndulo and D. Lee (eds), *Food and Financial Crises and Their Impacts on Achieving the Millennium Development Goals in Africa*, Athens, OH: Ohio University.

4   The historical institutionalism subfield of political economy has hinted at the instrumental value of such institutions in the stabilization and perpetuation of indigenous capitalist institutions.

5   For a rich discussion on the state of neoliberal reforms in South America and, more specifically, on the limited transformation of the preexistent model of development, see Laura Macdonald and Arne Ruckert (eds), 2009, *Post-Neoliberalism in the Americas: Beyond the Washington Consensus?* New York: Palgrave Macmillan.

6   For a thorough discussion on the role of developmentalism in the Third World during the second half of the twentieth century, see V. Prashad, 2007, *The Darker Nations: A People's History of the Third World*, New York: New Press.

7   For a thorough review of the development of government corporations in the Americas after the authoritarian period, see B. R. Schneider, 1992, *Politics within the*

State: Elite Bureaucrats and. Industrial Policy in Authoritarian Brazil, Pittsburgh, PA: Pittsburgh University Press, p. 337.

8   The model subsequent to this, the free market economy paradigm actively promoted by Bretton Woods institutions in the 1980s, was based on the following idea: "the core of this paradigm is the conviction that reducing state control of the economy and increasing private sector investment are keys to generating economic growth, and that growth is an essential first step on the path to broader development goals". See J. Burdick, P. Oxhorn, and K. Roberts, 2009, *Beyond Neoliberalism in Latin America? Societies and Politics at the Crossroads*, Basingstoke: Palgrave Macmillan.

9   Most of these transformations took place during the second half of the 1940s, but mostly throughout the 1950s and the 1960s.

10   As proven by Brazil's model of strong state intervention. See H. Shapiro, 1994, *Engines Of Growth: The State and Transnational Auto Companies in Brazil*, New York: Cambridge University Press, pp. 1–27.

11   The metallurgic industry and the creation of steelworks by the Pacific Steel Company is a good example of this.

12   One of the least known chapters of recent Chilean economic history pertains to the privatizations of public firms—mostly created in the 1940s and 1950s by CORFO. Yet the very format of these privatizations is open to controversy today as CORFO helped both to privatize the bulk of these public firms while subsidizing many of those who became the property of economic elites close to the military government.

13   They would merge in 1982 under the name of BNDESPAR.

14   The consortium, Siderbras, remains one of the most emblematic examples of this privatization period.

15   The initial project intended to obtain 5 percent economic growth per annum while ensuring that a direct intervention by the BNDES on the finances of strategic sectors would cap the population expenses on these items. See www.bndes.gov.br/SiteBNDES/bndes/bndes_pt/Areas_de_Atuacao/Infraestrutura/pac.html.

16   This renewal has been both the consequence of a quantitative expansion of the BNDES' personnel and an important renewal of old cadres during in the period 2006–9. See A.C. Além and R. Madeira, 2010, *O BNDES em um Brasil em transição*, Rio de Janeiro: BNDES, p. 129.

17   The Bank opened a new office in South America (Montevideo) in 2009 as well as a new subsidiary in Europe (London) in order to seek new alternatives to develop in a globalized and interconnected world.

18   A good example of this was the adoption by the Chilean authorities of a counter-cyclical fiscal rule since 2000 that proved quite effective in times of financial instability. By 2006 this rule was translated into an effective legislation (Ley de Responsabilidad Fiscal/2006), which reinforced some of the initial provisions that allowed for, thanks to accumulated surpluses, the running of fiscal deficits in times of crisis.

19   See J. Santiso, 2006, *Latin America's Political Economy of the Possible: Beyond Good Revolutionaries and Free-Marketeers*, Cambridge, MA: MIT Press.

20   Chile remains to this day the country that has signed the most PTAs in the world, with countries from the USA, the EU, Japan, Korea, and Canada, to mention a few. See Ricardo French-Davis, 2004, "Macroeconomic Growth under Financial Globalization: Four Strategic Issues", in Ricardo French-Davis (ed.), *Seeking Growth under Financial Volatility*, Economic Commission for Latin America and the Caribbean (ECLAC)/Ford Foundation, Palo Alto, CA: Stanford University Press.

21   The Banco Bilbao Vizcaya Argentaria (BBVA) and the Banco de Chile are the most important ones participating into this scheme.

22   Another important instrument developed by the Chilean government backed up by CORFO's expertise is the Pro Crédito program. The plan aimed at spurring the availability of bank credit, with a special track for SMEs, as well at increasing the

competition in the banking industry in order to ensure a faster and more efficient implementation of the interest rate cuts decreed by the Chilean Central Bank.

23   This in spite of a downturn in the last quarter of 2008 and the first quarter of 2009, as a consequence of markets contractions related to the international financial crisis.

24   These impressive growth rates were not quite similarly repeated in the following and present year as a result of the attempts by Dilma Rousseff's government to cool off the economy in the face of the risk of inflation.

25   Programa de Aceleração do Crescimento, or "Growth Acceleration Program." See www.brasil.gov.br/pac.

26   BNDESPar (BNDES Participacoes SA, fund implementation of BNDES) is in possession of 6.8 percent of the shares.

27   The controlling interest of Vale, at the beginning of 2012, was held Valepar, with a 53.5 percent stake.

28   A good example of this being the legal framework approved in 1997, allowing for the outsourcing of prospecting operations. See Lei no. 9.478, August 6, 1997.

29   See A. Mineiro, 2010, "Desenvolvimento e inserção externa: algumas considerações sobre o período 2003–2009 no Brasil," in *Os Anos Lula: contribuições para um balanço crítico 2003–2010*, Rio de Janeiro: Garamond, p. 157

30   See Petrobras Strategic Plan 2020, available at www.senado.gov.br/.../ AP20090324_Petrobras.pdf.

31   The creation of the Pacific Alliance between Chile, Peru, Colombia, and Mexico in 2012 was based on open markets and competitive environments, and sought to counterbalance more industrialist inward-driven development strategies in the region.

32   The Brazilian government approved in August 2012 an unprecedented public works reform package, intended to solve the long-lasting issue of structural bottlenecks as well as to revitalize an increasingly depressed economy. The format of concessions to private investors is in sharp contrast with traditional infrastructure development projects carried out in Brazil.

33   This is consistent with Peter Evans's findings on embedded autonomy. See Peter Evans, 1995, *Embedded Autonomy: States and Industrial Transformation*, Princeton, NJ: Princeton University Press.

34   See www.brasilmaior.mdic.gov.br.

35   For a good historical review of this problem, see M. Doctor, 2002, "Business and Delays in Port Reform in Brazil," *Brazilian Journal of Political Economy* 22(2): 79–101.

36   Estudo IPEA N°52, (2011) Rio de Janeiro.

37   As suggested by the preferential access of automotive association to trade ministries in the 1990s. See Laura Gomez-Mera, 2007, "Macroeconomic Concerns and Intrastate Bargains: Explaining Illiberal Policies in Brazil's Automobile Sector," *Latin American Politics and Society* 49(1): 113–40.

38   See Alvaro Artigas, 2012, "La régulation du secteur du lithium au Chili: d'une matrice traditionnelle d'exportations à la constitution d'un secteur stratégique," in Mathieu Arès and Eric Boulanger (eds), *L'investissement et la nouvelle économie mondiale*, Brussels: Brulyant.

References

Albuquerque, A., Rodrigues, G., and de Araujo, P. (2009) "Mercado de Crédito no Brasil: Evolução Recente e o Papel do BNDES (2004–2008)." *Revista do BNDES* 16(31): 41–61.

Além, A. C., and Madeira, R. (2010) *O BNDES em um Brasil em transição*. Rio de Janeiro: BNDES.

Artigas, A. (2012) "La régulation du secteur du lithium au Chili: d'une matrice tradition-nelle d'exportations à la constitution d'un secteur stratégique." In Mathieu Arès, and Eric Boulanger (eds), *L'investissement et la nouvelle économie mondiale*. Brussels: Brulyant.

Burdick, J., Oxhorn, P., and Roberts, K. M. (2009) *Beyond Neoliberalism in Latin America? Societies and Politics at the Crossroads*. New York: Palgrave Macmillan.

Cavalcante, L. R. and Uderman, S. (2009) "Regional Development Policies, 2003–2006." In J. L. Love and Werner Baer (eds), *Brazil under Lula: Economy, Politics, and Society under the Worker-President*, 263–82. New York: Palgrave Macmillan.

Doctor, M. (2002) "Business and Delays in Port Reform in Brazil." *Brazilian Journal of Political Economy* 22(2): 79–101.

Evans, P. (1995) *Embedded Autonomy: States and Industrial Transformation*. Princeton, NJ: Princeton University Press.

French-Davis, R. (2004) "Macroeconomic Growth under Financial Globalization: Four Strategic Issues." In Ricardo French-Davis (ed.), *Seeking Growth under Financial Volatility*. Palo Alto, CA: Stanford University Press.

Gomez-Mera, L. (2007) "Macroeconomic Concerns and Intrastate Bargains: Explaining Illiberal Policies in Brazil's Automobile Sector." *Latin American Politics and Society* 49(1): 113–40.

Guillen, M., and Tschoegl, A. (2008) *Building a Global Bank: The Transformation of Banco Santander*. Princeton, NJ: Princeton University Press.

Gumede, V. (2008) "Social Protection in Latin America and Africa." *Africa Notes* (Summer). Ithaca, NY: Institute for African Development, Cornell University.

Gumede, V. (2011) "The Role of Public Policies and Policy Makers in Africa: Responding to the Global Economic Recession." In M. Ndulo and D. Lee (eds), *Food and Financial Crises and Their Impacts on Achieving the Millennium Development Goals in Africa*. Athens, OH: Ohio University.

Guillen, M., and Tschoegl, A. (2008) *Building a Global Bank: The Transformation of Banco Santander*. Princeton, NJ: Princeton University Press.

Macdonald, L., and Ruckert, A. (eds) (2009) *Post-Neoliberalism in the Americas: Beyond the Washington Consensus?* New York: Palgrave Macmillan.

Mineiro, A. (2010) "Desenvolvimento e inserção externa: algumas considerações sobre o período 2003–2009 no Brasil." In *Os Anos Lula: contribuições para um balanço crítico 2003–2010*, 157. Rio de Janeiro: Garamond.

Munoz Goma, O. (ed.) (2009) *Desarrollo productivo en Chile: La experiencia de Corfo entre 1990 y 2009*. Santiago: CORFO y FLACSO-Chile.

Ollaik, L. G., and Medeiros, J. J. (2011) "Instrumentos governamentais: reflexões para uma agenda de pesquisas sobre implementação de políticas públicas no Brasil." *Revista de Assuntos Publicos Rio de Janeiro* 45(6): 1943–67.

Prashad, V. (2007) *The Darker Nations: A People's History of the Third World*. New York: New Press.

Prochnik, M., and Machado, V. (2008) "Fontes de Recursos do BNDES 1995–2007." *Revista do BNDES* 14(29): 3–35.

Santiso, J. (2006) *Latin America's Political Economy of the Possible: Beyond Good Revolutionaries and Free-Marketeers*. Cambridge, MA: MIT Press.

Schneider, B. R. (1992) *Politics within the State: Elite Bureaucrats and Industrial Policy in Authoritarian Brazil*. Pittsburgh, PA: Pittsburgh University Press.

Shapiro, H. (1994) *Engines of Growth: The State and Transnational Auto Companies in Brazil*. New York: Cambridge University Press.

Sobreira, R., and Montani Martins, N. (2011) "Os Acordos de Basileia e bancos de desenvolvimento no Brasil: uma avaliação do BNDES e do BNB." *Revista de Administração Pública—RAP* 45(2): 349–76.

Stallings, B. (2006) *Finance for Development: Latin America in a Comparative Perspective*. Washington, DC: Brookings Institution Press.

Index

capitalism: dependent capitalism 149n35; in emerging countries 152; *Guanxi* capitalism 46; heterogeneity of 7; historical perspective for public enterprises 82; need for public enterprises 82; in Poland 146; rational perspective for public enterprises 82; various forms of worldwide 7–8; VoC (varieties of capitalism) 7

capital, patient 61

Career Technology and Information Promotion Agency for SMEs 94

Center-Satellite Factories Program 65, 71–2

Central Public Sector Enterprises (CPSEs) *see* CPSEs

CETRA (China External Development Trade Council) 77n4

chaebols 2, 8, 62; growing power of 88; pressure on ruling coalition 88; supported privatization of GLCs 88

Chandler, Alfred Jr. 8

Chang, G.: on Chinese authoritarianism 39

Chang, H.-J.: organizational reforms of GLCs 95

Chile: broad strategy 164–6; countercyclical responses to the Financial Crisis 2008 157–62, 167n18; density of foreign trade and capital market integration 158, 167n20; developmental agencies *see* CORFO; economic program to promote innovation and entrepreneurship 155; fiscal stimulus package 158; industrialization program 154; measures to counter the Financial Crisis 2008 158; outstanding macroeconomic status and consolidated domestic financial market 158; privatization of public companies 155, 167n12; resilience of development agencies 162–3; small and medium export companies (EMT) 159; stress on international competition 159

Chilean Economic Development Agency (CORFO) *see* CORFO (Chilean Economic Development Agency)

China: 12th Five Year Plan 51; banks' support for SMEs 50; confronting bank losses 52; credit expansion 50–1; economic and enterprise development 8; historical context of the Chinese state 40; industrialization driven by

GLCs 9; overinvestment in the housing sector 51, 55n18; paradoxes of industrial organization for Western economic theorists 44; rapid economic growth 39; resilience of financial sector after global financial crisis 50; slowdown in financial reform 51, 55n19; *see also* Chinese state; Chinese state enterprises

China Banking Regulatory Commission 42

China Construction Bank 41, 55n16

China Import and Export Bank 41

China International Marine Containers Corporation 45

China Petroleum 6

China Securities Regulatory Commission (CSRC) 42

Chinese National Standards (CNS) 66

Chinese state: authoritarianism of 39; centralized control of the economy 40–1; civilization state 54n2; criticism of 39; criticism of policy to expand 49–50; defence of the realm and its citizens 40; defined by long history and cultural identity 40; evolution 53; historical context of 40; perceptions of 39–40; strong relationship with Chinese society 40

Chinese state enterprises: ambiguous ownership of 44; Bank of China 51–3; "central enterprises" (*yangqi*) 43; changing role of 40–2; corporate governance 44–6; courting of foreign strategic investors 42; criticism of policy to expand the state 49–50; decline in numbers of 42; economic growth 46; and the economy 46–9; employment losses 50; enlargement of management autonomy 41; examples of good corporate practice 45; falling exports 50; *Guanxi* capitalism 46; housing provision for workers 49; impact of the Financial Crisis 2008 49–51; lack of incentives 41; large-scale redundancies 41; market socialism 40; non-performing loans (NPLs) 42; ownership 42–4; paradoxes of performance 54; price reform 41; promoting innovation 46; reform of the financial sector 41–2; retention of largest enterprises 41; rural migrant unemployment 50, 55n15; seed money 44, 55n6; shift in industrial production 47, 48; social security experiments

increased investment by business
enterprises in India 28; increase in in-
house R&D in India 29; investment in
Asia 15; in Poland 15; professional
testing centre at BIRDC 73–4; reduced
government investment in India 28;
reduced role of PSEs in India 28–32;
research intensity of BHEL 36
Reagan, President Ronald 3
regulatory institutions 10
Renault 8
revolving door 11, 97
RHB Bank 117, 119
Rzeszow 142

Sabah Credit Corporation (SCC) 111
Sabah Development Bank (SDB) 111
samorzad 148n22
Samsung 95
Sappinton-Stiglitz Fundamental
Privatization Theorem 91
SAPs (structural adjustment programs):
activities aiding MNCs 5; imperative of
a liberalized private sector 4; private
monopolies by MNCs 5
Schwinn 69–70
Securities Commission 118, 120
self-management, Poland 148n22
Seoul Trust Bank 88
SEZs (Special Economic Zones):
advantage of geographical proximity in
Walbrzych 144; Aviation Valley 142–3;
clusters 141, 142–3, 143–4, 143n43;
commitment to innovation and research
in Walbrzych 143–4; competitive labor
force in Walbrzych 143; cooperatives in
Lublin 141; creation of 137; defining
137; fiscal incentives 137; industrial
relations in Lodz 140–1; influx of
international companies in Walbrzych
143; intermediaries with foreign
partners 140–1; job creation 137–8; job
creation in Walbrzych 143; local
produce from Lublin 141; public aid
150n41; research firm created in
Walbrzych 143–4; self-employment
141; social capital 140; success criteria
145; tax exemptions 136–7; textile
industry in Lodz 140–1; workers
selling products in Lodz 140–1
Shanghai stock exchange 41
Shenzhen stock exchange 41
Shields, Stuart: on foreign capital taxation
136; on working-class defeat 133

Shimano 72, 72n11
Shirley, Mary 96
Sime Darby Berhad 120
Singapore: influence of GLCs 8–9; invited
FDI to encourage manufacturing 9
Singapore Airlines 6
Singapore Telecom 6
SME Bank 106, 108
SMEs (small and medium-sized
enterprises): access to a professional
testing centre at BIRDC 73–4;
alleviation of R&D burden 75; benefits
of export quality inspection scheme 68;
domination of economic system in
Taiwan 62; domination of the economy
in Poland 145; encouraged to learn 75;
nurtured by GLCs 12; prioritized by
CORFO 159; technological learning
through standardization 65, 66–7
social compacts 10–12
social expenditure: target-based initiatives
13
social security, China 46–7
SOEs (state-owned enterprises): end of
political economic model 3; investment
in Central and Eastern Europe 3
Solidarnosc: disbandment 134; divergent
sensitivities 130; mobilization and
electoral victories 135
Soskice, David 7
South Korea: *chaebols* 2, 8, 62, 88;
changing roles of GLCs 93–4;
competition between public and private
enterprises 96; competition between
public enterprises 96–7; competitive
edge in product development created
by GLCs 85; confusion in neoliberal
ruling coalition 91–3; contradiction
between public investment programmes
and privatization of GLCs 91;
controlling society through GLCs 85–6;
control of money supply dilemma
89–90; corruption in private companies
95; creation of GLCs as agents of neo-
mercantile industrialization 83–6;
creation of public banks 85; definition
of GLCs 99–100n1; destruction of
industrial facilities during Korean War
84; dimensions of government failure
86–7; division of country after Korean
War 84; effects of the Financial Crisis
2008 89–91; employment of GLCs for
neo-mercantilist industrialization
strategy 84; "enemy properties" 83;

For Product Safety Concerns and Information please contact our
EU representative GPSR@taylorandfrancis.com Taylor & Francis
Verlag GmbH, Kaufingerstraße 24, 80331 München, Germany